The Jewish Pope
Myth, Diaspora and Yiddish Literature

THE EUROPEAN HUMANITIES RESEARCH CENTRE

UNIVERSITY OF OXFORD

Director: Martin McLaughlin
Fiat-Serena Professor of Italian Studies

The European Humanities Research Centre of the University of Oxford organizes a range of academic activities, including conferences and workshops, and publishes scholarly works under its own imprint, LEGENDA. Within Oxford, the EHRC bridges, at the research level, the main humanities faculties: Modern Languages, English, Modern History, Classics and Philosophy, Music and Theology. The Centre stimulates interdisciplinary research collaboration throughout these subject areas and provides an Oxford base for advanced researchers in the humanities.

The Centre's publications programme focuses on making available the results of advanced research in medieval and modern languages and related interdisciplinary areas. An Editorial Board, whose members are drawn from across the British university system, covers the principal European languages. Titles currently include works on Arabic, Catalan, Chinese, English, French, German, Italian, Portuguese, Russian, Spanish and Yiddish literature. In addition, the EHRC co-publishes with the Society for French Studies, the Modern Humanities Research Association and the British Comparative Literature Association. The Centre also publishes a Special Lecture Series under the LEGENDA imprint, and a journal, *Oxford German Studies*.

Further information:
Kareni Bannister, Senior Publications Officer
European Humanities Research Centre
University of Oxford
76 Woodstock Road, Oxford OX2 6LE
enquiries@ehrc.ox.ac.uk
www.ehrc.ox.ac.uk

LEGENDA

Chairman of the Editorial Board
Professor Martin McLaughlin, Magdalen College

STUDIES IN YIDDISH

Editorial Committee
Professor Malcolm Bowie (General Editor)
Christ's College, Cambridge
Professor Marion Aptroot
Heinrich Heine University, Düsseldorf
Dr Gennady Estraikh
Oxford Centre for Hebrew and Jewish Studies
Dr Mikhail Krutikov
Oxford Centre for Hebrew and Jewish Studies
Professor David Roskies
Jewish Theological Seminary of America, New York
Dr Joseph Sherman
Oriental Institute, University of Oxford

Volume Editor
Professor Ritchie Robertson, St John's College

Published in this series:
1. *Yiddish in the Contemporary World*
2. *The Shtetl: Image and Reality*
3. *Yiddish and the Left*
4. *The Jewish Pope: Myth, Diaspora and Yiddish Literature*
5. *The Yiddish Presence in European Literature: Inspiration and Interaction* (forthcoming)

LEGENDA/STUDIES IN YIDDISH are published
with support from the Mendel Friedman Fund

LEGENDA

European Humanities Research Centre
University of Oxford

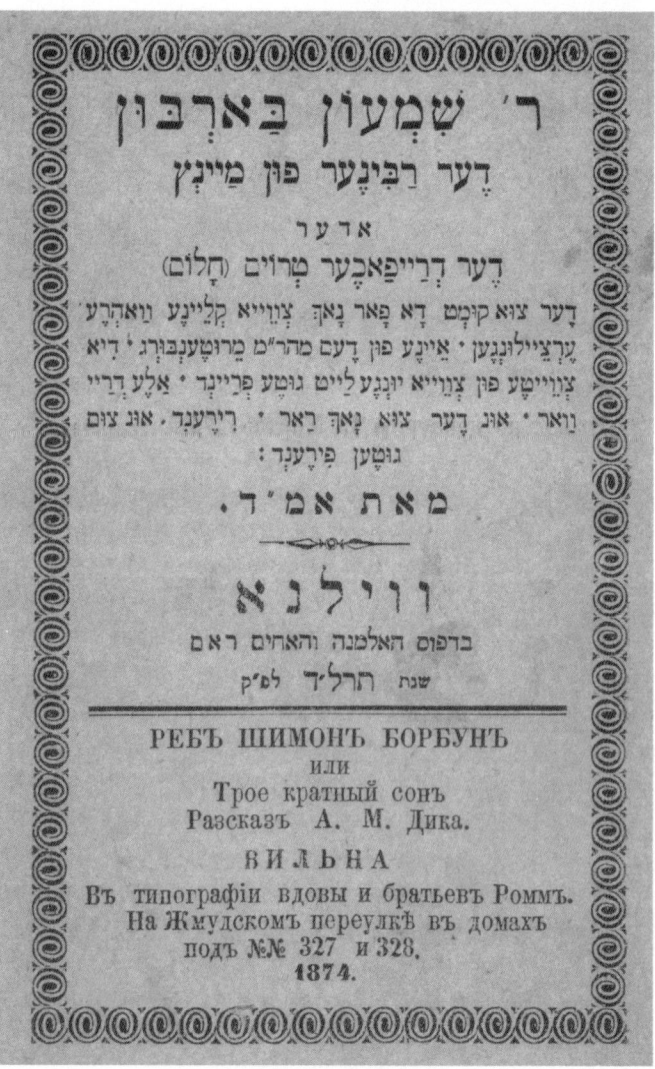

Title page of the original edition of *R. Shimen Barbun, der rabiner fun maynts, oder der drayfakher troym* (Vilna: Romm, 1874) by Ayzik-Meir Dik (see p. 90). From the Harvard College Library Judaica Collection, with the permission of the Harvard College Library.

The Jewish Pope
Myth, Diaspora and Yiddish Literature

Joseph Sherman

European Humanities Research Centre
University of Oxford
Studies in Yiddish 4
2003

Published by the
European Humanities Research Centre
of the University of Oxford
47 Wellington Square
Oxford OX1 2JF

LEGENDA *is the publications imprint of the*
European Humanities Research Centre

ISBN 1 900755 77 7
ISSN 1474–2543

First published 2003

All rights reserved. No part of this publication may be reproduced or disseminated or transmitted in any form or by any means, electronic, mechanical, photocopying, recording or otherwise, or stored in any retrieval system, or otherwise used in any manner whatsoever without the express permission of the copyright owner

British Library Cataloguing in Publication Data
A CIP catalogue record for this book is available from the British Library

© *European Humanities Research Centre of the University of Oxford 2003*

LEGENDA *series designed by Cox Design Partnership, Witney, Oxon*
Printed in Great Britain by
Information Press
Eynsham
Oxford OX8 1JJ

Copy-Editor: Nigel Hope

CONTENTS

1	Why?	1
2	The Master-Narrative and its Ambiguities	26
3	The *Mayse-bukh* and the Debut of the Myth	67
4	Ayzik-Meir Dik, Reformer through Fiction	83
5	Y. Y. Trunk and the Myth after the Holocaust	106
6	Radical Subversion with Isaac Bashevis Singer	121
7	The Case of Israel Zangwill	137
8	A Kind of Closure	157
	Appendix: R. Shimen Barbun, the Rabbi of Mainz	167
	Select Bibliography	195
	Index	199

DEDICATION

TO THE BLESSED MEMORY OF
ARCHIE BOROWITZ (1929–1982)
AND
LEVI SHALIT (1916–1994)
BELOVED TEACHERS AND FRIENDS

simha la-ish be-ma'aneh-fiv ve-davar be-ito mah-tov

A man hath joy by the answer of his mouth:
and a word spoken in due season, how good is it!
Proverbs 15:23

CHAPTER 1

Why?

For four centuries, between 1602 and 1958, Yiddish literature produced no fewer than four separate reworkings of a myth that one day a Jewish apostate might come to rule the world as pope. The roots of this fantasy lie deep in the biblical story of Joseph, from which it branches out into numerous quasi-messianic longings informing Jewish existence through two thousand years of exile. The biblical story of Joseph, its *midrashim* or narrative extensions adduced by the earliest rabbinical commentators, and the similarities and differences in each of the four versions of the myth derived from it, all offer absorbing insights into the nature of a Jewish identity evolving among a people exiled from their homeland and scattered among the nations of the earth to whose beliefs and values their own stood opposed.

For the Jews, 'Diaspora' was both a physical and a metaphysical state of existence: the restored Zion they longed for was simultaneously a geographical locality and a spiritual condition. As the yoke of exile grew ever more onerous, the story of Joseph, the gifted Jewish boy snatched from his homeland and sold into foreign slavery who yet rose to rule over his masters, seemed increasingly to preoccupy Diaspora Jews. This tale could be read as a consolatory assurance that patient confidence in God's providence would be rewarded, or as a wish-fulfilment fantasy that one day a Jew would rule over the Gentile world and bring deliverance to his people, or—more starkly—as a cautionary tale about the evil effects of assimilation into Gentile culture, and therefore as an object lesson in what pious Jews should avoid in their oppressive life under Gentile domination. In essence, the Joseph story is concerned with the nature of identity—the identity of an individual, of his tribe, his people, and his nation. It explores how far that identity is predicated upon collective norms and mores, mutual language, and above all shared faith. It questions how far an individual, born into and brought up to bear one national-cultural and spiritual identity, can acculturate himself to another; how far he might acquire different cultural values and yet retain both personal and national integrity; how far, indeed, he can live a dual existence.

Hellenism—the influence of Greece and its related secular culture on Jews, which endured from 331 BCE until the rise of Islam in the seventh century CE—presented the first great challenge to Jewish integrity by tendering to the world an alternative mode of perception that seemed both greater and stronger. For many centuries, it seemed as if the institutions of Judaism would be swallowed up by those intellectual and artistic achievements that continued to erode exclusive Jewish identity long after the militantly nationalist, anti-Hellenistic uprising of the Maccabees in the second century BCE. Paradoxically, though, while many of the teachings of the early rabbis were influenced by Hellenism—an influence manifest even in the Hebrew they wrote, which bore the impress of the Greek language and its syntax—these were nevertheless single-mindedly directed towards restating and reinforcing the continuity of the Jewish tradition as expressed in the Hebrew Scriptures.[1] Although Hellenism exerted a powerful influence on the thought, language, and even the religious observance of the Jews, and while the rabbis could not entirely efface it, they were to a large extent able to counter it through judicious accommodation of what the teachings of Judaism could ideologically absorb without total betrayal.

By the fourth century CE, however, with the conversion of the Roman emperors from Constantine onwards, the ascendancy of Christianity posed a still greater threat. The Hellenistic ideal had been founded upon human reason, which could be exposed as inadequate to encompass the full range of human experience. Christianity, by contrast, claimed to have sprung from the spiritual roots of Judaism, and to have fulfilled in the person of Jesus all the prophetic promises of salvation found in the Hebrew Scriptures. It relegated these to the status of an 'old' testament or covenant, claiming that a 'new' covenant had been entered into with all mankind, through which the particularity as God's chosen formerly enjoyed by the Jewish people had been superseded, and could now be extended to all who accepted the messiahship of Jesus. Where Hellenism had been rooted *a priori* in paganism, Christianity by disturbing contrast laid claim to the holy texts of Judaism, and identified its saviour and his disciples from among the Jews themselves. How was it now possible for rabbis to teach the truth of their own faith in the light of a new teaching that claimed to be offering an improved and completed version of it? How could exegetical explanations, known in Hebrew as *midrashim*,[2] be devised that would uphold Jewish orthodoxy in a Diaspora dominated by the ruling ideology of Christianity, which steadily came to gather unto itself all the temporal power of the earth?

*

> I was envious of the Church sceptre because I thought that the Synagogue clings to a broken sceptre.
> FRANZ ROSENZWEIG (1916)[3]

Rosenzweig's 'envy', and the language in which it is formulated, draws from and refers back to the iconographic distinction drawn by medieval Christianity between the Church (*ecclesia*) and the Synagogue (*synagoga*). In the earliest Christian painting and sculpture, dating from the ninth century, these were depicted as two women at the foot of the cross bearing the crucified Jesus, the former receiving power and authority over the world with the blood of Jesus dripping into a vessel she held; the latter a white-haired, powerless figure standing at a distance. Later thirteenth-century representations, like those on the south façade of the cathedral of Strasbourg or over the eastern entrance of the cathedral of Bamberg, for instance, developed these images into those of a majestic crowned woman holding a cross in her right hand and a chalice in her left, and a downcast, bareheaded and blindfolded woman supporting a broken spear in her right hand and inverted stone tablets in her left. Sometimes the chalice was replaced with a drawn sword, and the broken spear with a wanderer's staff, but the visual message was always the same—the Church was triumphant and the Synagogue defeated.[4]

Though the presence of Israel in Europe from the fourth century on was tolerated—the existence of Jews, as Augustine first argued, could in various ways be made to demonstrate the truth of Christianity, and from time to time the continent's Christian rulers found having Jews among them economically useful[5]—Jews nevertheless lived a precarious existence. The role they could play in society was strictly curbed to ensure that they did nothing to hinder the conversion of Europe. The medieval Church increasingly demanded that Jewish populations be confined to limited areas of residence, urging the removal of Jews from small towns and villages so as to eliminate contact between Jews and Christians. Medieval legal enactments made the figurative distinction between *ecclesia* and *synagoga* literal by prohibiting synagogue buildings from being taller than church buildings.[6] To obviate the possibility of their giving offence to Christians, Jews were curtailed in the public expression of their religious observances and were compelled to hide themselves from Christian sight during the commemoration of Christian festivals. They were banned from proselytising their own religion, forbidden to occupy any position of power or influence over Christians, disqualified from owning Christian slaves and disbarred from holding any public office. Legislation designed to make Jews identifiable at all times later made the wearing of distinguishing badges compulsory.[7]

Clearly evident in all these impositions is the operation of what Louis Althusser has identified as 'Ideological State Apparatuses'.[8] In pre-capitalist Europe, State and Church were intertwined in a mutually determining history, so that when the ideological functions of the Church were gradually usurped by capitalist secular powers, they were informed, in varying degrees of bias, by the dictates of Christianity. By presenting the conflict between Judaism and Christianity in a metonym of political power, Rosenzweig's remark startlingly illustrates the degree to which, as a Jew, his consciousness continued to be shaped by Christian definitions of reality. As late as the twentieth century, he remained what Althusser has defined as a 'subject' of a dominant ideological system that, to maintain its power, sets everyone up in a series of imaginary relations to the real relations in which they live.[9] This process of 'interpellation', as Althusser calls it, is designed to affect every utterance within the social formation, and the social formation of Europe was—and to some extent continues to be—avowedly Christian. All the discourse employed to underprop and maintain that society is consequently Christian in ideology.

In no sphere of human functioning is the operation of ideology through discourse more readily apparent than in adherence to the dictates of religions, all of which are committed to attaining comparable ideological objectives. Thus where Althusser cites, in illustration of the process he has identified, the Christian formula of Pascal which says, in effect, 'Kneel down, move your lips in prayer, and you will believe',[10] Jews may adduce the Talmudic precept which insists that the regular performance of external rituals leads by degrees to an awareness of the inner spiritual realities which these purportedly represent (*Pesahim* 50b). Since no ideology takes shape outside a struggle with some opposing ideology, the doctrines of the ruling and the ruled are formed in antagonistic relation to each other.[11] Hence the parallel developments of Christianity and Judaism are marked through all their stages with ineradicable evidence of what each is resisting or restructuring. Living as barely tolerated sojourners wholly at the mercy of varying repressive laws enforced by state-sanctioned and popular regimes of violence and control, Jews were for nearly two millennia engaged in an ongoing struggle to resist domination by alien teachings and institutions, while simultaneously fighting to create and enforce their own. This ceaseless resistance to having their identity determined for them by hostile outside forces, while at the same time creating a system by which they themselves could define who and what they were, is indelibly inscribed on both Jewish and Christian literary texts, testifying to the ideological cognizance each faith was compelled to take of the other, and identifying the structures created by each for negating or neutralizing the threats posed by the other's existence.

Both Christian and Jewish ideologies adopted as their master-text the Hebrew Scriptures, and undertook the task of explicating these books to their adherents in ideologically consistent terms. The tradition of biblical exegesis became, for both Jews and Christians, an ideological process of imposing coherence upon contradictions, interrogations and imponderables inherent within this master-text, with the purpose of accommodating faith to the realities of current experience. Conscious of its ambivalent origins in Judaism, Christianity developed an obsessive attitude to the earlier religious ideology entirely disproportionate to the numbers or influence of Jews in Christendom.[12] In its determination to appropriate to itself, yet at the same time to distinguish itself from, the teachings of Judaism, Christianity employed Jewish exegetical techniques to construct a doctrine radically antagonistic to Judaism. To begin with, Christian self-definition came to depend foremost upon undermining the self-definition Judaism gave itself. In response, Judaism employed similar strategies to achieve antithetical ends. Rabbinical exegesis, from the earliest times a central pivot of Jewish teaching, was obliged to fashion a discourse that would serve two interrelated functions. It had to create Jews as its own subjects who freely accepted an imaginary role in the real world, and it had to establish a powerful mechanism of what Pêcheux has defined as 'disidentification', a process of working on and against the dominant Christian mode of ideological subjection by transforming and displacing it.[13]

The core assertion of Jewish identity may be said to reside in the command of Leviticus 18:2–4, on which the whole canon of Jewish Law was built, and from which issued the Jews' total rejection of Christianity:

> I am the Lord your God. After the doings of the land of Egypt, wherein ye dwelt, shall ye not do; and after the doings of the land of Canaan, whither I shall bring you, shall ye not do; neither shall ye walk in their statutes. Mine ordinances shall ye do, and My statutes shall ye keep, to walk therein: I am the Lord your God. (trans. J. H. Hertz, *Pentateuch and Haftorahs*)

Jewish adherence to this commandment was chiefly what incited Christian Jew-hatred, primarily an expression of the antagonism provoked by Israel's refusal to accept the Gospels, and an assertion of the Church's claim to be the new heirs of that divine election which had first lighted on the Jewish people. Though this hatred of Jews had been manifest from the earliest days of the new faith, it developed fully only in the fourth century, when the spiritual and doctrinal advocates of Christianity found it essential to elucidate the absolute rejection with which the Jews treated the message originally intended for them. They drew from the Bible they shared with the Jews material to support their condemnations of these stubborn people who, they believed, had crucified Christ and repulsed his call. Christian Jew-hatred thus came to be warranted on strictly theological grounds, and the Church Fathers sought scriptural proof texts to bear witness that the death of Christ was the inevitable end of an uninterrupted series of grave sins and crimes that laid bare Israel's unworthiness. This contention, endlessly repeated throughout patristic literature, first emerged in the second century with the appearance of the tract *Adversus Judaeos*, Tertullian's refutation of the tenets of Judaism. Patristic writers extended this anti-Jewish polemic in the succeeding two centuries, until it reached its most vituperative expression in the eight denunciatory sermons preached by John Chrysostom (354–407), bishop of Antioch.[14] Chrysostom's malevolence was reiterated by other Church leaders. Jerome (345–c.419) insisted in a letter to Augustine that 'the ceremonies of the Jews are pernicious and deadly; and whoever observes them, whether Jew or Gentile, has fallen into the pit of the Devil. For Christ is the end of the Law.'[15] In 388, Ambrose, bishop of Milan, denounced the emperor Theodosius for attempting to punish arson on Jewish synagogues, asserting in both letters and public preachments that it was legitimate for Christians to set fire to synagogues, that if the laws forbade this, then the laws were injurious and it was a Christian duty to disobey them, and that if he, Ambrose, had known earlier of such prohibitions, he would himself have felt compelled to set fire to the synagogue of Milan.[16]

Ideologically speaking, the systematization of both Jewish and Christian teaching may be read as historical necessities, constantly reinforced for Christians by increasing material power, and for Jews by dwindling material security. These necessities were reflected, *mutatis mutandis*, in different kinds of literature responding to shifting historical circumstances, but always under the same impetus. Max Weinreich places valuable emphasis on the fact that, from the earliest stages of its post-exilic development, Judaism strove for legitimation in two directions, the horizontal and the vertical. Jews who wanted horizontal legitimation for their faith sought to bring it into accord with an external model, usually an esteemed Gentile philosophical system, in sincere conviction that, as Judaism was continually being weakened by attacks from outside itself, it needed to be strengthened with the spiritual weapons of the stronger power, a process that ran the danger of accepting acculturation as a prelude to the even greater peril of assimilation. However, as Weinreich notes further, until the eighteenth century and progressive Jewish emancipation, such attempts were resisted by a powerful ideological resolve among orthodox rabbis to legitimate their faith and define the identity of its adherents by exclusive reference to the tenets of Judaism itself. This process sought to preserve Judaism intact by rigorously upholding the authority of its Sages to the total exclusion of all non-Jewish influence.[17]

As Christian ideology came steadily to dominate the socio-political and ideo-cultural apparatuses of Europe's social formations from the fourth century onward, Christians came to see themselves as directing the course of history. By contrast, in proportion as Jews became more and more victims of events over which they exercised no control, they re-conceived the process of history in a way that removed ideological importance from contemporary events and placed it instead in mythical apocalypses in the remote past and the unknowable future, living in a self-created time-lag between the establishment of the Covenant and the expectation of the Messiah. Ways of perceiving the 'facts' of history were naturally coloured by these radical ideological differences. As a cardinal illustration, Jews interpreted the Destruction of the Second

Temple in 70 CE, part of the Roman attempt to obliterate Jerusalem and scatter the Jewish people, as part of the divine plan for Israel. God was understood to be mourning equally with His chosen people, and the thought that, 'Since the Destruction, the Holy One has not laughed' is repeated many times in the Talmud and related holy writings.[18] Destruction was also theologically linked to redemption, for the Talmud taught that, 'On the day the Temple was destroyed, the Messiah was born' (*Berakhot* 2.4). Accordingly, in the centuries of dispersion that followed, for Jews the sight of their brethren braving every kind of hardship to worship at the Western Wall in Jerusalem was eloquent testimony to the certainty of the ultimate rebuilding of the Temple at the Messianic End of Days. For Christians, however, as Jerome insisted, hordes of ragged Jews clustered around a decaying pile of stones offered clear proof of divine judgement against a people forever branded with the mark of Cain:

> On the day of the Destruction of Jerusalem, you see a sad people coming to visit, decrepit little women and old men encumbered with rags and years, showing both in their bodies and their dress the wrath of the Lord. A crowd of pitiable creatures assembles, and under the gleaming gibbet of the Lord and his sparkling resurrection, and before a brilliant banner with a cross, waving from the Mount of Olives, they weep over the ruins of the Temple. And yet they are not worthy of pity.[19]

On the question of the Messiah, since it had been raised in the master-text, Jews and Christians shared a belief that their salvation was linked to his coming, but they were ideologically sundered in defining his nature. For Christians he had arrived in the person of Jesus to fulfil the prophecies of Scripture, had died on the cross for the redemption of all mankind, and had made all men equal sharers in the Covenant:

> For through faith you are all sons of God in union with Christ Jesus. Baptized into union with him, you have all put on Christ as a garment. There is no such thing as Jew and Greek, slave and freeman, male and female; for you are all one person in Christ Jesus. But if you thus belong to Christ, you are the 'issue' of Abraham, and so heirs by promise. (Galatians 3:26–9, *New English Bible*)

For Jews, however, Jesus had been a false messiah, since his coming had not changed the corrupt nature of the world. Instead they continued to pray for the coming of their own saviour who would restore them to their homeland, gather in their exiles from under foreign oppression, and rebuild the Temple in true realization of the same scriptural prophecies. The events of history were once more invoked and interpreted according to two conflicting ideological demands. Rome, which had been the awesome capital of the greatest empire of the pagan world, became for Christians the fitting capital of the Church Triumphant, the seat of Christ's Vicar on Earth, and the centre of the world. Jews controverted this conception by teaching that the Messiah had been born on the day of the Destruction of the Temple, and waits in hiding for the proper moment of his appearance, when all Israel is free from sin. In the interim, the Messiah dwells, according to the Talmud (*Sanhedrin* 98a), among the lepers and beggars at the very gates of Rome itself:

> Rabbi Joshua ben Levi met [the Prophet] Elijah standing by the entrance to the cave of Rabbi Simon bar Yohai [a second-century Sage who spent thirteen years hiding from the Romans in a cave] [...] He asked him: 'When will the Messiah come?'—He replied: 'Go and ask him.'—'And where is he sitting?'—'At the entrance to the city of Rome.'—'And by what sign may he be recognized?'—'He is sitting among the poor lepers. But whereas they untie their bandages all at once and tie them back together, he unties and ties each separately, thinking: "Perhaps I will be summoned. Let me not be delayed."'
>
> Rabbi Joshua went to the Messiah and said to him: 'Peace upon you, my master and teacher.'—'Peace be upon you, son of Levi,' he replied.—He asked: 'When will you come, master?'—He answered: 'Today!'
>
> Rabbi Joshua returned to Elijah. The latter asked him: 'What did he say to you?' [...] He replied; 'He lied to me, for he said that he would come today, yet he has not come.'—Elijah answered: 'This is what he said to you—*Today, if ye would but hearken to his voice* [Psalm 95: 7].'[20]

This rabbinic *midrash*, as Gershom Scholem notes, arose in the second century, long before Rome became the seat of Christendom, but '[t]his symbolic antithesis between the true messiah sitting at the gates of Rome and the head of Christendom, who reigns there, accompanies Jewish messianic thought through the centuries.'[21]

Although ideological subjection may construct individual consciousness, contradiction and struggle keep the process within history, and so make change and revolt possible.[22] History had to be made to bolster the rival claims of Christianity and Judaism as the sole source of revealed truth, a precondition essential for the self-definition of each in the world. Central here is the mutually contradictory interpretation offered by each of the same historical reality, the Dispersion. Traditionally, rabbinical Judaism taught acceptance of exile as the punishment of God on an erring people, and insisted on a rigorous practice of the Law in the faith that renewed devotion would hasten redemption. The binding force of the rabbinical teaching that all suffering was a punishment for sinfulness, to be averted only by acts of penitence, is painfully illustrated in two documents dating from the eleventh and twelfth centuries, the period of the Crusades. Significantly, in the light of the Ashkenazi setting for the Jewish pope myth, these documents both derive from the massacres suffered by the Jews of Germany. In May 1096, a band of crusaders led by the German Count Emico forced its way into the city of Mainz (Mayence) and then into the archbishop's palace where the Jews had sought refuge. Faced with the inevitability of slaughter, the Jews responded in the only way for which their religious instruction had prepared them: they killed their children and then committed suicide.

The children of the holy covenant who were there, martyrs who feared the Most High, although they saw the great multitude, an army numerous as the sand on the shore of the sea, still clung to their Creator. Then young and old donned their armour and girded on their weapons. [...] Yet because of the many troubles and the fasts which they had observed they had no strength to stand up against the enemy. Then came gangs and bands, sweeping through like a flood, until Mayence was filled from end to end.

The foe Emico proclaimed in the hearing of the community that the enemy be driven from the city and be put to flight. Panic was great in the town. Each Jew in the inner court of the bishop girded on his weapons, and all moved towards the palace gate to fight the crusaders and the citizens. They fought each other up to the very gate, but the sins of the Jews brought it about that the enemy overcame them and took the gate.

The hand of the Lord was heavy against His people. [...] When the children of the holy covenant saw that the heavenly decree of death had been issued and that the enemy had conquered them and had entered the courtyard, then all of them—old men and young, virgins and children, servants and maids—cried out together to their Father in heaven and weeping for themselves and their lives, accepted as just the sentence of God. [...] With a whole heart and with a willing soul they then spoke: 'After all it is not right to criticize the acts of God—blessed be He and blessed be His name—who has given us His Torah and a command to put ourselves to death, to kill ourselves for the unity of His holy name.'[23]

A century later, when a third crusade was mounted to repulse the victorious Muslim commander Saladin, the violence of the mob was again turned upon the Jews in their path, and in January 1188 the Jews of Mainz were once again threatened with mass carnage:

When we heard [of the victories of Saladin and the Christians' vow of vengeance], a very great trembling seized us, and we took up the arts of our forefathers, decreeing fasting, weeping and mourning. On Friday, the twenty-eighth of the month of Shevat [24 January 1188], the Christians gathered to kill us and came into the Jews' street. [...] Our sages and elders told us: 'Let us fast and beseech our God. Perhaps our God will come to our aid.' Then at the afternoon service of the Sabbath, on the thirteenth day of Adar I [13 February], after the Torah scroll had been rolled up, my father R. Judah b. Kalonymus ascended the wooden platform and said: 'Let every man repent of his wicked ways. Perhaps the Lord, in His mercy and grace, will deal kindly with us. Let us accept upon ourselves a fast and let us seek mercy.' Likewise R. Moses b. Mordechai and all our elders and my brother-in-law R. Moses the cantor exhorted tearfully, enjoining the Jews to fast every Monday and Thursday until the month of Nisan [a period of two months], to give charity on the nights of these fasts, to utter the penitential prayers, and to seek forgiveness—every man from his friend and every woman from her neighbour. Thus we begged tearfully for our lives, for our wives, and for our children, lest the wicked kill them or baptize them with their impure waters.[24]

Equally traditionally, the Church taught that exile was God's righteous punishment on the Jews as deicides who were condemned to eternal wandering, but who—despite ferocious periodic assaults—were not to be wholly wiped out or forcibly converted, but rather to be preserved alive as a reprobate nation, serving as a miserable example that would eternally demonstrate the truth of Jesus and the triumph of his Church.[25] Bernard of Clairvaux restated this central Church teaching in the letters he dispatched to the rulers of Western Christendom in 1146, calling for the Second Crusade. Though he uncompromisingly called for Muslim blood to be shed, he also specifically warned against a repetition of the earlier attacks upon the Jews. The Jews were to be kept alive, Bernard argued, for the negative reason that in their oppressed and outcast state they bore witness to the truth of Christianity:

The Jews are not to be persecuted, killed, or even put to flight. Ask anyone who knows the Sacred Scriptures what he finds foretold of the Jews in the Psalm: 'Not for thy destruction do I pray,' it says. The Jews are for us the living words of Scripture, for they remind us always of what our Lord suffered. They are dispersed all over the world so that by expiating their crime they may be everywhere the living witnesses of our redemption. Hence the same Psalm adds, 'only let Thy power disperse them.' And so it is: dispersed they are. Under Christian princes they endure a hard captivity, but 'they only wait for the time of their deliverance.' Finally we are told by the Apostle [Paul] that when the time is right all Israel shall be saved. But those who die before will remain in death. [...] If the Jews are utterly wiped out, what will become of our hope for their promised salvation, their eventual conversion? [...] It is an act of Christian piety both 'to vanquish the proud' [the Muslims] and also 'to spare the subjected' [the Jews], especially those for whom we have a law and a promise, and whose flesh was shared by Christ Whose name be forever blessed.[26]

Common to both these Jewish and Christian ideological interpretations is a concept of punishment that, in terms of subsequent history, led each ideology to believe that the condition in which it found itself *vis-à-vis* the other was the immutable will of God. The dominant position accorded in the strictures of Judaism to its acceptance of culpability made it vulnerable to acquiescence in the subjection exercised over it by the hegemony of the Church. For centuries, Jews were thus forced to cling to the ideal of their Covenant in the teeth of the reality that the world was dominated by those with whom a supposedly New Covenant had been joined. Confronted with a terrifying division of spiritual from temporal experience, they had not only socially to accept, but also ideologically to justify, the inescapable fact that they were powerless and the Christians were powerful; that their religion was despised while the religion of the Jesus they had rejected was triumphant. Christianity's political dominance consequently led both to perceive the Jews as inferior 'subjects'.

This imposed inferiority was given outward and visible form. During the twelfth century, Christendom took over from Islam laws compelling Jews to wear identifying badges, illustrated, among other markers, by the 'Jewish hat' in pictorial and allegorical representations of the *synagoga*. The Fourth Lateran Council of 1215 established the first sealed-off areas of habitation for Jews and, to prevent sexual congress between believers and infidels, ruled that both Jews and Muslims were to wear signifiers on their dress. In 1218, Pope Honorius III added to these demands the rule that all Jews were to pay tithes to their local churches, statutes frequently reaffirmed by successive popes. In 1555, when Pope Paul IV instituted the ghetto with his bull *Cum nimis absurdum*, he also enforced the wearing of the 'badge of shame', and these discriminatory laws remained in force in Europe until the French Revolution of 1789, and in the Papal States until these were incorporated into the newly unified Italian state in 1870. As is well known, the Nazis followed a practice established long before by the Church when it compelled German Jews to wear the yellow badge in 1933. Thus on 4 April 1933, when the *Jüdische Rundschau*, the organ of the German Zionist Organization, urged its readers to 'wear it with pride, this yellow badge',[27] it too was evoking and repeating a centuries-old Jewish response.

Missionary sermons preached for the conversion of the Jews were introduced by the newly established Dominican order in 1216, and throughout the thirteenth century spread steadily to Spain, France, Austria and Lombardy. In the sixteenth century, these sermons were made mandatory by papal law when Pope Paul III built the first *casa dei catechumeni*, 'God's house of the catechumens', in Rome to receive and house converts from Judaism. In 1543 Pope Julius III imposed a tax of ten gold ducats on each of the 115 synagogues in the Papal States to cover the costs of maintaining the converts in this house. Subsequently the tax was borne by the Jews of Rome alone. Later, other such houses were established in all Italian cities in which there was a ghetto. Compulsory missionary sermons were rigorously enforced by Pope Gregory XIII (1572–85), who also compelled the Jews to pay the costs of the apostate preacher as well as those of the house of the catechumens. In 1577, Gregory XIII issued a bull demanding that a specific quota of Jewish men and women attend these sermons on particular occasions, and he made the law still stricter with another bull, *Sancta mater ecclesia*, issued in 1584, which stipulated that 100 Jewish men and 50 Jewish women were obliged to attend such an enforced sermon every week, on Saturday afternoons, the Jewish Sabbath. Beadles armed with rods patrolled the congregation to ensure that the Jews paid attention, and these watchmen were empowered to examine the ears of those attending to ensure that they were not plugged. These compulsory missionary sermons were only abolished as late as 1846, during the first liberal year of the pontificate of Pius IX.

In one way or another, a great deal of the literature produced by Jews in the Diaspora reflects these measures and the consequent installation of themselves as subjects by Christians, most evidently that written in Yiddish. As Max Weinreich has shown, Ashkenazi Judaism, the normative orthodoxy of Western and Eastern European Jewry, has two living languages: Hebrew, the mediated language of its writing; and Yiddish, the unmediated language of its oral communication. Venerated as *loshn-koydesh*, 'the language of holiness', the discourse of Hebrew is accorded a privileged status so ideologically entrenched that no change of any kind is permitted to its pronouncements. Though Yiddish, the vernacular, served as 'the supply language in which Jewishness is brought to the individual',[28] its discourse could not lay claim to the same authority, so as the medium of daily interaction it was capable of developing independent strategies of resistance to the dominant discourse—first to that of Christianity, but later to that of normative Judaism itself. These resistances are well illustrated in the recurrent appearance, across four centuries, of the Jewish pope myth. The different Yiddish texts to which it gives rise defy subordination to Christianity, challenge the historical necessity imposed upon Jews to disidentify themselves from their ideological adversaries, and, at root, question the destabilizing biblical master-text itself. The conflicting claims of history and ideology for both Christians and Jews produce a 'myth' whose contradictions, while located in literature, can be explained in terms of both history and ideology. Rosenzweig's 'envy' can thus baldly be seen as that of a 'subjectified' modern Jewish intellectual still trying to come to terms with the unconscious but still unconquerable fear that Christianity may be right to claim that it alone propagates the revealed truth, so that clinging to the tenets of Judaism may be sheer stupidity.

David Levine Lerner has investigated the implications of the Jewish pope legend from a structuralist perspective.[29] He compares the earliest Yiddish version found in the *Mayse-bukh* (1602) with three even earlier Hebrew treatments of the same theme—originally identified and explored by Avraham David (1983)[30]—among other things to 'demonstrate the adaptation of the story, not only to different locations and characters, but to the different circumstances of Ashkenazic and Sephardic Jewish life' (p. 150). The central difference between the earlier Hebrew texts and that of the *Mayse-bukh* which Lerner notes is that in all of the earlier texts, the rabbi-father demands suicide-martyrdom or *kiddush ha-Shem* (Sanctification of the Holy Name) from his pope son as the only fitting atonement for apostasy or *hillul ha-Shem* (Desecration of the Holy Name) (p. 156). The fact that in the Yiddish (Ashkenazi) *Mayse-bukh* version the rabbi-father urges penitence and return to the true faith of Judaism instead seems to me to confront an issue more complex and disquieting than what Lerner regards simply as 'tolerance on the part of R. Shim'on [which] reflects a conscious rejection by the LAV [*Mayse-bukh*] author of the harsh demand of personal self-sacrifice present in the earlier version of the legend' (p. 154). I would argue rather that this radical alteration reflects not 'tolerance' but desperation to survive.

WHY? 15

To be sure, the alternative Ashkenazi response certainly reflects conditions very different from those of their Sephardi brethren under which Ashkenazi Jews were forced to live. In this respect it parallels, in minor secular mode, the modifications made, for example, by the Ashkenazi R. Moshe Isserles (*c.* 1520–72) to the *Mapah* (Tablecloth), his commentary and notes on the *Shulhan Arukh* (Prepared Table), the code of Jewish Law compiled during the second half of the sixteenth century by the Sephardi R. Joseph ben Ephraim Caro (1488–1575). I would argue, however, that in this difference lies the far more fundamental pattern of subjectification to the demands of the non-Jewish world in which the Ashkenazim lived, from which the Sephardim were for a long time relatively free. While proud and publicly dignified Sephardim, whose existence was not daily threatened on account of their faith, might well insist upon the penitential suicide of their renegade sons, oppressed and terrified Ashkenazim could hardly afford to lose gifted children from among their harried and decimated people. Consequently they would inevitably seek to save them by invoking the Talmudic principle that 'a Jew, even if he sins, remains a Jew', and would certainly hope to reclaim an apostate son for their faith.[31] For this reason, all Yiddish versions of the pope myth emphasise that, unlike the twelve sons of the patriarch Jacob, the abducted Jewish boy is the precious only child of a devout rabbi father who has been childless for many years. This, I hope to show, demonstrates not that we are dealing with what Lerner takes to be a 'defiant story [that] expresses the confidence of medieval Jewry both in the ultimate truth of Judaism and the Jews' potential for success in the Gentile world' (pp. 148–9), but rather with a terror-stricken response to the possibility that their faith might be misplaced, and a recognition that the powerful temptations offered to gifted Jewish children by the Christian world might conceivably express true divine favour. This, I would suggest, is the same crucial ambiguity surrounding both the composition and the content of the disturbing Yom Kippur meditation *untaneh tokef*, 'We will celebrate the mighty holiness of this day'. The martyrdom of its author, Rabbi Amnon—significantly also of Mainz, and also as a result of his brief temptation to embrace Christianity—reflects the same fear of spiritual obliteration powerfully expressed in the prayer he composed in the last moments of his life.[32]

Briefly summarizing the evidence to demonstrate that '[t]he Judeo-Christian opposition, reinforced by repeated incidents of forced conversion, disputation and instances of martyrdom, had considerable influence on the evolution of the Jewish pope legend' (p. 161), Lerner identifies the myth as an attempted 'mediation between binary oppositions' and applies to it the structuralist theory of Lévi-Strauss, only to discover that it in fact denies the possibility of mediation: 'The legend [...] expresses the impossibility of compromise in matters of faith; in Lévi-Straussian terms, no possibility exists for mediation of the main binary opposition' (p. 156). This conclusion seems to offer unequivocal proof of the very forces of fear and subordination that my own study is concerned to investigate. Therefore I reject Lerner's conclusion that 'The Jewish reaction to this opposition between religions, as expressed in the legend, was one of complete confidence in the ultimate truth of their faith and in the eventual reward that they could expect for their loyalty' (p.164). My study aims to prove quite the contrary, certainly in respect of the Yiddish (Ashkenazi) texts I examine. I would argue that in these stories the entire situation of the Jewish boy-convert to Christianity and its interpretation belong exclusively to the domain of Ashkenazi, not Sephardi, Jewry. It seems to me a matter of considerable significance that, although Spanish Jewry was no less exposed to the pressures of Catholic Christian hegemony, and many of the most prominent Church leaders in medieval Spain were converted Jews, this legend of the Jewish pope was a purely Ashkenazi creation. Why this should have been so is a matter of some complexity that my individual analyses of the different tales hopes to treat, but one suggestion may be made here. In all the persecutions visited upon Jews by the Catholic Church in Spain—the rigged Talmud disputations, the laws against Jewish observance, the forced conversions, and the torments of the Inquisition—Jewish converts to Christianity played leading roles, often outdoing their Catholic masters in fanatical zeal. Is it not probable that the horror of what these converted Jews in Spain did to their Jewish brethren might have goaded terrified Ashkenazi Jews to intensify their warnings about the dangers of assimilation and conversion, to provide even the simplest of Jews with parables and moral instruction about how to avoid this danger?

The schizoid condition of simultaneously conflicting with and acquiescing in an imposed inferior identity could not but evince its pathology in many aspects of Jewish consciousness and in many outward expressions of its faith across diverse histories, communities and periods of the Jewish Diaspora in Europe. Thus in times during which the temptations of apostasy held out by the Christian powerful to the Jewish powerless were at their most alluring, the possibility that a convert from Judaism might one day come to rule the Christian world became for Jews the most terrifying betrayal of their continued spiritual witness, firstly because it offered Christians what they could view as proof and use as propaganda that, by rejecting the claims of Jesus, Jews continue to live in blindness and error. Secondly, the example of one such renegade might corrupt other Jews of uncertain faith or worldly ambition. On both counts, apostasy threatened the organic unity and collective survival of a people for whom religious vocation and national identity had from their earliest history been made ideologically inseparable. From the point of view of Christian ideology, on the other hand, the persistent refusal of Jews to admit their error was a constant affront, since the Gospel had been preached to them before all other peoples; the Jews' own acknowledgement of their blindness would consequently be far weightier proof of the truth of Christianity than the testimony of pagans. Since Christianity had appeared long after much of Jewish history had already unfolded, the claims of the younger sibling to have superseded the older could only be fully legitimated by the acquiescence of the older[33] who could, in turn, be rewarded with the highest office in the new social formation. At the same time, however, for both Judaism and Christianity, the idea of a Jew as ruler of the world is a symbol thoroughly invested with the most contradictory significance, embedded as it is in the highly ambiguous master-text story of a Jewish son who rose to hold in his hands the power of life and death over his brethren.

The biblical tale of Joseph, the first-principle paradigm for the pope myth, is fraught with complexities that rabbinical commentators have for centuries, and from the earliest times, been at pains to reconcile, most conspicuously in those hermeneutic extrapolations known collectively as Midrash. For Jews, the chief question raised by the Genesis story is that of assimilation. Is it possible for a Jew to rule over a heterogeneous world without losing those distinguishing essentials by which the ideology of Judaism defines what truly constitutes a Jew? For Christians, a Jew *qua* Jew could not possibly rule over a world that, unlike that of Pharaoh, had been enlightened by the Gospel. Given its primary textual and historical sources, the meaning of the 'Jewish ruler' myth had therefore to be appropriated by Jews in accordance with both historical and ideological necessity. When the Church appeared to have triumphed absolutely, Judaism reconstructed this apparent victory of its enemies into a promised assurance that from it would spring the true redemption. The assimilation into Egyptian culture of Joseph, the master-text archetype, was ideologically justified not only by scriptural exegesis, but also by midrashic extension. The imagined harbinger of the End of Days was to be a descendant of the house of Joseph, who would willingly undergo apostasy and suffer death at the hands of the Gentiles to bring about that final battle with the powers of the world which was an essential precondition of the destruction of history and the arrival of the true descendant of the house of David.[34]

Since the ideologies of both Judaism and Christianity accepted providential causality in human affairs, when the great-grandson of a Jewish apostate, Petrus Pierleone, was actually elected to the Throne of Peter as Anacletus II in 1130, each religion was forced to interpret the meaning of this ideologically destabilizing occurrence in terms that would continue to validate the particular apprehension of revelation nurtured by each. Although no objection had been raised to Pierleone's Jewish descent when he served as an influential cardinal and papal legate, his majority election to the papacy created a schism in the Church, with a minority body of cardinals simultaneously electing a rival in Innocent II. Urged on by Bernard of Clairvaux, the rulers of Europe turned their support to Innocent, and Anacletus, though powerfully defended in Rome itself, lived as a virtual prisoner there, abandoned by the rest of Christendom from his election until his death eight years later. His Jewish ancestry was unquestionably a major factor governing the hostility towards him. Bernard was simply upholding received Catholic dogma when in a letter to the emperor Lothar he deplored Pierleone's election with the outcry, 'To the shame of Christ a man of Jewish origin was come to occupy the chair of St Peter.'[35] The fact that the Pierleone family had, like many other contemporary contenders for the papal throne, made use of lavish bribe was denounced as typical Jewish venality. His opponents accused Anacletus of having unscrupulously acquired wealth enough to buy the papacy by melting down gold and silver church vessels, apart from having raped nuns, kept a prostitute for a mistress, and enjoyed incestuous relationships with his sister and other close female relatives.[36] All-powerful Catholic Christendom reconstructed him as an anti-pope and hence outside the apostolic succession. Thus, in the official view of the Church, from the time of the death of Anacletus until the present, there has never been a 'Jewish' pope.

For its part, impotent Jewry invented a fantasy that there might one day be crowned a truly Jewish pope—not an apostate, but a crypto-

Christian—who, by remaining true to the faith of his people, would help to reverse that people's powerlessness. This fantasy was usefully reworked over four centuries to address Jewish needs during different centuries. Fictional appropriation of the meaning of this myth in accordance with historical, and consequently ideological, necessity became, in both religious and secular branches of Jewish writing, a means of self-protection against Christian calumnies such as the rigged Talmud Disputations and the Blood Libel.

The Talmud Disputations were enforced in Christian Europe between the thirteenth and fifteenth centuries by a succession of popes who wished to eliminate what they regarded as the blasphemous lies Jews supposedly disseminated in the Talmud. The Church had little direct knowledge of what post-biblical Judaism actually taught until the middle of the thirteenth century, when its opportunity to gain first-hand knowledge was advanced by the appearance of knowledgeable Jewish converts to Christianity. The first of these was Nicholas Donin (thirteenth century) who reported that the Talmud repeatedly vilified the Christian faith and its followers. Pope Gregory IX (1227–41) decided to investigate the charge and root out the evils, and in 1239 he dispatched Donin to Paris with letters to the French king, Louis IX (1226–70), the archbishops of France, and the Dominicans and Franciscans of Paris, in which he ordered the seizure and examination of the Talmud and other 'blasphemous' books:

> If what is said about the Jews of France and other lands is true, no punishment would be sufficiently great or sufficiently worthy of their crime. For they, so we have heard, are not content with the old law which God set forth in writing through Moses; they even ignore it completely and affirm that God set forth another law which is called 'Talmud', that is, 'Teaching', handed down by Moses orally. Falsely they allege that it was implanted within their minds and, unwritten, was there preserved until certain men came, whom they call 'Sages' and 'Scribes'. Fearing that this law might be lost from the minds of men through forgetfulness, they reduced it to writing, and the volume of this by far exceeds the text of the Bible. In this is contained matter so abusive and so unspeakable that it arouses shame in those who mention it and horror in those who hear it.
>
> Wherefore, since this is said to be the chief cause that holds the Jews obstinate in their perfidy, we, through apostolic letters, order you to have the Jews [...] forced by the secular arm to give up their books. Those books in which you will find errors of this sort you shall cause to be burned at the stake. You will silence all opponents through use of ecclesiastical censure without right of appeal. You will also report to us faithfully what you have done in this matter.[37]

Following this injunction, the first Talmud debate was held in Paris in 1240, where predictably the defence mounted by R. Yehiel was dismissed as mendacity and the Talmud was burnt. More disputations followed, in which stringent controls were exercised over speakers appearing for the prosecution: they were normally Jewish converts to Christianity, chosen to fulfil the Church's avowed purpose of humiliating Jewish spokesmen in such a way as to persuade the Jewish masses to convert. The most vigorous of these debates was held in 1263 in Barcelona, Spain. The chief Jewish defendant was the great scholar Nahmanides, whose defence proved so successful that he was forced into exile. The lengthiest debate, held at Tortosa, also in Spain, lasted for several months during 1413–14, and led to mass Jewish conversions. The last of these rigged debates was held as late as 1759 in Lvov, Poland, where the chief speaker on the Christian side was the notorious false messiah Jacob Frank; during this disputation the question of the Blood Libel as well as the messianic role of Jesus were both debated, and it again issued in the burning of the Talmud.[38]

The Blood Libel was the most savage and longest-lasting of the accusations levelled against the Jews. This vilification, propagated from the twelfth century on, insisted that Jews used Christian blood, especially the blood of children, for their religious rituals, especially in the baking of unleavened bread for Passover and in the making of Passover wine. It became linked to the libel of poisoning wells during the Black Death raging in Europe in 1348, and expanded to include the accusation that Jews stole the consecrated wafers used in the communion service of Catholic churches. Historians count the appearance of 154 major libels of this kind between the twelfth and the twentieth centuries, most of them in Eastern Europe, but several in Austria, Italy and France as well. Among the later libels, received with international outrage, was the Damascus Affair of 1840, which was denounced, among others, by the governments of Britain and the United States. The last case to come to court was the notorious Beiles Affair of 1913, held in Russia, where the defendant was acquitted as a result of a spirited investigation by the Russian prosecutor.[39]

In orthodox ideological terms, the myth of the Jewish pope could thus validate a variety of Jewish sufferings. On the one hand, it could be made to uphold the absolute moral authority of the *Halakhah* by postulating the possibility that if a boy, brought up strictly within its parameters, were to achieve rule over the Christian world, he would use his powers, not as the apostate Talmud disputants had done, to destroy Judaism, but to preserve it. On the other hand, it could invert the Blood Libel by showing that not Jews but Christians wickedly 'ate' children by seducing Jewish boys into conversion. The materials of the legend could be self-justifyingly manipulated.

However, unquestioning pious acceptance of the subjection imposed by orthodox rabbinical teaching in the face of intensifying oppression grew steadily less acceptable to European Jews situated in a world which seemed to move relentlessly forward, forcibly leaving them behind. As I intend to show, events of contemporary history between 1602 and 1958 revived the deeply embedded 'Jewish pope' myth as a frame within which to set up not *dis*-identification, which displaced and transformed the dominant ideology to which Judaism stood in antagonistic relation, but *counter*-identification, a means through which Jewish subjects, exhausted and frustrated at being variously subjectified by conflicting ideologies, could attempt openly to reject that identity, even though those who attempted this rejection might remain unconsciously complicit with the definition it prescribed.[40] Literary texts once more essayed the rejection of both history and ideology by offering a reinterpretation, in Jewish terms, of the parable of God, suffering the loss of a beloved son—the People of Israel, who abandon His ways—and discovering after years of grief that the son returns from whoring after false gods penitent and with renewed faith in the One and the True. This revision, by tapping the Christian as much as the Jewish unconscious, built a Jewish hope on a Christian nightmare, for if this parable were extended into the realm of recorded history, it deconstructed the core Christian myth itself. Reading history in Jewish, rather than in Christian terms, why might not the apostate son be Jesus himself, whose martyrdom might testify not to the triumph of a new covenant but to the eternal validity of the old? Then the trial and crucifixion of Jesus might become a metonym for the unending agony of his people, and the suffering image of the Jew on the cross might come to symbolize the meek endurance and unmerited torture of the people from whom he was born, and who, like him, remain chosen witnesses to the validity of Revealed Truth. In this way the threat posed by the rivalry of Christianity might be neutralized, and Jewish self-construction itself might either be disidentified through homiletic vindication, or counter-identified through ironic reinterpretation.

The post-Marxist theories regarding the creation of political identity that I draw on can be applied equally usefully to the investigation of contexts in which religious identity is created. Evidence for this can be adduced both intra- and extra-textually: firstly, from the language and narrative strategies employed at different stages by each of the writers who chose to return to this theme; secondly, from the events of recorded history at each of the particular periods in which the tale recurs. This analysis will consequently proceed from a brief outline of the theoretical basis on which it is founded, given here, to an examination of the discourse used, consciously or unconsciously, by each writer; and then to a close reading of key linguistic and structural devices in each successive remodelling of the Jewish pope myth. Answers to some unresolved questions raised by each text will be sought through reference to specific historical details in order to suggest, in conclusion, what tentative implications the results of such an investigation might hold for a Jewish literature that seeks to express the nature and complexity of Jewish identity.

This study examines first the biblical narrative of Joseph (Genesis 37–50) and those *midrashim* and rabbinical commentaries on it that explore its ambiguities, to establish motifs that are either employed or discarded in the reworkings that follow. In seeking to track a variety of *midrashim*, compiled and edited at widely different periods of Jewish history, I have found it expedient for my present purpose to use and to cite from *Legends of the Jews*, the massive seven-volume work compiled by Louis Ginzburg over a period of nearly thirty years between 1908 and 1938, though I am well aware of the limitations of using this source. Since Ginzburg's great work attempts to record all the extant *midrashim* in one seamless narrative sequence, it of necessity elides significant variations in the midrashic tradition, and does not make clear the fact, indispensable to students of Midrash, that this exegetical tradition is long, varied, and the work of many hands responding to numerous different pressures. *Midrashim* were composed at sundry times and developed diverse motifs, whereas Ginzburg's work gives the deceptive impression that there is only one tradition of Midrash. Moreover, Ginzburg designates as 'legends' the *midrashim* he weaves together, a description, as James Kugel has pointed out, that is highly misleading:

[Ginzburg's work] as a matter of policy, sought to submerge utterly the exegetical character of these expansions [the *midrashim*]. [...] The great work of generations and centuries of Jewish exegetes was thus fundamentally distorted into being what it certainly was not, popular 'legends' that simply sprang up in the minds of the common folk just as the 'legends' of ancient Greece or the folklore of other civilizations.[41]

Nor is it the case that the Yiddish writers who drew on Midrash for their reworkings of the pope myth used only one midrashic tradition. Nevertheless, my purpose here is not to make a scholarly examination of Midrash and its various motifs *per se*. As I hope will become clear, my focus is chiefly on those aspects of the biblical portrayal of Joseph that have caused problems or embarrassment to the exegetes, and which have therefore been most prominently to the fore in the tales that derive from it. In this general respect, I have found Ginzburg's narrative handy in providing the essence of midrashic encounters with the biblical Joseph, and thus useful in broadly enabling me to deploy some of its hermeneutic practices in illuminating disquieting reservations arising from the biblical story of Joseph, and the bearing these have on the Jewish pope myth.

The main thrust of my study is an examination, through close reading, of the four Jewish pope myth offshoots in Yiddish: the earliest, found in the *Mayse-bukh* (1602); the nineteenth-century version by Ayzik-Meir Dik, *R. Shimen Barbun, der rabbiner fun maynts, oder der drayfakher troym* (1874); and two twentieth-century reworkings, Isaac Bashevis Singer's radical reconstruction, *Zeydlus der ershter* (1943), and Y. Y. Trunk's version, *Der yidisher poypst: historishe dertseylung* (1958). For reasons I hope will become clear in the course of my argument, I shall examine these tales in thematic rather than in chronological order. The final story I examine is 'Joseph the Dreamer' (1898), by Israel Zangwill. Although this variation on the pope myth was written in English, not in Yiddish, it deals strikingly with related thematic materials. The study concludes with some tentative suggestions about the problems inherent in this material and its legacy.

As an appendix, I have included my own translation of Ayzik-Meir Dik's version, which is difficult to obtain even in Yiddish, and which has never before been translated into English. Since the other three Yiddish versions are all readily available in published English translations, including Dik's important variation in this volume will ensure that all the texts discussed here can be consulted by interested readers who have no Yiddish. The myth of the Jewish pope, I believe, has not yet spoken its last word.

Notes to Chapter 1

1. James L. Kugel, *In Potiphar's House: The Interpretive Life of Biblical Texts* (San Francisco, 1990), 6–7.

2. The way these exegetical explanations or *midrashim* were conceived, and their central importance to the Jewish theological tradition, is explained and discussed more fully in Chapter 2.
3. Franz Rosenzweig, in one of the famous series of letters of disputation exchanged with Eugen Rosenstock-Huessy, written between May and December 1916. Quoted in *Encyclopaedia Judaica* (Jerusalem, 1971), 6:100.
4. Wolfgang Seiferth, *Synagoge und Kirche im Mittelalter* (Munich, 1964), text and illustrations.
5. Robert Chazan (ed.), *Church, State, and Jew in the Middle Ages* (West Orange, NJ, 1980), 1–14.
6. Max Weinreich, *History of the Yiddish Language*, trans. Shlomo Noble, with the assistance of Joshua A. Fishman (Chicago and London, 1980), 204–5.
7. Chazan, *Church, State, and Jew*, 5–7.
8. Louis Althusser, 'Ideology and Ideological State Apparatuses' (1971), cited in Catherine Belsey, *Critical Practice* (London and New York, 1980), 56–8.
9. Diane Macdonell, *Theories of Discourse* (1986; Oxford and New York, 1989), 27.
10. Ibid. 38.
11. Ibid. 33.
12. Todd M. Endelman (ed.), *Jewish Apostasy in the Modern World* (New York and London, 1987), 1–2.
13. Cited in Macdonell, *Discourse*, 39–30.
14. Marcel Simon, *Verus Israel: A Study of the Relations between Christians and Jews in the Roman Empire (135–425)*, trans. H. McKeating (Oxford, 1986), 207–11.
15. Ibid. 93, trans. p. 509.
16. Ibid. 226–7.
17. Weinreich, *Yiddish Language*, 206–7.
18. For example *Avoda Zara* 3b, *Berakhot* 59a, *Zohar:* Genesis 61b.
19. Quoted in Paul Johnson, *A History of the Jews* (London, 1987), 143.
20. Quoted in this translation in Yosef Haim Yerushalmi, *Zakhor: Jewish History and Jewish Memory* (New York, 1989), 23.
21. Gershom Scholem, *The Messianic Idea in Judaism* (1971; New York, 1978), 11–12.
22. Macdonell, *Discourse*, 35–6.
23. Jacob R. Marcus (ed.), *The Jew in the Medieval World: A Source Book 315–1791* (New York, 1974), 115–16.
24. Chazan, *Church, State, and Jew*, 118–20.
25. The reasons for the Church's decision in this regard are explored by Yosef Haim Yerushalmi, 'Response to Rosemary Ruether', in Eva Fleischner (ed.), *Auschwitz: Beginning of a New Era? Reflections on the Holocaust* (New York, 1977), 97–107.
26. Chazan, *Church, State, and Jew*, 101–4.
27. *Encyclopaedia Judaica* (Jerusalem, 1971), iv. 62–73.
28. Weinreich, *Yiddish Language*, 252–9.
29. In his interesting essay, 'The Enduring Legend of the Jewish Pope', *Judaism* 40/2 (Spring 1991), 148–70.
30. Abraham David, 'Jewish–Christian Relations, Past and Present: Notes on the Legend of the Jewish Pope', *Immanuel* 15 (Winter 1982/3), 85–96.
31. *Teshuvot Rashi*, 173 and 175; cited by Lerner, 'Enduring Legend', 159.

32. See H. M. Adler (trans.), *Mahzor le-Yom ha-Kippurim/Service of the Day of Atonement* (New York, 1938), 149 and note on p. 288.
33. Endelman, *Apostasy*, 2–3.
34. Scholem, *Messianic Idea*, 18, 96–9.
35. Salo W. Baron, *A Social and Religious History of the Jews*, iv (Philadelphia, 1957), 10–11.
36. See, *inter alia*, Nathan Ausubel (ed.), *A Treasury of Jewish Folklore* (New York, 1948), 576; *Encyclopaedia Judaica*, ii. 916–17; Philip Hughes, *A History of the Church*, 3 vols. (London, 1979), ii. 292–5; J. N. D. Kelly (ed.), *The Oxford Dictionary of Popes* (Oxford, 1986), 169–70; J. McCabe, *A History of the Popes* (London 1939), 318–19; Joachim Prinz, *Popes from the Ghetto: A View of Medieval Christendom* (New York, 1966), 197–237; Rappaport, 'Anacletus II – Pope from the Ghetto', *Perspectives in Judaism* (Johannesburg, 1985), 186–90.
37. Chazan, *Church, State, and Jew*, 223–4.
38. *Encyclopaedia Judaica*, xv. 768–71.
39. Ibid. iv. 1120–31.
40. Michel Pêcheux, *Language, Semantics and Ideology: Stating the Obvious* (1975), cited in Macdonell, *Discourse*, 39–40.
41. Kugel, *Potiphar's House*, 9.

CHAPTER 2

The Master-Narrative and its Ambiguities

The myth of the Jewish pope, and the prototype of its chief character, a Jewish boy who rises to supreme power, derives ultimately from the biblical story of Joseph, the longest single narrative in Genesis (Genesis 37–50). This story, the earliest record of dualism in Jewish identity, is—like so many other narratives in the Bible—shot through with lacunae, disruptions and ambivalences that the earliest rabbinical commentators were at pains to reconcile with the received teachings of Judaism. These exegetical attempts issued in a hermeneutic tradition known as Midrash.

Midrash, a word deriving from the Hebrew root *daresh*, 'to seek out', developed chiefly as an oral tradition over a long period. From the second or third century BCE on through the Middle Ages,[1] these interpretations were collected, edited and published by many different hands, in order urgently to accommodate into the ideology of Judaism the presence of cultural or religious tensions generated by the laconic style of biblical narrative. Midrash, a series of narrative expansions, sought to answer troubling questions, to clarify confusions, and to resolve apparent contradictions in the biblical text. More significantly, however, Midrash sought to reconcile with the teachings and traditions of Judaism the exigencies of changing socio-political realities, and discontinuities imposed by such violent socio-political change as the Destruction of the Second Temple in 70 CE, and the ensuing dispersion of the Jewish people.

In making the interpolations known collectively as Midrash, the rabbis were sustained by an unshakable belief that, since the Torah was the revealed word of God, and hence eternally true, everything to be found in it, or extrapolated from it, had been there from the very beginning, and required only scholarly diligence to search it out.

They therefore boldly asserted that any 'deductions' they made from the biblical text, in respect of such elements as background details, conversations, or even entire incidents not openly stated in the biblical narrative, had in fact accompanied what the Bible recorded.[2] Although this radical process of literary creativity often involved the rabbis in significantly changing the meaning of the Bible—the Torah—itself, they certainly did not view their project in this way. In their own minds, they were not *changing* the Torah—a blasphemous idea—but only uncovering its hidden depths of meaning. All possible interpretations that the learned might deduce from the sacred text were already embedded in it, they believed; Midrash, in other words, was already in God's mind when the Torah was conceived, a conviction they expressed in their exegetical ground principle, 'Turn it [the Torah], and turn it again, for everything is contained therein.' It has therefore been suggested that that 'we can rightfully call almost all Jewish writing, at least until the nineteenth century, a kind of Midrash', because it all found its source, inspiration and motive in the sacred text of the Bible.[3] The myth of the Jewish pope, I shall argue, performs this kind of midrashic function in Yiddish literature.

In their imaginative attempts to fill in narrative fissures, explicate motive and meaning, and clarify the slightest grammatical, syntactical or verbal irregularities in the biblical text, the midrashists consciously or unconsciously highlighted the troubling actions of characters that Scripture ostensibly seeks to hold up as irreproachable moral models. As a result, the extensive *midrashim* on the Joseph story transform it into an exposure of the dangers posed by assimilation to a gifted Jewish youth. What would happen if Joseph, unswervingly called in the rabbinical tradition *Yosef ha-tzadik*, 'Joseph the Righteous', were not to remain faithful to his people, but were, on the contrary, to use his great power to escape from his background, reject his father and his traditions, punish his brothers, and wholly embrace a hostile culture?

A long rabbinical tradition criticizes Joseph,[4] even as it exerts its hermeneutic skills to justify, in normatively orthodox terms, all the ironies embedded in the biblical account of his life. In doing so, Midrash, the product of a long engagement with the constraints of life in the Diaspora, offers revealing insights into the theological, moral and social concerns of those dispersed rabbis who were grappling with the anxieties of a subaltern nation. Since the Joseph story is not only revelatory in itself, but is also the master-text underpinning the Jewish pope myth, it is worth exploring in some detail. In outlining here the progress of the biblical narrative, and highlighting some of the more challenging midrashic and exegetical interpretations of its key moments, I seek first to call attention to ambiguities; second, to point up those disquieting elements in the master-narrative that are carried over into the Jewish pope myth, as well as those that are omitted or deliberately avoided; and finally, to suggest reasons for these inclusions and omissions. Because the story of Joseph and its derivatives dramatize the Jewish reaction to acculturation and assimilation in a condition of dispersion, the way Christian exegetes have viewed Joseph is not germane to my study. I examine only the commentaries and interaction with biblical text and Midrash of the medieval rabbis.

Joseph's Vanity

Joseph is introduced as a mere youth, remarkable for physical beauty and the privileged status he enjoys in consequence of his father Jacob's blatant favouritism:

> Joseph, being seventeen years old, was feeding the flock with his brethren, being still a lad, even with the sons of Bilhah, and with the sons of Zilpah, his father's wives; and Joseph brought evil report of them unto their father. Now Israel loved Joseph more than all his children, because he was the son of his old age; and he made him a coat of many colours. And when his brethren saw that their father loved him more than all his brethren, they hated him and could not speak peaceably unto him. (Genesis 37:2–4)[5]

The rabbis infer from the narrative remark, 'being still a lad', that Joseph was narcissistic and acted irresponsibly. RaShI (R. Shlomo Itzhaki, 1040–1105) notes that in befriending Jacob's two sons by his concubines Bilhah and Zilpah—whom his brothers despised as illegitimate, and thus inferior to themselves—Joseph further provoked their anger, already kindled against him because, by persisting in wearing his 'coat of many colours' all the time, he daily flaunted his favoured position in their faces. Joseph also intensified his brothers' resentment by tale-bearing, a mean practice encouraged by his doting father, as Scripture explicitly records (Genesis 37:13–14). Midrash develops its censure of a vain and effeminate Joseph as follows:

> In spite of his scholarship [according to Midrash, Joseph spent the first seventeen years of his life anachronistically deep in Torah study], there was something boyish about Joseph. He painted his eyes, dressed his hair carefully, and walked with a mincing step. These foibles of youth were not as

deplorable as his habit of bringing evil reports of his brethren to his father. He accused them of treating the beasts under their care with cruelty [...] and he charged them with casting their eyes upon the daughters of the Canaanites, and giving contemptuous treatment to the sons of the handmaids Bilhah and Zilpah, whom they called slaves. (G 5)[6]

Joseph's youthful self-importance emerges from his haste to disclose to his brothers the nature of his two dreams: in the first, all his brothers' sheaves bow down to his sheaf (Genesis 37:7), and in the second, the sun, the moon and eleven stars make similar obeisance (Genesis 37:9). Scripture twice stresses that for this arrogant disclosure, his brothers 'hated him yet the more' (Genesis 37:5, 8), viewing the scenario his dreams create as intolerable evidence of Joseph's insolent ambitions. After the second dream, which Joseph relates also to his shocked father, 'his brethren envied him' (Genesis 37:11), though his father 'kept the saying in mind'. The rabbis remark that although Jacob rebuked Joseph for his presumption in order to avert increased hatred from his brothers, he was secretly proud of his favourite son's leadership abilities. By 'keeping the saying in mind', the commentators go on, Jacob was instinctively aware that a great destiny awaited Joseph. The biblical narrative itself emphasizes that everything which befalls Joseph is part of a providential design. Thus when his father sends him to report on the conduct of his brothers, he is guided on the right road to Dothan, where they are, by 'a certain man [who] found him [...] wandering in the field' (Genesis 37:15), evidently an angel who, by directing Joseph to his brothers, ensures that he takes another necessary step in the fulfilment of God's plan.

Several of these establishing narrative elements are transposed directly into the pope myth, notably Joseph's capacity for learning and leadership, his shrewdness, and the sense that he is an agent of God's purposes, however mysterious. Unpleasant personality traits, when they exist, are subtly hinted at rather than explicitly spelled out, since the polemical purpose of the pope tales demands that their subject remains faithful to the Jewish people, and makes a wholly credible penitential return. The biblical Joseph's physical beauty is transformed into the Jewish pope's spiritual beauty, associated with holiness and the Torah, the scrolls of which are called in Yiddish *di reynikeyt*, 'the purity'. The rabbinical commentators on the Bible, however, are alive to the manipulative advantages of Joseph's extraordinary physical beauty. Midrash enlarges on the Bible's terse remark that his brothers 'stripped Joseph of his coat, the coat of many colours that was on him'

(Genesis 37:23) to explain that Joseph was naked when the slave-traders found him: '[n]ot satisfied with exposing Joseph to the snakes and scorpions [in the pit], his brethren had stripped him bare. [...] They took off his coat of many colours, his upper garment, his breeches, and his shirt' (G 13) with the result, Midrash goes on, that when the passing Midianite merchants hear Joseph's cries and look down into the pit, they 'saw a youth of beautiful figure and comely appearance', whom they at once draw up and take with them. The unmistakable suggestion that these traders were attracted to Joseph's body nicely anticipates the lustful attentions of Potiphar's wife later in the narrative. Midrash even makes the Midianites boldly challenge the overbearing brothers: 'What, this lad, you say, is your slave, your servant? More likely is it that you are all slaves unto him, for in beauty of form, in pleasant looks and fair appearance, he excelleth you all.' The Midianites buy Joseph for twenty shekels of silver, a sum which, Midrash goes on, '[f]or so handsome a youth as Joseph [...] was too low by far' (G 17). Sold again to a group of Ishmaelites, Joseph is packed off in a caravanserai transporting perfumes from Gilead (Genesis 37:25), goods, according to Midrash, that both literally and metaphorically complement his youth and beauty:

> These aromatic substances were well suited to Joseph, whose body emitted a pleasant smell, so agreeable and pervasive that the road along which he travelled was redolent thereof, and on his arrival in Egypt the perfume from his body spread over the whole land, and the royal princesses, following the sweet scent to trace its source, reached the place where Joseph was. (G 19)

On the one hand, Joseph's singular beauty can be read as the distinguishing mark of divine favour. On the other hand, however, it is the prime cause of Jacob's favouritism for, as Midrash notes, 'Joseph's beauty of person was equal to that of his mother Rachel, and Jacob had but to look at him to be consoled for the death of his beloved wife' (G 6–7). Later it feeds the suspicion that, since Joseph is sexually desirable to both women and men, he might consciously exploit his allure to advance himself. On the very few occasions in which beauty is ever attributed to the Jewish pope, it is—in a decidedly Christian manner—transformed into an outward and visible sign of inward and spiritual grace; it is never valued as an attribute for its own sake.

Joseph and Sex

Once in Egypt—for the medieval rabbinical commentators a metonym for everything alien to Jewishness—Joseph is snatched up by Potiphar, the captain of the guard, who, Midrash suggests, 'was willing to pay as much as four hundred pieces of silver, for, high as the price was, it did not seem too great for a slave that pleased him as much as Joseph' (G 23). From the Bible's ambiguous narrative comment that 'Joseph found favour in [Potiphar's] sight, and he ministered unto him. And he [Potiphar] appointed him [Joseph] overseer over his house, and all that he had he put into his hand' (Genesis 39:4), Midrash intimates that Potiphar 'had secured possession of the handsome youth for a lewd purpose, but the angel Gabriel mutilated him in such a manner that he could not accomplish it' (G 43). Another Midrash, however, building on later events in the Genesis narrative, argues that his wife urges Potiphar to buy Joseph, because as soon as she saw him, she lusted for his body.

Such overt sexuality is frightening to a religious value system that valorizes chastity. Hence the rabbinical exegetes take pains to stress that Joseph achieves rapid advancement and great favour in Potiphar's house because God is with him. Possibly they emphasize divine providentiality to discredit the human alternative, since Joseph is obviously possessed of excellent managerial skills that could as readily be employed for his own advancement as for his master's affairs. Scripture itself, introducing the lustful attentions of Potiphar's wife, re-emphasizes that Joseph has command of everything in Potiphar's house: 'And [Potiphar] left all that he had in Joseph's hand; and having him, he knew not aught save the bread which he did eat' (Genesis 39:6), and pointedly restates the extent of Joseph's beauty: 'And Joseph was beautiful of form, and fair to look upon (*va-yehi yosef yefey to'ar vifey mar'eh*)'. The twice-repeated emphasis that Potiphar 'knew not aught save the bread which he did eat' is a remarkable manifestation of total trust rare in a master, and potentially an opportunity of the greatest temptation to a slave. RaShI, following Midrash, suggests that the phrase 'the bread' (*ha-lehem*) is a euphemism for the woman of the house: Potiphar entrusted everything, except his wife, to Joseph. Midrash also pictures Joseph primping and titivating to maintain his position amid the sophisticated luxury of life in Egypt, in the process suggesting that a handsome and talented young man might feel great thankfulness to be removed from the persecutions of envious brothers, and from the puritanical restrictions of his father's house:

> Free from anxieties, [Joseph] turned his attention to his external appearance. He painted his eyes, dressed his hair, and aimed to be elegant in his walk. But God spake to him saying, 'Thy father is mourning in sackcloth and ashes, while thou dost eat, drink and dress thy hair. Therefore I will stir up thy mistress against thee, and thou shalt be embarrassed.' (G 44)

Joseph's response to the unbridled lust of Potiphar's wife (given the personal name Zuleikah in Midrash but not in Scripture) naturally preoccupies the commentators. They are at some pains to explain that her violent advances are a direct punishment from God to chastise Joseph for his vanity. Encoded in the narrative of this sexual temptation are always subversive possibilities: firstly, that Joseph might well surrender to these explicit blandishments, and secondly, that in resisting them, Joseph is motivated as much by self-interest as by piety: 'Behold, my master, having me, knoweth not what is in the house, and he hath put all that he hath into my hand; he is not greater in this house than I, neither hath he kept back any thing from me but thee, because thou art his wife. How then can I do this great wickedness and sin against God?' (Genesis 39:8–9). The fear thus piously expressed here may actually mean 'I am not prepared to lose all I have gained in this house for a momentary and illicit sexual encounter that may be used against me'; in other words, Joseph may be acting out of sound worldly self-interest. The real possibility that Joseph, a young man with healthy sex drives, might well yield to temptation may be implicit in Scripture's description of his arrival in Potiphar's house on the very day Potiphar's wife is preparing her final assault: 'And it came to pass on a certain day, when he went into the house to do his work, and there was none of the men in the house there within, that she caught him by his garment, saying: "Lie with me"' (Genesis 39:11–12). In commenting on this verse, RaShI cites the opinion of an earlier commentator, who interpreted the phrase 'to do his work' (*la'asot melakhto*) as a euphemism, meaning that Joseph entered the house with every intention of accommodating Mrs Potiphar, but drew back at the last minute. Midrash enlarges on the devastatingly seductive possibilities of this scene:

> Then Zuleika stood before him suddenly in all her beauty of person and magnificence of raiment, and repeated the desire of her heart. It was the first and the last time that Joseph's steadfastness deserted him, but only for an instant. When he was on the point of complying with the wish of his

mistress, the image of his mother Rachel appeared before him, and that of his aunt Leah, and the image of his father Jacob. (G 53)

Narratively significant is the fact that in fleeing from the all too nearly successful embrace of Potiphar's wife, Joseph leaves behind his garment in her hand (Genesis 39:12). Here is an unmistakable suggestion that Joseph is again stripped naked, a parallelism that, by correlating physical with moral nakedness, is designed to remind us that just as his conceit in boasting of his dreams to his brothers led to his being driven naked into a desert pit, so his narcissistic temptation to lie with Potiphar's wife deprives him of clothing, shelter and protection, forcing him outside into a hostile world where he must again fend for himself.

None of these sexual motifs are employed in developing the pope myth: priestly celibacy meshes conveniently with Jewish chastity to render them inoperable, but their patent emphasis in both the biblical narrative and its midrashic extensions add a useful dimension to the potential for wrongdoing in Joseph that, given other manifestations in the pope myth, help to cast dark shadows over the whole tale.

Joseph Interprets Dreams

Scripture relates that, in response to his wife's accusations of attempted rape, Potiphar commits Joseph to prison (Genesis 39:19–20). Significantly, as Nahmanides (R. Moshe ben Nahman, 1194-*c.*1270) notes, Potiphar did not put Joseph to death, suggesting either that he did not believe the accusations, or that loving Joseph too greatly, he could not bear to lose him. Sforno (R. Ovadyah ben Yakov Sforno, *c.*1475–1550) adds the suggestion that only to save his wife's honour did he put Joseph in prison. What constitutes 'honour', and to whom it is due, becomes one of the minor motifs in the pope tales.

Once in prison, Joseph once again employs his considerable charms, as Midrash relates:

Seeing the youth's zeal and conscientiousness in executing the tasks laid upon him, and under the spell of his enchanting beauty, [the jailer] made prison life as easy as possible for his charge. He even ordered better dishes for him than the common prison fare, and he found it superfluous caution to keep watch over Joseph, for he could see no wrong in him. (G 59)

Once again Joseph's beauty and his efforts to please are explicitly made to suggest that side by side with any innate virtue in Joseph, or any divine plan of which he is the agent, is his skill at securing the best possible arrangements for himself under the most adverse circumstances.

In prison, confronting the disturbing dreams of Pharaoh's baker and his butler, Joseph has the opportunity to use his skill in interpreting dreams. He rightly advises that in three days' time the butler will be restored to royal favour, while the baker will be hanged, and so it happens. But here the commentators pause to censure Joseph. Having prophesied a bright future for the butler, Joseph asks a favour of him: 'But have me in thy remembrance when it shall be well with thee, and show kindness, I pray thee, unto me, and make mention of me unto Pharaoh, and bring me out of this house' (Genesis 40:14). Understandably, Joseph seeks some reciprocal advantage for himself, but in all too human a fashion, once the butler is restored to favour, he forgets his debt and 'did not [...] remember Joseph, but forgot him' (Genesis 40:23). Noting that Scripture reports Pharaoh being troubled by dreams only 'at the end of two full years', Midrash suggests that as a punishment for putting his trust in human flesh and blood, rather than in God, Joseph was obliged to spend a further two years in the prison where he had already languished for ten years as a punishment for slandering his brothers.

When the butler finally does remember Joseph, the terms in which he recommends him to Pharaoh have been read as rancorous: 'There was with us there [in prison] a young man, a Hebrew, servant to the captain of the guard; and we told him, and he interpreted to us our dreams; to each man according to his dream he did interpret' (Genesis 41:12). RaShI, following Midrash, reads the butler's presentation of Joseph thus: 'a young man' (*na'ar*), therefore ignorant and unfitted for distinction; as 'a Hebrew' (*ivri*) and therefore a foreigner who does not understand the Egyptian language; and as 'a slave' (*eved*) and therefore excluded by law from ever occupying any distinguished place in the land, forbidden even to wear the garments of a nobleman. On the one hand, this insightful reading may be pointing to Joseph's ineradicable Hebrew identity, and in this way tries to anticipate his loyalty to his father and his brothers. On the other hand, however, it can also be read as indicating how far Joseph will have to acculturate himself to the norms and mores of the Egyptians if he hopes to be accepted as a leader among them.

The scriptural narrative is not blind to this possibility. As soon as Pharaoh's summons comes to Joseph, 'they brought him hastily out of the dungeon (*vayiritsuhu min ha-bor*) and he shaved himself, and changed his raiment, and came in unto Pharaoh' (Genesis 41:14). Now while it is obviously true that out of respect for the royal presence, an unkempt prisoner should tidy up his appearance, the narrative details suggest more egocentric motives. Pharaoh has sent for the one person, he has been told, who can correctly interpret the dreams that are acutely troubling him. Joseph is brought out of prison 'hastily', since the king cannot be kept waiting. Yet despite the seeming urgency of the royal summons, Joseph finds time not only to change his garments, but also, it must be assumed, to bathe. He sees quite clearly the necessity, quite apart from any considerations of personal freshness, for him to appear before Pharaoh looking as close to an Egyptian as possible, hence—contrary to Hebrew custom—he shaves himself, perhaps hoping that his physical beauty, thus improved after his ungroomed stay in prison, will seduce Pharaoh as much as it has seduced Potiphar and the jailer earlier. On the Bible's use of the expression 'brought him hastily', Sforno remarks that divine salvation always comes unexpectedly. It might just as easily be added that having waited so long for his deliverance from prison, and having been summoned to do for Pharaoh what he knows he can do so well, Joseph here sees the arrival of his main chance, and seizes it as eagerly as possible. He is not going to let this most brilliant of opportunities slip out of his reach through neglecting merely to shave, bathe and change his clothes. If Pharaoh has any reward in mind for the person who can relieve his anxieties, let him at least see before him a young man who looks like an Egyptian and thus belies the begrudging introduction he has been given by the butler.

Having brilliantly interpreted Pharaoh's dreams as foretelling seven years of plenty in the land to be followed by seven years of famine (Genesis 41:25–32), Joseph then boldly advises the ruler: 'Now therefore let Pharaoh look out a man discreet and wise (*ish navon ve-hakham*), and set him over the land of Egypt' (Genesis 41:33) with full authority to harvest and store grain. This advice proves 'good in the eyes of Pharaoh', who instantly decrees, 'there is none so discreet and wise as thou (*ayn navon ve-hakham kamokhah*). Thou shalt be over my house, and according unto thy word shall all my people be ruled; only in the throne will I be greater than thou' (Genesis 41:35). Since Pharaoh uses the exact words with which Joseph has a short time before defined the qualities of the man who will save Egypt from starvation—*navon* having the meaning in Hebrew of 'understanding', in the sense of knowing how to provide for the needs of the Egyptians themselves and to sell the surplus for profit to other countries, and *hakham*, 'wise' in the knowledge of how to store the grain so that it would not rot—Nahmanides infers that Joseph offered this job description with himself in mind, yet another indication that, virtuous or not, Joseph has considerable personal ambition and the intelligence to fulfil it.

This resolve to do well in the corridors of Gentile power becomes a central motive for the Jewish pope, and in every rewriting of this myth, it is treated in some depth, though with differing degrees of emphasis. The secular writers who develop the tale are each faced in sundry ways with a pressing need to come to terms with so human and natural a passion as ambition, and to accommodate—or reject—it within the parameters of normative Judaism. The extent to which Midrash hints at this quality in the biblical figure of Joseph provides the foundation on which the later secular tales build.

Joseph Assimilates

In interpreting Scripture's account of Joseph's rise to great power, the rabbis take some trouble to show how Joseph is able to overcome prejudice and legal restrictions against aliens holding office in Egypt. First, Nahmanides calls attention to the way in which Pharaoh opens his proclamation of Joseph's advancement: 'Can we find such a man as this? (*hanimtzah kazeh ish*)' to explain that, by thus expressing his astonishment and his approval in this dramatic way, Pharaoh desired to abolish the traditional xenophobia. Scripture's description of the absolute authority with which Joseph is invested supports this inference:

And Pharaoh took off his signet ring from his hand, and put it upon Joseph's hand, and arrayed him in vestures of fine linen, and put a gold chain about his neck. And he made him to ride in the second chariot which he had; and they cried before him 'Abrekh'; and he set him over all the land of Egypt. And Pharaoh said unto Joseph: 'I am Pharaoh, and without thee shall no man lift up his hand or his foot in all the land of Egypt.' (Genesis 41:42–4)

The signet ring and the gold chain have been understood to symbolize ultimate legal sovereignty, the outward signs of which are the highly prized linen robes, the sign of aristocratic eminence. Pharaoh's earlier proclamation that 'according to thy word shall all my people be ruled [*al pikhah yishak kol ami*]' (Genesis 41:40) is taken by both RaSHbaM (R. Shmuel ben Meir, 1085–1174) and Ibn Ezra

(R. Abraham Ibn Ezra, 1092–1167) to mean that Joseph is also made commander-in-chief of the Egyptian armed forces.

Nevertheless a great problem remains for Joseph. How are xenophobic people to be brought to accept an outsider in supreme authority over them? Up to a point, Egyptian homage can be enforced by fear. Midrash, having given a glowing description of the great pomp and ceremony that accompanies Joseph on his triumphal progress though the land, explains that 'Twenty heralds walked before him, and they proclaimed: "This is the man whom the king has chosen to be the second after him. All the affairs of state will be administered by him, and whoever resisteth his commands, or refuses to bow down to the ground before him, he will die the death of the rebel against the king and the king's deputy" ' (G 74). In the same way, some rabbinical commentators connect Scripture's strange word 'Abrekh' with the Hebrew word *berekh*, 'knee', implying that all are commanded to bend the knee before Joseph. Midrash also inventively solves the problem of Joseph being unable to speak the language of the Egyptians. It relates—with no scriptural basis whatever—that when Pharaoh is enthroned in his state, he sits at the top of seventy steps, representing the seventy languages of the earth. Only one who knows all seventy languages can ascend to the royal presence, and only such a one can rule over Egypt. Making a useful narrative pause before Joseph is fully invested with royal power, and thereby giving Pharaoh's counsellors the opportunity to disparage Joseph, Midrash adroitly creates a night's break during which Joseph can acquire the requisite skills:

The angel Gabriel appeared unto Joseph, and taught him all the seventy languages [...] The next morning, when he came into the presence of Pharaoh and the nobles of the kingdom, inasmuch as he knew every one of the seventy languages, he mounted all the steps of the royal throne, until he reached the seventieth, the highest, upon which sat the king, and Pharaoh and his princes rejoiced that Joseph fulfilled all the requirements needed by one that was to rule over Egypt. (G 72)

Elaborate midrashic hermeneutics are not wholly necessary to indicate how far the Egyptians demand complete assimilation, or how rapidly Joseph complies. Moreover, this mastery over languages moves Joseph's assimilationism into the realm of cosmopolitanism; it enables him simultaneously to belong everywhere and—ironically—also nowhere. The biblical narrative explicitly tells us that Pharaoh changed Joseph's name and gave him an Egyptian wife, a woman not only high-born but the daughter of an Egyptian priest, and therefore, in Jewish terms, an idolater: 'And Pharaoh called Joseph's name Zaphenath-paneah; and he gave him to wife Asenath the daughter of Poti-phera priest of On. And Joseph went out over the land of Egypt' (Genesis 41:45).Only after he has been renamed and given a pure-bred Egyptian wife with whom to beget Egyptian children is Joseph fully equipped to 'go out' over the land of Egypt as its supreme governor whose word is law. This transformation lies at the heart not only of the ambivalences of the Joseph story, but also of the pope myth. Is it possible for a Jew to rise to supreme rule over a Gentile nation and yet retain the defining attributes of Jewishness? The special pleading of Midrash, in addressing the problems inherent in the biblical narrative, becomes the basis for a variety of other responses to this key question in the reworkings that follow the master narrative.

A Hebrew now thoroughly assimilated into the Egyptian court, Joseph names his first-born son Manasseh and his second son Ephraim, Hebrew names, to be sure, but highly equivocal in meaning: 'And Joseph called the name of his first-born Manasseh ["making to forget"]: 'for God hath made me forget all my toil, and all my father's house.' 'And the name of the second called he Ephraim ["to be fruitful"]: for God hath made me fruitful in the land of my affliction' (Genesis 42:51–2). Does the name of his elder son sound suspiciously like a kind of prayer, 'O God, make me forget'? And forget what? Not only the persecutions of his violent brothers, but perhaps also the primitive life he led among them, a shepherd in his father's nomad home, bound to rigid customs and far from the elegance, sophistication and power he now commands in Egypt. Though he signalizes Egypt as 'the land of [his] affliction' in the name of his second son, it is the land in which he has been fruitful beyond all counting, so that the emphasis in the second son's name might fall on the fruitfulness, the gain and status he has achieved, rather than on any sense of the afflictions through which he has passed. If Joseph does think of these sufferings, on the other hand, who but his envious and brutal brothers were the authors of them? Joseph was seventeen when his brothers sold him; he is thirty when he assumes the office of regent (Genesis 41:46), so he has passed thirteen years of humiliation and danger. Is now not the proper time for him to be thinking of a full and satisfying revenge on the authors of his hardships? Moreover, Joseph now lives in luxury and honour. It is quite likely that he has forgotten—or has chosen to forget—his origins and his past. He has integrated his two sons into the culture of Egypt, and has told them nothing about his birth, his heritage, his past life, or their Jewish grandfather. As though to stress even more emphatically how powerful Pharaoh was determined to make Joseph, and thus how great was Joseph's potential capacity for revenge, Midrash extrapolates a scenario in which, by Pharaoh's explicit command, Joseph is personally enriched not only by the king himself, but also—coercively—by every citizen of Egypt:

> The king commanded [...] that every Egyptian give Joseph a gift, else he would be put to death. A platform was erected in the open street, and there all deposited their presents, and among the things were many of gold and silver, as well as precious stones, carried thither by the people and also the grandees, for they saw that Joseph enjoyed the favour of the king. Furthermore, Joseph received one hundred slaves from Pharaoh, and they were to do all his bidding, and he himself acquired many more, for he resided in a spacious palace. Three years it took to build it. Special magnificence was lavished upon the hall of state, which was his audience chamber, and upon the throne fashioned of gold and silver and inlaid with precious stones, whereon there was a representation of the whole land of Egypt and of the river Nile. (G 75)

This is only one of several lavish descriptions given in Midrash of the great state in which Joseph lived in Egypt. The exotic fantasy in which these descriptions indulge expresses exactly that blend of admiration and terror that is carried wholesale from Midrash into the pope myth to explore the potentially devastating consequences for the People of Israel were they to be ruled over by an apostate nurtured from their own seed. Midrash aside, the Bible itself is quite specific about the fact that the Hebrew Joseph is given awesome authority over the entire kingdom of Egypt, and over life and death when the famine comes, since the giving or withholding of food lies exclusively in his hands:

> And when all the land of Egypt was famished, the people cried to Pharaoh for bread; and Pharaoh said unto all the Egyptians: 'Go unto Joseph; what he saith to you, do'. And the famine was over all the face of the earth; and Joseph opened all the storehouses, and sold unto the Egyptians; and the famine was sore in the land of Egypt. And all countries came into Egypt to Joseph to buy corn; because the famine was sore in all the earth. (Genesis 41:55–7)

Joseph and Revenge

The famine Joseph predicted soon spreads to Canaan, as Joseph must undoubtedly know. Yet he shows himself in no hurry to send food to his father who might well still be alive and dying of hunger there. Instead Joseph waits until his brothers are forced to come to him and, once they have arrived, Joseph, so far from hastening to make himself known to them, sets in motion a protracted series of ruses to test the ruffians who treated him so badly so long before. By making Jacob refuse to send Benjamin with them, the biblical narrative (Genesis 42:3–4) ensures that only those ten brothers who hated Joseph and sold him into slavery are the first to confront him. As RaShI notes, the narrative emphasis on there being a full ten brothers in the delegation to Egypt stresses that although they had earlier been divided in the extent of their resentment towards the boy Joseph, by the time they face him again they are unanimous in their urgent need for food. To underscore how deeply they are at their brother's mercy, the commentators infer that Joseph took particular care to ensure that he would attend to his brothers' transaction personally. The drama of this personal confrontation becomes a key motif in every reworking of the pope myth, particularly in view of the fact that the outcome is fundamentally uncertain.

Midrash develops the biblical narrative's confrontation between Joseph and his brothers by suggesting that in entering Egypt, the ten brothers followed their father's instructions to travel separately and not in a group, for fear that their handsome appearance and heroic stature might attract hostile attention. They consequently entered Egypt in what might easily be construed as furtive aggression. They are therefore doubly at a disadvantage when they appear before Joseph:

And Joseph was the governor over the land; he it was that sold to all the people of the land. And Joseph's brethren came, and bowed down to him with their faces to the earth. And Joseph saw his brethren, and he knew them, but made himself strange unto them; and spoke roughly with them; he said unto them: 'Whence come ye?' And they said: 'From the land of Canaan to buy food.' And Joseph knew his brethren, but they knew not him. And Joseph remembered the dreams which he dreamed of them, and said unto them: 'Ye are spies; to see the nakedness of the land ye are come.' And they said unto him: 'Nay my lord, but to buy food are thy servants come. We are all one man's sons; we are upright men, thy servants are no spies.' And he said unto them: 'Nay, but to see the nakedness of the land ye are come.' (Genesis 42:6–12)

The narrative fully realizes the dramatic irony of this moment by repeating information about Joseph's absolute power as both ruler and supplier that we have already been given at some length (Genesis 41:54–7) because it wishes to stress the fulfilment of Joseph's two boyhood dreams: of the many sheaves of grain bowing down to the one (his role as victualler), and the sun, moon and eleven stars bowing down to his star (his role as supreme governor). The brothers enact the abject gesture foreseen in Joseph's dream, bowing down before him 'with their faces to the earth (*veyishtakhavu lo apayim artzah*)'. Ironically, we and Joseph both know who they are and what their obeisance signifies, while they do not. And in this situation—their ignorance opposed to his knowledge—lies the fraught possibility of great danger. What will Joseph choose to do with the authors of his early trauma?[7]

The rabbis comment that in the narrative's double emphasis, 'Joseph saw his brethren, and he knew them (*va-ya'ar yosef et ekhav va-yakireym*)', we are being told that Joseph first recognized his brothers collectively ('he saw them') and only then distinguished each of them individually ('he recognized them'), because they were as bearded now as when he, a beardless youth, had first known them, and their appearance had not greatly changed. Significantly, however, while he knew them, 'they knew him not'. This is only partly explained by Joseph's forbidding manner; more significantly, in appearance Joseph looks wholly like an Egyptian prince, as Midrash extrapolates: 'A large crown of gold on his head, apparelled in byssus and purple, and surrounded by his valiant men, Joseph was seated upon his throne in his palace. His brethren fell down before him in great admiration of his beauty, his stately appearance, and his majesty' (G 82). His brothers' assertion, 'we are all one man's sons (*kulanu bnei ish ehad*)' (Genesis 42:11), is thus doubly ironic. RaShI remarks that because the divine spirit entered into them, they unwittingly included Joseph in this affirmation. However, the biblical narrative also suggests that the brotherhood between them remains sundered by the extent to which Joseph is no longer outwardly—and perhaps inwardly as well—a Hebrew. This appalling possibility, so clear in both Bible and Midrash, is made a dramatic cornerstone of the confrontation between the Jewish pope and his rabbi father.

The biblical narrative emphasizes the extent of Joseph's assimilation by showing him swearing by the name of Pharaoh. Twice he strengthens his accusations with the oath 'as Pharaoh liveth (*hai far'o*)' (Genesis

42:15, 16), a disturbing pagan usage that the midrashists are at pains to bring into line with normative Jewish observance: 'The expression "by the life of Pharaoh" might have betrayed Joseph's real feeling for his brethren, had they but known his habit of taking this oath only when he meant to avoid keeping his word later' (G 84). This is a piece of special pleading that does little to cancel out the menacing alternative possibility, as the pope tales will demonstrate. The normally spare biblical narrative itself foreshadows this alternative by giving us a rare moment of interiority, pregnant with unspoken implications: 'And Joseph remembered the dreams which he dreamed of them (*va-yizkor yosef et hahalamot asher halam lahem*)' (Genesis 42:9). This cryptic narrative observation has called forth conflicting interpretations. Nahmanides argues that Joseph must use subterfuge to bring his father and youngest brother to Egypt in order to fulfil the prophecy and bring his brothers to full repentance, otherwise he would be guilty of a grave double wrong in unjustly holding Simeon to ransom and thus causing his aged father great disquiet. This also explains, Nahmanides argues, why Joseph did not send a letter to his father telling him that he was alive and well as soon as he arrived in Egypt, something even a slave might easily have done, since Egypt was only six days' journey from Hebron. According to Nahmanides, Joseph realized that the prophetic import and divine purpose of his dreams could only be fulfilled after he had achieved his full eminence.

The alternative, more disturbing possibility is that Joseph deliberately did not write to his father because he wished to forget both his father and his father's house, and that, far from wishing to reform his brothers, he wished to punish them. Given the lack of more explicit motivation in the biblical narrative, is it not equally possible that the sight of his boorish brothers prostrate before him awakens in Joseph painful memories of their past cruelty towards him, and consequently a deep mistrust of their present motives? Midrash boldly confronts just such a possibility, suggesting that, at their first appearance before him, Joseph 'was inclined to make himself known to them as their brother, but an angel appeared unto him, the same that had brought him from Shechem to his brethren at Dothan [Genesis 37:15–17], and spoke, saying: "These came hither with intent to kill thee" ' (G 82). As Robert Alter suggests, there may also be in Joseph's mind a clear connection between the deceptiveness of espionage, the seemingly random charge he levels against his brothers, and the deceptiveness of fraternal treachery,[8] for in the Hebrew text, Joseph accuses them of being *meraglim* [...] *lir'ot et ervat ha-aretz*, 'spies [...] come to see the nakedness of the land' (Genesis 42:9), the action of spying being denoted by a form of the verb 'to see' with which the Bible identifies the very moment at which the brothers set eyes on the boy Joseph coming to them in the field and plot to kill him him: *vayiru oto meyrakhok* [...] *vayitnaklu oto lehamito*, 'and they saw him afar off [...] and they conspired against him to slay him' (Genesis 37:18). Moreover in his accusation Joseph twice repeats the suggestive phrase, 'the nakedness of the land', *ervat ha-aretz*, which seems to equate its defencelessness with his own when they left him naked in the pit. These ruffians, having taken advantage of their young brother's defencelessness and planned to kill him, might just as easily take the same advantage of the defencelessness of Egypt for their own greed and gain. Men who can plot to kill their own brother can do anything, after all. Nahmanides, alive to all these possibilities, suggests that something about the appearance of the brothers made the accusation of their being spies plausible. Possibly they came richly dressed as chieftains, an immediate cause for mistrust since chieftains would normally send their servants, not come in person. Nahmanides also suggests that since Joseph asks them where they come from before he accuses them (Genesis 42:7), no one else from their country had yet come foraging in Egypt, indicating that since the famine was not yet so severe there, their motives in coming were doubtful.

It is certainly possible to read in Joseph's harsh accusations a reflex of anger and resentment at their inherent treachery. In protesting their innocence as twelve branches of one tree, the brothers needlessly incriminate Benjamin and equivocate over the fate of Joseph: 'behold, the youngest is this day with our father, and one is not (*ve-ha-ehad eynenu*)' (Genesis 42:13). This prevarication must raise grave doubts about their attitude to their youngest brother, Rachel's second son, hence Joseph's brutal reply: 'That is it that I spoke unto you, saying: Ye are spies' (Genesis 42:14), an accusation the Bible makes him repeat three times. Liars and prevaricators can easily be spies as well.

In demanding that Benjamin be brought to him, Joseph therefore puts his brothers to a test that reveals the complexity of his own motives. This test is shaped not only by his eagerness to see his only full brother once again and thus bring his prophetic dream to ripe fruition, but also because he cannot trust the other brothers not to do away with Benjamin as they did away with him, out of the same envy of their father's unjust favouritism. The logic behind Joseph's ruthless demand is clear: if they have not harmed Benjamin all these years past, they are now speaking the truth, and can repair the sundered bonds of brotherhood.[9]

Hence Joseph inflicts on his ten brothers first a reversal and then a repetition of what they originally did to him. In return for casting him into a desert pit, where he lay terrified and uncertain of his fate, he throws them into a dungeon for three days, during which they experience the same fear of their unknown future.[10] Brought before the all-powerful ruler of Egypt after their ordeal, the brothers confront a mirror-image of their past—one brother is separated from the rest, who must return to an already broken old father to demand from him the second of those two sons on whom he has bestowed immoderate love, and they disproportionate envy. Facing this grim future, they recognize that what has befallen them is the operation of a principle of retaliation that gives exact measure for measure: 'We are verily guilty concerning our brother, in that we saw the distress of his soul, when he besought us, and we would not hear; therefore is this distress come upon us' (Genesis 42:21). When Reuben accuses them to their faces of fratricide, and asserts that 'his blood also is required (*ve-gam damo hiney nidrash*)' (Genesis 42:22), none of them denies this accusation, for all recognize that selling Joseph was tantamount to killing him.

Here the narrative opens questions about the way 'peoplehood' is created. Does it depend upon filiation, a blood tie between members of the same family who must develop national characteristics of their own, or upon affiliation, an adoption of an established nation whose characteristics are assimilated? The story of Joseph's dealings with both his brothers and with Egypt can, on an important level, be read as an allegory of 'peoplehood', and therefore as an exploration of the respective imperatives of filiation as against affiliation. This is certainly one of the central motifs carried over from the biblical masternarrative to its extrapolations in the pope myth reworkings. On the other hand, the motif of personal guilt is either wholly absent from, or severely attenuated in, all the pope myth narratives, since the pious rabbi father of the apostate boy never willingly gives his child away; the boy is forcibly abducted by over-zealous proselytizing Gentiles. What does remain, however, is the dark shadow of the potential collapse of reconciliation and restitution, deriving directly from the biblical narrative. It is always possible, until the very last moment, that Joseph's ten brothers will prove as merciless to Benjamin as they were to him; there is no absolute certainty that they will be chastened by their testing. Similarly, confronting his apostate son in the pope myth narratives, the rabbi father can never be certain that the renegade will turn back to the faith of his people. There is never any guarantee, in other words, that filiation will prove the stronger binding force of peoplehood than affiliation.

Hearing his brothers confront their guilt, Joseph, Scripture records, 'turned himself about from them, and wept' (Genesis 42:24). This is the first of three times that Joseph is overcome. Since the biblical narrative paints each of these occasions with an unusual number of personal details, each is given particular weight. On this first occasion, Joseph's tears—shed in private—may well be those of anger or chagrin: how is it possible to erase bitter feelings of resentment built up over two decades in a single moment? Joseph returns determined to prosecute his trial: first he speaks to them—presumably harshly— and then chooses his hostage, Simeon, and has him bound before their eyes in a blatant demonstration of his power. Midrash, always alive to the possibility of Joseph's vengeful feelings breaking through, explains why Simeon was chosen:

> Joseph decided to keep Simeon as hostage in Egypt, for he had been one of the two—Levi was the other—to advise that Joseph be put to death, and only the intercession of Reuben and Judah had saved him. [...] Also he preferred Simeon to Levi, because Simeon was not a favourite among the sons of Jacob, and they would not resist his detention in Egypt too violently. [...] Besides, it was Simeon who had lowered Joseph into the pit, wherefore he had a particular grudge against him. (G 86)

RaShI, following Midrash, suggests that Joseph wished to separate Simeon from Levi, because the two of them had plotted together to kill him. Simeon and Levi have a long history of vengeful violence behind them; they destroyed Shechem, his father Hamor, and all their tribe to avenge the rape of Dinah (Genesis 35:25–31), and Midrash consistently presents them both as brutal men. Joseph clearly knows his brothers, perhaps because he shares their vengeful nature, which he may find it possible to control but which they certainly do not.

In sending them back with their money returned in the mouths of the sacks of grain they have bought, Joseph offers them a subtle reminder of another transaction in which they received money. As Sforno notes, this money in the sacks will furnish the pretext on which to rearrest them and sell them as slaves, as he himself was once sold. To ensure that his brothers would have no need to open their doctored sacks until they stood in Jacob's presence, when they would feel the full extent of their discomfiture, he also gives instructions 'to give them provision for the way' (Genesis 42:25). The care Joseph takes in planning his test leaves nothing to chance, and certainly provokes feelings of unease—he is so much cleverer as well as so much more powerful than his brothers, that were he after vengeance rather than penitence, they could hardly survive. Judged from his brothers' viewpoint, Joseph's actions increasingly appear to be motivated by heartless capriciousness and vindictiveness.

According to Scripture, Jacob, as oblivious to the feelings of his other sons now as he was twenty-two years previously, melodramatically refuses to part with Benjamin, to whom he has transferred the partiality he earlier felt for Joseph. 'He only is left (*hu levado nishar*)', he insists, thus creating again the impression that Rachel's sons alone count as his offspring.[11] Jacob refuses to consider sending Benjamin, even when their food runs out, and orders his sons back to Egypt to 'buy us a little food (*shivru lanu me'at okhel*)', as though this were a simple matter. Sforno reads Jacob's evasion of reality as indicating that he disbelieved the brothers' story, imagining that they wanted only an opportunity to dispose of Benjamin as they had disposed of Joseph earlier. The passionate intensity of Judah's arguments given in the biblical narrative makes Jacob reluctantly agree, and he instructs his sons to carry down a rich gift to the regent of Egypt in addition to the money that was returned to them, and twice that money again (Genesis 43:11–12). This instruction ironically brings restitution for the sale of Joseph full circle. Money—in Hebrew *kesef*, 'silver'—was given by the Ishmaelites in exchange for their slave Joseph, who was carried down to Egypt; now it is to be carried back to Egypt by the brothers. The rest of the gift Jacob has prepared ironically parallels the Ishmaelite spice caravan, which the brothers must now, in reparation, reconstitute, going down themselves as potential slaves to Egypt to confront, unknown to them, the brother they had so cruelly wronged.[12]

The Bull and the Lion

The way Midrash dramatizes the confrontation between Judah and Joseph over Joseph's determination to keep Benjamin with him is among Judaism's most explicit rabbinical expressions of Jewish powerlessness in the face of Gentile oppression during the Middle Ages.

This scene is not only crucial in itself, but is also the chief crux carried over from the biblical master-narrative into the pope myth deriving from it. It is remarkable both for the arguments it adduces, and for the degree to which it imaginatively creates a wish-fulfilment fantasy that seeks to assuage medieval Jewish powerlessness through an appeal to a mythical vision of past Hebrew might.

The biblical narrative gives Judah a speech of touching humility in pleading for the return of Benjamin (Genesis 44). Midrash, by startling contrast, develops the character of Judah along wholly different lines. It presents him as a fiercely aggressive man 'determined to use in turn the three means of liberating Benjamin at his disposal. He was prepared to convince Joseph by argument, or move him by entreaty, or resort to force in order to accomplish his end' (G 103). In Midrash, Joseph dismisses his brothers, carries Benjamin off 'by main force, and lock[s] him up in a chamber'. Judah immediately breaks down the door and belligerently confronts Joseph with the frenzied accusation that he has violated the accepted manner of dealing with thieves for the specific purpose of using Benjamin for illicit purposes, 'and in this lustfulness thou resemblest Pharaoh' (G 103), an accusation he repeats twice in the course of vilifying Pharaoh and his duplicity. Once again the alien mores of Egypt are characterized in terms of sexual promiscuity and deviance, with Joseph, as an Egyptian prince, now accused of the same criminal motives Midrash earlier attributed to Potiphar. The midrashists consistently link Joseph's physical beauty to sexual licentiousness as their means of identifying what is most alien and most dangerous to Jewish values in the lifestyle of Egypt. To counter these perils they make Judah into a ranting bully who, giving Joseph no time for reply, yells out ferocious threats that he and his brother will destroy Egypt as they destroyed Shechem, that he will call down pestilence on Egypt, that he will 'hew thee down first, and then Pharaoh'. Judah furiously calls Joseph's attention to the way 'from the very beginning thou didst resort to all sorts of pretexts in order to embarrass us' with personal questions, exclaiming that his personal commitment to Benjamin's safety comes from the pledge he has given his father. The tart reply Midrash gives Joseph—which is not to be found in Scripture—explicitly reminds Judah that he was not always a moral paragon:

Why wast thou not a surety for thy other brother, when ye sold him for twenty pieces of silver? Then thou didst not regard the sorrow thou wast inflicting upon thy father, but thou didst say, A wild beast hath devoured Joseph. And yet Joseph had done no evil, while this Benjamin has committed theft. Therefore, go up and say to thy father, The rope hath followed after the water bucket. (G 106)

This reply, throwing Judah's hypocrisy in his face and tarring the innocent Benjamin with the same brush as his morally reprehensible older brothers, produces a remarkable reflex of guilt and rage in the Judah of Midrash. He breaks into a loud outcry of frustration, joined in his yelling from a great distance away by 'Hushim the son of Dan', so that 'the whole land was on the point of collapsing from the great noise they produced. Joseph's valiant men lost their teeth, and the cities of Pithom and Ramses were destroyed' (G 106). Following Judah's call to them to 'demean yourselves as men, and let each one of you show his heroism', his brothers all resolve to destroy Egypt, and they outdo one another in threats of destruction and vaunts of their physical strength. A scene of bitter conflict is set by a midrashic narrative voice that invests the struggle between Judah and Joseph with cosmic dimensions: 'Even the angels descended from heaven to earth to be spectators of the combat between Joseph the bull and Judah the lion, and they said, "It lies in the natural course of things that the bull should fear the lion, but here the two are engaged in equal, furious combat"' (G 105). This amazing extrapolation grows even more fantastic, as Judah's bullying transforms him into a monster of Frankenstinian proportions: 'Then Judah's towering rage began to show signs of breaking out: his right eye shed tears of blood; the hair above his heart grew so stiff that it pierced and rent the five garments in which he was clothed; and he took brass rods, bit them with his teeth, and spat them out as fine powder' (G 107). Frightened by this outburst, Joseph in Midrash is made to link moral to physical strength, since Judah cannot understand any language but that of force, and can respect none but the physically mighty. So Joseph 'pushed with his foot against the marble pedestal on which he sat, and it broke into splinters', a device that captures the momentary attention of the bully Judah, and enables Joseph to level his accusation again:

JUDAH: If I pluck out a single hair from my body, I will fill the whole of Egypt with its blood.
JOSEPH: Such it is your custom to do; thus did ye unto your brother whom you sold, and then you dipped his coat in blood, brought it to your father, and said, An evil beast hath devoured him, and here is his blood.
(G 108)

In Midrash, this is the final straw for the guilty Judah, and in his rage he sets about breaking huge rocks and calling his brutal brothers to arms. Joseph, not to be outdone, issues the same call to his son Manasseh, and a massive war breaks out between Judah's brothers and Joseph's son, in which a great deal of noise is made on both sides, and in which, astoundingly, Judah is victorious:

> [Judah] drew his sword, and uttered a wild cry, which threw all the people into consternation, and in their disordered flight many fell over each other and perished, and Judah and his brethren followed after the fleeing people as far as the house of Pharaoh. Returning to Joseph, Judah again broke out in loud roars, and the reverberations caused by his cries were so mighty that all the city walls in Egypt and in Goshen fell in ruins, the pregnant women brought forth untimely births, and Pharaoh was flung from his throne. Judah's cries were heard at a great distance, as far off as Succoth.
>
> When Pharaoh learnt the reason of the mighty uproar, he sent word to Joseph that he would have to concede the demands of the Hebrews; else the land would suffer destruction. 'Thou canst take thy choice,' were the words of Pharaoh, 'between me and the Hebrews, between Egypt and the land of the Hebrews. If thou wilt not heed my command, then leave me and go with them into their land.' (G 109–10)

What can this extraordinary midrashic interpolation possibly mean, so utterly removed as it all is from the actual words that pass between Joseph and Judah in the biblical narrative, so utterly at variance with the penitent tenor of the scene depicted there? Here the transgressive nature of Midrash can most clearly be seen, 'the nonchalance with which it consistently violates the boundaries between text and commentary'.[13] Viewing the entire Bible as a seamless whole, Midrash draws its personifications of Joseph and Judah from elsewhere in dramatizing the conflict between the lion of Judah, from whom 'the sceptre shall not depart nor the ruler's staff' (Genesis 49:10), and the bull of Joseph, who 'shall gore the peoples, all of them, even the ends of the earth' (Deuteronomy 33:17). In its determination to give the victory to Judah, not to Joseph, Midrash seeks spectacularly to reverse the actual situation in which the people of Israel find themselves *vis-à-vis* the might of Egypt. It insists that Benjamin is released through a display of Hebrew power, not through Egyptian magnanimity. In presenting both Joseph and Pharaoh as terrified of the might of Hebrews roused to ungovernable rage by injustice, the midrashist entirely subverts the moral weight of the confrontation recorded in Scripture, undermining the ethical necessity of the trial Joseph has imposed on his brothers.

By depicting the Hebrews overthrowing Pharaoh, destroying his cities, and laying waste his land, the midrashist shifts the moral high ground from Joseph to his brothers, exalting their capacity for brute force over their guilt and need for repentance. He also undermines Joseph's authority by making a frightened Pharaoh accuse him of dual loyalty and demand that he choose between being a Hebrew and being an Egyptian. Midrash permits Joseph to make himself known to his brothers only as a response to having been intimidated into this invidious position. The propriety of Judah's moral regeneration tenderly emphasized in the biblical narrative (Genesis 44) is replaced in Midrash by the rightness of might, and Joseph, in complete antithesis to both spirit and letter of Scripture, is forced to reveal himself to his brothers not because he judges them morally ready to receive this revelation, but because he has been bullied by their superior show of strength.

The incredible piece of moral subversion perpetrated here by the medieval midrashists manifests the wish-fulfilment fantasy of an oppressed and subaltern people seeking to accomplish through fiction what they cannot accomplish in the reality of their lived experience. This extravagant midrashic undermining of the crucial recognition scene between Joseph and his brothers is significant not only because of the light it sheds on a Jewish response to Diaspora exile, but also because it rejects the idea that Joseph is a fit person to impose moral tests upon the People of Israel. Behind the text of this conflict lurks a subtext of resentment at the extent of Joseph's assimilation. As Midrash slants its narrative, the ruffian brothers are to be victorious because they alone, not Joseph the assimilationist, are the true bearers of the faith of Israel, for they alone have never abandoned the mores of Israel, and they alone are clothed with the moral strength—metonymically bodied forth in physical muscle—to enforce them. The power Joseph wields in Pharaoh's name is shown to be a false power that can have no dominion over the Hebrews; only the unassimilated sons of Jacob will protect the Hebrew people and free them from unjust bondage. Few other incidents in the Midrash display more clearly the extent to which it is unmistakably the product of impotence, the fantasy expression of hope for a reversal of the degraded Jewish condition. It is therefore only to be expected that this crucial confrontation is made the linchpin of all those subsequent fictional responses to Gentile power that issue in the Jewish pope myth.

The biblical narrative itself, of course, is far from indulging such wish-fulfilment fantasies. When Joseph finally makes himself known to his now contrite brothers, it records that 'his brethren could not answer him; for they were affrighted at his presence (*ki nivhalu mi panav*)' (Genesis 45:3). The 'affright' here originates not in fear of brute force, but in moral shame, something Joseph is at pains to encourage when he repeats for a second time: 'I am Joseph your brother whom ye sold into Egypt' (Genesis 45:4). He is determined to show his brothers how their impulses of jealousy, anger and self-assertion violated primal familial bonds, to him as their brother, and to Jacob as their father. For one terrifying moment the biblical narrative seems to throw the shadow of vindictive revenge ominously over the jealous, mean-minded brothers. But then, by striking contrast with the narrative in Midrash, it is Joseph's magnanimous spirit of forgiveness that brings the guilty to repentance and recognition of the true nature of brotherhood.

However, even in this moment of *éclaircissement*, the biblical narrative is capable of equivocal interpretation. Joseph orders the room cleared so that 'there stood no man with him while [he] made himself known unto his brethren' (Genesis 45:1). Why is this necessary? Ever alive to Joseph's ambivalent position in Egypt, Nahmanides suggests that it might have been dangerous to let the Egyptians know all that had transpired in Joseph's past. Firstly, they might then have refused such vicious Hebrew ruffians permission to settle in Egypt, for if they had treated their own kin in this way, how would they treat the Egyptians, who were strangers and foreigners to them? Secondly, they might lose complete confidence in the hitherto unchallenged capabilities of Joseph, who could save Egypt from famine but could not avert the ruthless designs of his own siblings. Having revealed himself once to his brothers in complete privacy, why does Joseph then find it necessary to ask them, '"Come near to me, I pray you." And they came near' (Genesis 45:4), after which Joseph emphatically tells them for a second time who he is? Are they so disbelieving that one announcement is not enough? RaShI, following Midrash, suggests that here Joseph exposed himself to his brothers, to show them that he was circumcised and therefore not an Egyptian but a Hebrew, something they would certainly not have been able to tell from the rest of his outward appearance. Sforno suggests further that he brings them closer so that the Egyptians standing outside, who heard him weeping, would not hear about his sale into slavery. Both readings stress the extent of Joseph's ambivalent position—to the Egyptians he is a foreigner, always on his guard against xenophobia; to his brothers he is an Egyptian and therefore, to their minds, capable of all manner of duplicity. Hence he is obliged to go to great lengths to prove his true identity. Since, as the biblical narrative relates, no interpreter is present, Joseph speaks to his brothers in their own language, but this is not in itself proof, since as ruler of Egypt he knows all languages. Apart from the physical proof of his circumcision, he reminds them that they sold him into slavery, an incident about which only the real Joseph and they themselves could know, and it is shared guilt rather than kinship that seems to convince them.

Although in revealing himself, Joseph speaks pridefully of the great height he has attained: 'And ye shall tell my father of all my glory in Egypt (*kol kvodi bemitzraim*), and of all that ye have seen' (Genesis 45:13), his Hebrew birth clearly limits his authority. For fear of being suspected of private trading, he cannot keep sending large supplies of Egyptian food to Hebrew Canaan, so he brings Canaan to Egypt. To demonstrate the extent of his magnanimity, the biblical narrative makes Joseph, defining himself as 'a father to Pharaoh, and lord of all his house, and ruler over all the land of Egypt' (Genesis 45:8), invite his brothers to bring their father and all their households to settle in the land of Goshen, the richest pasture land in all Egypt, 'lest thou come to poverty' for there are still five years of famine to run (Genesis 45:11). Contrary to the Midrash's extrapolation, which makes Pharaoh act out of fear (G 113), the biblical narrative specifically makes Pharaoh second Joseph's invitation with even greater generosity: 'Come unto me; and I will give you the good of the land of Egypt (*tuv eretz mitzraim*), and ye shall eat the fat of the land (*helev ha-aretz*) [...] regard not your stuff; for the good things of all the land of Egypt are yours' (Genesis 45:18, 20). Why should Pharaoh respond so munificently? In the biblical narrative, when the news reaches him that Joseph's brothers have come, 'it pleased Pharaoh well (*va-yitav be'eyney par'o*)' (Genesis 45:16). Nahmanides explains that the Egyptians had found it humiliating to be governed by an ex-slave and jailbird, and only now do they have proof that, as Joseph had told them, he was not born in servitude but to a family of high standing in Canaan; hence they were pleased. Pharaoh himself may well be especially gratified because, having had such abundant proofs of Joseph's great ability, he is delighted to welcome more talented members of the same tribe to enrich his kingdom. With Joseph's family settled in Egypt, Sforno adds, Joseph would regard himself no longer as a stranger in Egypt, but rather as a citizen with all his personal and professional interests vested in the country, and this pleased the Egyptians.

While this influx of foreign Hebrews might have delighted Pharaoh, his feeling was not necessarily shared by the Egyptian majority, who from the moment of his elevation resented Joseph for being an alien, and who are now forced to watch the very best part of their fertile land turned over to that alien's entire family at the whim of a thoughtless ruler. This is certainly the possibility that Midrash dramatizes: 'Not all the servants of Pharaoh were in agreement with their master concerning this invitation to the Hebrews. Many among them were disquieted, saying "If one of the sons of Jacob came hither, and was advanced to a high position over our heads, what evil will happen to us when ten more come hither?"' (G 113). Joseph, moreover, shows himself every bit as prone to favouritism as his father Jacob. Presenting gifts to all his brothers, he gives Benjamin, his only full brother, five times as many as any of the others. At the same time, he reveals just how little he thinks his brothers have changed their mean-spirited, envious natures when he warns them, just as they are setting off to fetch Jacob and their families, 'See that ye fall not out by the way (*al tirgzu ba-derekh*)' (Genesis 45:24), either by recriminating each other or through bile at Benjamin's evident position of privilege. In this respect, it is significant that they never tell Jacob what really happened to Joseph. When the brothers report the events in Egypt, 'they told him [their father] all the words of Joseph, which he had said unto them' (Genesis 45:27), from which Nahmanides infers that, through their reticence, Jacob was allowed to believe only that Joseph had been kidnapped by strangers. Midrash, however, anticipates the possibility that Jacob will not believe his inherently devious sons, so it introduces a secret code between Joseph and his father:

Joseph had a premonition that his father would refuse to give his brethren credence, because they had tried to deceive him before, and 'it is the punishment of the liar that his words are not believed even when he speaks the truth.' He had therefore said to them, 'If my father will not believe your words, tell him that when I took leave of him, to see whether it was well with you, he had been teaching me the law of the heifer whose neck is broken in the valley.' When they repeated this, every last vestige of Jacob's doubt disappeared [...]. (G 116–17)

As James Kugel explains, this interpolation is derived from a play on words in the Bible's Hebrew text, the homonyms *agalah*, 'wagon', and *eglah*, 'heifer'. The pun links the phrase, *va-ya'ar et ha-agalot asher shlah yosef laseyt oto*, 'and he [Jacob] saw the wagons (*ha-agalot*) which Joseph had sent to carry him' (Genesis 45:27) to the phrase *ve-arfu sham et ha-eglah be-nahal*, 'and they shall break the heifer's neck there in the valley' (Deuteronomy 21:4) in order to read the sentence in Genesis, 'And he [Jacob] saw the *heifers* which Joseph had sent'. Through this transhistorical reading of the Torah, Midrash makes Joseph send an encoded message that only his father would understand. It transforms the biblical Joseph into a medieval *yeshiva* student who recalls the last lesson in which his teacher Jacob was instructing him before sending him off to enquire after his brothers.[14] Once Joseph is established as the true son of Jacob, bound to him by a shared secret, the stage is set for Jacob's mass emigration to Egypt.

This motif of the secret code between father and son becomes a decisive stratagem in the pope myth reworkings, for it is the only means by which the son can convince his father of his identity. In itself, of course, it cannot persuade the father that the apostate condition of his only child is temporary. Instead, it remains a potentially double-edged device, for to the enemies of the alien Jewish renegade, it could provide proof of the dissident and duplicitous intentions of Jews, who in their eyes always operate by means of cryptic devices to gain power. This, after all, is one of the chief canards of Jew-hatred through the ages, and it finds its origins deep in Midrash.

Joseph, Ruler of Egypt

To emphasize Jacob's religious integrity, Midrash insists that, in coming to Egypt, the patriarch would have no truck with the trappings of assimilation. It assumes that the wagons sent at Pharaoh's command were ornamented with idolatrous images, so Judah burnt them, and Joseph replaced them with 'eleven other wagons, among them the one he had ridden in at his accession to office' (G 114), now specifically employed to transport his father. For the medieval rabbinical commentators, of course, Egypt was not a geographical locality but a spiritual condition, a metonym for everything that stood in opposition to Judaism and Jewish values. Nor did they conceive of the Bible as existing in any kind of 'historical' time-frame; for them the events it described were coterminous with their own lives, the people and places one and the same with those they themselves knew and inhabited, the lessons it taught directly applicable to their own immediate condition. The statements the Midrash makes about 'Egypt' and 'Egyptians', for example, must consequently be read as metaphorical, not literal, assertions, referring not to situations located in other people's remote past, but alive in their own contemporary present. The project which engaged the rabbis was the necessity continually to bolster the values of Judaism in an anti-Jewish world.

For this reason, Midrash understands only too well the possibility that the Egyptians must have been resentful of the arrival of these Hebrew interlopers, so it postulates the probability that, in order to ensure that all Egypt welcomed his father with honour, Joseph was compelled to issue 'a proclamation throughout the land, threatening with death all that did not go forth to meet Jacob' (G 120). The same coercion that Pharaoh was obliged to apply to obtain public honour for Joseph must now be applied to obtain a token of public welcome for his father.

Jacob himself is evidently well aware that his arrival is offensive to the Egyptians, which explains why, as the biblical narrative relates, 'he sent Judah before him unto Joseph, to show the way before him unto Goshen' (Genesis 46:28). Jacob did not want to appear like some greedy interloper arrogantly taking advantage, so he sends Judah, the son he has selected to lead his family after his death, humbly to ask instructions from the Egyptian ruler.[15] Such instructions are clearly necessary for, as the biblical narrative makes clear, the Hebrews are not only outsiders, but as herders of cattle, they also belong to a despised caste. As vegetarians who protected sheep and worshipped the Sign of the Ram, the Egyptians despised as uncouth those who tended sheep in the fields, and held them in repugnance for eating these animals' flesh and drinking their milk. Thus Joseph is at pains to instruct his brothers about what to say when they are presented to Pharaoh: they are to report that they have been 'keepers of cattle from our youth' (Genesis 46:32), meaning that they have been cattle-breeders and not simply herdsmen, for Joseph is painfully aware that 'every shepherd is an abomination unto the Egyptians (*to'avat mitzraim*)' (Genesis 46:34). He therefore instructs his brothers to tell Pharaoh openly how they supported themselves, for by bringing candidly to the fore that aspect of their lives most distasteful to the Egyptians, Joseph will be able to gain for them an entirely separate province in which to settle and prosper,[16] and so be prevented from assimilating, as Joseph himself has assimilated. Behind Joseph's shrewd manipulation of Egyptian prejudice to the advantage of his family may perhaps also be discerned a more self-interested motive: by settling his family in Goshen, far from the capital over which he rules, he can put distance between himself and these uncouth cattlemen who are his close relatives.

The biblical narrative exposes Joseph's shrewd ambiguity of motives even more explicitly: Joseph chooses only five of his brothers to present to Pharaoh (Genesis 47:2). RaShI, following Midrash, declares these five to have been the weakest, in order that Pharaoh might not be tempted to retain them in his own service as warriors—or as rivals to Joseph's own eminence—and the plan works: Pharaoh grants them 'the best of the land', the rich pastures of Goshen, and even finds some royal work for them, telling Joseph: 'If thou knowest any able men among them, then make them rulers over my cattle' (Genesis 47:6). These favours may be regarded, as the rabbinical commentators insist, as signs of Pharaoh's gratitude to Joseph; they may equally be read as subtle means of bringing importunate foreign relatives under the control of the Egyptian government and at the same time putting them at a great distance from any possibility of embarrassing their viceregal brother. Certainly, Joseph is magnanimous. He was under no absolute necessity to reveal his identity to his crass brothers, still less to invite them to live in his adoptive country; yet once they are settled, through his careful manipulation, in the land of Goshen, he 'sustained his father, and his brethren, and all his father's household' (Genesis 47:12). Nevertheless, an element of self-interest may be detected in all of this: instead of nobility of character, Joseph's actions might equally bespeak his old desire to control and dominate. His brothers, stricken with guilt, now know that Joseph is alive and holds over them their undisclosed crime of the past. Settled in Goshen, and wholly dependent on Joseph's protection, they are now truly subservient to him, just as his youthful dreams foretold.

The biblical narrative explicitly records how Joseph uses the power to give or withhold food—the absolute power over life and death—to augment the supremacy of Pharaoh. As the famine grows more severe, hunger intensifies among the people of Egypt and its neighbouring countries. During the seven years of plenty, Joseph not only took control of one fifth of the land of Egypt, but also collected a major proportion of all harvests, not by purchase but probably by a tax levy in kind, and thus amassed the stores that filled the granaries he built (Genesis 41:34–5, 47–9). When the famine came, however, the biblical narrative specifically notes that the people who came to get food were obliged to buy back, with ready money, the very harvests they themselves had grown: 'And Joseph gathered up all the money that was found in the land of Egypt, and in the land of Canaan, for the corn which they bought; and Joseph brought the money into Pharaoh's house' (Genesis 47:14). Money was thus removed from circulation, so that when the people came to ask again for food, having no cash with which to purchase the means of their survival, they were obliged to pay Joseph with their cattle, 'and he fed them with bread in exchange for all their cattle for that year' (Genesis 47:17). Having no more cattle, when they came yet again for food, Joseph took their land, and acted on their offer to turn themselves into 'bondmen unto Pharaoh', stipulating that they should continue to work the land for ever as tenants and pay one fifth of their produce as rent, in this way subjecting them completely to the feudal rule of Egypt (Genesis 47:23–4). Joseph's authoritarian ruthlessness goes even further, for he also organizes a massive transfer of population, removing and resettling people 'city by city, from one end of the border of Egypt even to the other end thereof' (Genesis 47:21). The clear purpose of this resettlement policy was to demonstrate that the people no longer owned the land, so as to forestall any future claim to its ownership on the grounds of occupation (Genesis 47:20). Only the priestly class is exempt from this wholesale dispossession, 'for the priests had a portion from Pharaoh, and did eat the portion which Pharaoh gave them' (Genesis 47:22).

In this way, the text of the Bible sets Joseph up as the prototype of a long succession of despotic rulers who claim personal possession of the entire land they rule, have at their beck and call a tame clergy who owe them their very sustenance, and who persuade the people they govern of the ultimate beneficence of their rule, for which their subjects should be ever ready to pay the tribute demanded of them: 'And [the people] said [to Joseph]: "Thou hast saved our lives. Let us find favour in the sight of my lord, and we will be Pharaoh's bondsmen" ' (Genesis 47:25). As for Joseph's brothers, 'Israel dwelt in the land of Goshen; and they got them possessions therein, and were fruitful, and multiplied exceedingly' (Genesis 47:27). RaShI, following Midrash, calls attention, perhaps unwittingly, to the extent of Joseph's self-interest in these policies: he suggests that in resettling the Egyptian population after gaining possession of their land, Joseph's purpose was to remove all possible causes of reproach that might be levelled against his brothers as alien interlopers, since he reduced all the Egyptians to aliens in their own land.[17] In this scriptural presentation of the ostensibly righteous Joseph single-mindedly operating on the principles of appropriation and absolutism, one may—paradoxically—locate in Scripture itself the root of key anti-Semitic accusations down through history, for in Joseph's conduct here, after all, can be found a prototype of the so-called international Jewish conspiracy to undermine and control the Gentile world through cunning financial manipulation. Significantly, Midrash lends unwitting support to this negative perception of Joseph's conduct, even as it seeks to praise Joseph for his foresight and compassion through a series of assertions that read entirely like special pleading:

> The people cursed Pharaoh, who kept the stores of corn in his treasure chambers for his own use, and they blessed Joseph, who took thought for the famishing, and sold grain to all that came. The wealth which he acquired by these sales was lawful gain, for the prices were raised, not by him, but by the Egyptians themselves. [...] The wealth of the whole world flowed into Egypt at that time, and it remained there until the exodus of the Israelites. They took it along, leaving Egypt like a net without fish. (G 125)

The oppressed and degraded condition of medieval Jewry leads its midrashists to transform the Egyptian Pharaoh—quite contrary to Scripture's presentation of him—into a selfish tyrant, in order to make the Jewish Joseph the exemplar of human kindness—again quite contrary to Scripture's account. After Hitler's poisonous accusations, no Jewish reader of Midrash can feel anything but discomfort in encountering in this narrative interpolation a deliberate falsification of the biblical narrative that simultaneously gives Joseph absolute power over food supplies yet places the blame for exploitative profiteering on 'the Egyptians themselves', or that takes smug pride in asserting that the Israelites bankrupted the state of Egypt when they left it.

Joseph's questionable conduct in public becomes even more disturbing in private. During all the time he is busy augmenting the power of Pharaoh, acting with high *realpolitik* as the chief statesman of the realm, he makes no effort to see his father. Although the biblical narrative specifically states that Jacob dwelt in Egypt for seventeen years (Genesis 47:28), the old man never gets to see his Egyptian daughter-in-law or his Egyptian-born grandsons. Joseph, whom his father held in such excessive affection, never comes to visit his family in what is effectively the ghetto of Goshen, and they assuredly did not come to him. This is obviously why, when Jacob falls into his final illness, 'one said to Joseph [*va-yomer le-yosef*, literally 'and Joseph was told']: Behold, thy father is sick' (Genesis 48:1). Joseph did not know, and had to be told by a third party. Midrash seeks to whitewash Joseph's motives by suggesting that he wanted to avoid giving Jacob the opportunity of asking how his lost son had come to Egypt because 'he was apprehensive that Jacob might curse his sons and bring death upon them, if he discovered the facts connected with their treacherous dealings with Joseph', and so he arranged 'a courier service' between himself and his father to keep in touch with his father's welfare (G 132). This is certainly a possibility; but equally so, in the absence of any contrary motivation offered by the biblical narrative, is the alternative—that having established his father and all his family in the Goshen Pale of Settlement, Joseph was only too willing to wash his hands of any further dealing with them.

Here, most clearly dramatized, is the inevitable consequence for the parents of assimilated children who wish only to escape the burden of a detested past and everything that recalls it. The scriptural narrative obliges Jacob to beg his son to visit him; the pope myth narratives make the pope son force his rabbi father into his presence through a series of cruel tricks. Though the situations are reversed, the import of the meeting remains the same—power vested in an assimilated son leaves the Jewish father a helpless victim, and if in both sets of narrative the ending satisfies received morality, the alternative possibility, in which the father and all he represents is mercilessly rejected, remains potentially ever-present.

The Death and Burial of Jacob

On his deathbed, Jacob significantly begs Joseph, not his other sons, to 'deal kindly and truly with me: bury me not, I pray thee, in Egypt' (Genesis 47:29). Though Jacob later lays the same sacred obligation upon his other sons (Genesis 49:29–32), it is to Joseph alone that he primarily addresses himself. Moreover, he is very persistent: not satisfied with Joseph's bare promise, he makes him swear a solemn oath that he will fulfil his father's dying wish (Genesis 47:29). Why does Jacob find this necessary? From the humble tone in which the old man speaks, he appears to know that Joseph might be reluctant to transport his father's body out of Egypt, and might perhaps even prevent his brothers from doing so. From the point of view of the

Egyptians, it would ill beseem their viceroy to encourage foreigners to eat the fat of Egypt's land, only to hurry out of it when they have made their pile. Those immigrants who demand to be buried out of Egypt openly proclaim that they have been temporary and exploitative sojourners in an alien land to which they owe neither loyalty nor duty. Thus it is to the viceroy himself, who alone of all Jacob's sons has the power to carry out his father's dying wish, that the dying man appeals. His son's exalted circumstances have transformed his patriarchal father into a subservient petitioner.

Midrash adds a significant extension to the biblical narrative's detail that, after Joseph had agreed, Jacob 'bowed himself down upon the bed's head (*va-yishtahu yisrael al rosh ha-mitah*)' (Genesis 47:31): 'Jacob [...] had to ask services of others while he was among strangers, and when Joseph promised to do his bidding, he bowed himself before his own son, for it is a true saying, "Bow before the fox in his day," the day of his power' (G 130). In paying homage to Joseph's illustrious position, Jacob is involuntarily forced to concede also that Joseph is bound to Egypt and its customs. For all the honour Jacob and his family have received in Egypt, they remain outsiders in an alien land, a situation in which, despite all the outward trappings of his complete assimilation, Joseph ironically also finds himself. Midrash emphasizes this point by making Joseph promise his father that when his own time comes to die, he too will beg his brothers to carry his body from Egypt to Canaan (G 130). Only in death will he be reunited with his kin, for in life, the biblical narrative makes clear, Joseph lived at a distance from his family, in which the physical denotes also the social and the cultural, bespeaking Joseph's desire to be in all worldly things an Egyptian, not a Hebrew. Midrash stresses that during the seventeen years Jacob lived in Egypt, he was never once allowed to meet Joseph's sons. Only on his deathbed does Joseph seek his father's blessing for them (G 133).

When these unknown grandsons are finally brought to him, Jacob does not know who they are, as Scripture relates: he is obliged to ask, 'Who are these (*mi eyleh*)?', not simply because his sight is failing, but more disturbingly because in all outward appearance they look like Egyptian princes. Joseph is embarrassingly obliged personally to assure his father, 'They are my sons whom God hath given me here' (Genesis 48:8–9). That Jacob remains perfectly capable of visual distinctions is made clear when, 'guiding his hands wittingly', he deliberately crosses them in order to place his right hand not upon

Manasseh, the older son who has been presented to him first, but instead upon the head of Ephraim, the younger son, to whom he wishes to give the precedence in his blessing (Genesis 48:14–19).

After his death, Jacob's body is embalmed according to the Egyptian custom (Genesis 50:2). Midrash recognizes this embalming as the act of an assimilationist son, and censures it accordingly: 'Joseph ordered the physicians to embalm the corpse. This he should have refrained from doing, for it was displeasing to God, who spoke, saying, "Have I not the power to preserve the corpse of this pious man from corruption?" [...] Joseph's punishment for this useless precaution was that he was the first of Jacob's sons to suffer death' (G 150). Jacob's fears that Pharaoh would be loath to allow the Hebrews to return to Canaan turn out to be well founded. The biblical narrative relates the puzzling detail that Joseph is obliged to ask, through an intermediary, permission of Pharaoh to accompany his father's funeral, concluding with the assurance 'I will come back' (Genesis 48:4–5). The rabbinical commentators' explanation—that one was not allowed to enter the royal presence while in mourning—is scarcely satisfactory, since it fails to account for the extraordinary humility of the way Joseph phrases his request. Why should Joseph, hitherto second only to Pharaoh himself, suddenly need the intercession of his subordinates? Cannot he himself make this request personally of a ruler for whom he has done so much and in whose favour he has lived for so long? Indeed, cannot Joseph act on his own authority in this matter of his father's burial? Joseph's fidelity to Pharaoh and his patriotism to Egypt should by now be beyond question, yet in his ascent to power he must undoubtedly have made influential enemies and envious rivals. These might well revive old xenophobic feelings and accuse him of divided or imperfect loyalty should he now come forward with his request to bury his father outside Egypt. His ill-wishers might argue that he has remained a hostile alien like his father who for seventeen years ate bread taken from the mouths of native-born Egyptians, yet refused to be buried in the soil of Egypt that had sustained him for so long. Clearly, Joseph was afraid that his request would be refused because Pharaoh and his advisers would regard it as demonstrating the rankest ingratitude.[18] Joseph, according to Scripture, is therefore obliged to beg in the most deferential terms, insisting that he is acting only under emotional compulsion: 'My father made me swear' (Genesis 50:5). Left to make his own decision, Joseph seems to be protesting, he himself would never voluntarily have thought of burial outside Egypt.

The inference is that without the oath wrested from him, he would not have complied with Jacob's dying wish, would not have had the courage to importune the king, nor would Pharaoh have agreed. His assurances to Pharaoh insist that his true home is in Egypt, not in Canaan.

Pharaoh accordingly grants permission, as the Bible narrates, and moreover lays on a magnificent funeral: 'And there went up with him [Joseph] both chariots and horsemen; and it was a very great company' (Genesis 50:9). Why, it must be asked, is a military funeral granted to this old Jew who lived in Goshen and is now to be buried in another land? Less, the answer must be, to honour Jacob than to make sure of Joseph. The soldiers are there to bring Joseph back to Egypt, for he is too valuable to be allowed to slip away—assuming he wanted to. The rest of the family must also give cast-iron guarantees to return: while all the adults are permitted to go up to Canaan to bury Jacob, 'their little ones, and their flocks, and their herds, they left in the land of Goshen' (Genesis 50:8), evidently as hostages against their assured return. These Hebrews are useful to the economy of Egypt but, always regarded as aliens, they cannot be relied on to return of their own free will. Even the supremely assimilated Joseph, after all he has done for Egypt, is not fully trusted to put that country's interests before his own.

Joseph is finally suspected both by the Egyptians and by his own family. After his father's death, Scripture relates, his brothers fear his delayed vengeance: 'It may be that Joseph will hate us, and will fully requite us all the evil which we did unto him' (Genesis 50:15). So they send supplicating messages to him, begging him in the name of their dead father to 'forgive the transgression of thy brethren, and their sin, for they did unto thee evil [...] forgive the transgression of the servants of the God of thy father' (Genesis 50: 15–17). In their guilty fear they offer once again to become Joseph's slaves. Joseph's response is to weep (Genesis 50:17). Why? Is he deeply disappointed that his brothers retain their old mean-spirited characters? Is he overcome with pity for their unreasonable terror? Is he ashamed of once having genuinely thought of a bloody revenge? Interestingly, Midrash offers a wholly self-interested motive for Joseph's repeated magnanimity:

> It is to my own good that I should treat you with fraternal affection. Before your advent, I was looked upon as a slave in this country—you proved me a man of noble birth. Now, if I should kill you, my claims upon an aristocratic lineage would be shown to be a lie. The Egyptians would say, He was not their brother, they were strangers to him, he but called them his brethren to

serve his purpose, and now he has found a pretext to put them out of the way. Or they would hold me to be a man of no probity. Who plays false with his own kith and kin, how can he keep faith with others? (G 168–9)

This rationale for being merciful, as Midrash conceives it, encapsulates the essential insecurity of the assimilated Jew. He can never be confident that he has done enough to be accepted by the Gentiles, he is constantly made aware that his own merits, however great, will never be sufficient to assure his acceptance among them, and he is obliged at all times to search for ways and means to prove to them that he is indeed worthy of trust and respect. At the same time, he must equally attempt to convince his own people that he is their friend, not their enemy. RaShI explains the biblical narrative's remark that, to still his brothers' fears, Joseph 'comforted them, and spoke kindly to them (*va-yidaber al libam*, literally, 'spoke to their heart')' (Genesis 50:21) as meaning that Joseph appealed to his brothers' reason, which clearly implies their own self-interest as well. Joseph and his brothers need each other as long as they dwell among hostile Gentiles. For all the eminence he has achieved in Egypt, Joseph remains essentially isolated—a dubious alien to the Egyptians, and a potentially hostile agent of retribution to his brothers. The price of assimilation is great, and its gains ambivalent. It is uncomfortable to live with a dual identity.

Joseph's own death and burial confirm the degree of his alienation. He knows that Pharaoh will not allow him to be buried outside Egypt, so he dare not disclose his dying wish. The fear of being accused of double loyalty haunts him even unto death. Having lived as an Egyptian for the greater part of his life, he must die as an Egyptian as well. Although he desires, like his father, to be buried in Canaan with his forebears, he dare not ask this of his own sons. Joseph understood the profound reasons for his dying father's desire, but his own, wholly assimilated sons would be quite incapable of comprehending a similar wish. He therefore turns to his brothers, and '[takes] an oath of the children of Israel', promising them the transactional reward that 'God will surely remember you' (Genesis 50:25) if they were to carry his body out of Egypt for ultimate burial in Canaan when they leave.

But what real reason can Joseph have for wanting to return to Canaan, even in death? There he had been persecuted by his malevolent brothers for seventeen years; for the rest of his life he has lived in Egypt, returning to his homeland only once, to bury his father.

In Egypt, by contrast, his talents and diligence enabled him to achieve the highest pinnacle of earthly success and the greatest fulfilment of all his many gifts. Second in rank only to Pharaoh himself, in Egypt he would be buried with all the honour due to a great man. Why did he not wish to lie in Egypt for ever, but instead strictly charged his brothers to take his body back with them? Perhaps behind his wish to lie with his fathers, behind some loyalty to the land of his birth and the scene of his childhood, is a harsher awareness that for all his assimilation into the ways of Egypt, he would always be a stranger to its people and to its customs, and that he could never wholly change his identity. If he could not achieve a wholly integrated identity in life, perhaps he might affirm it in death.

The biblical narrative of Joseph's life ends with a curious piece of information: 'So Joseph died. [...] And they embalmed him, and he was put in a coffin in Egypt' (Genesis 50:26). Why this emphasis on the fact that his body was put into a coffin, rather than buried? And why stress that this was done 'in Egypt'? One would hardly expect an Egyptian ruler to be buried anywhere else. Firstly, this makes clear that Joseph foresaw rightly that his body would not be permitted to be buried outside Egypt. Secondly, if his embalmed body was not buried, what became of it? The vague generalization, 'in Egypt', suggests that its exact location was unknown. As a result, his brothers' descendants would have experienced considerable difficulty in fulfilling their sworn oath to carry Joseph's bones with them when they left Egypt. The final reburial of Joseph's bones is a matter of considerable importance, for the biblical narrative subsequently refers to it twice. Firstly, it specifically notes that on leaving Egypt, 'Moses took the bones of Joseph with him' (Exodus 13:19); then it precisely records their final resting place: 'And the bones of Joseph which the people of Israel had brought up from Egypt were buried at Shechem, in the portion of ground which Jacob had bought from the sons of Hamor the father of Shechem for a hundred pieces of money; it became an inheritance of the descendants of Joseph' (Joshua 24:32). Why was the coffin's resting-place in Egypt kept secret? And why did it fall to no less a figure than Moses to seek it out and carry it away? In answer to the last question, all the medieval commentators agree that as a reward for his virtue, Joseph had the honour of being taken out of Egypt by Moses, the only Hebrew greater than himself. In answer to the first question, Midrash offers several elaborate

The Master-Narrative 65

explanations, one of which is of particular relevance to the troubling question of Joseph's ambivalent relationship with Egypt and its people: 'The bones of Joseph the Egyptians kept in the treasure-houses of the palace, since their wizards told them that at the departure of Joseph's bones there would be darkness and gloom in the whole land and a great plague on the Egyptians, so that even with a lamp no one could recognize his brother.'[19] As he is preparing himself for death, Joseph is well aware that his brothers will not be allowed to bury him outside Egypt, so he makes them swear an oath to do so at some future time when they will leave Egypt for good. He knows this partly as a result of his knowledge of Egyptian customs, partly because of his awareness of his own ambivalent position in Egypt, and partly—according to this Midrash—because he knows, as do all the other 'wizards' of Egypt, that when his bones are removed from their location in Egypt, ten plagues will fall upon the land, of which the ninth will be absolute darkness. Foreseeing this, the magicians of Egypt seek to prevent the disaster by keeping Joseph's bones hidden and tightly secured in a place known only to themselves. Joseph thus becomes as highly ambivalent in death as he was in life, belonging fully neither to the Egyptians nor to the Hebrews, but situated uneasily between them. Another Midrash on the same theme supports this conclusion with yet a further reason. In his search for Joseph's hidden coffin, Moses is led to the source of Egypt's fertility itself:

Serah [the aged daughter of Joseph's brother Asher] took him [Moses] to the Nile River, and told him that the leaden coffin made for Joseph by the Egyptians had been sunk there after having been sealed up on all sides. The Egyptians had done this at the instigation and with the help of the magicians, who, knowing that Israel could not leave the country without the coffin, had used their arts to put it in a place whence it could not be removed. (G 181–2)

In both *midrashim*, Moses, the only one of the Israelites to recall the oath sworn to Joseph, succeeds in raising the coffin and carrying it away, so that Joseph is finally laid to rest in the land God had promised to his great-grandfather Abraham. Although it would seem that at the end Joseph is returned to his people and their faith, the ambiguity surrounding this first and most dramatic exemplar of assimilation remains. From this ambiguity, in all its many dimensions, the myth of the Jewish pope draws its life.

Notes to Chapter 2

1. James L. Kugel, *In Potiphar's House: The Interpretive Life of Biblical Texts* (San Francisco, 1990), 2.
2. Ibid. 3–4.
3. Barry Hotz, 'Midrash', in Barry Hotz (ed.), *Back to the Sources: Reading the Classic Jewish Texts* (1984; New York, 1992), 178–9, 186.
4. Kugel, *Potiphar's House*, 125.
5. In this chapter all quotations in English from the Bible are given in the translation published in A. Cohen, *The Soncino Chumash* (London, 1979). Citations from the medieval rabbinical commentators are all taken from this edition.
6. All quotations from Midrash are cited from Louis Ginzburg, *The Legends of the Jews*, trans. Henrietta Szold, vol. 2, *From Joseph to the Exodus* (Philadelphia, 1913). Ginzburg's masterly work, compiled over a period of thirty years and published in seven volumes, collects, organizes and retells all the *midrashim* on the whole of the Bible. Ginzburg cites all the Hebrew sources of various *midrashim* on the Joseph story in vol. 5 (Philadelphia, 1925). Henceforth, all citations from Ginzburg appear after the letter G, followed by the relevant page number.
7. See Robert Alter, *The Art of Biblical Narrative* (New York, 1981), 162–3.
8. Ibid. 164.
9. Ibid. 165.
10. Ibid. 166.
11. Ibid. 170.
12. Ibid. 172.
13. David Stern, *Midrash and Theory: Ancient Jewish Exegesis and Contemporary Literary Studies* (Evanston, IL, 1996), 4–5.
14. Kugel, *Potiphar's House*, 102–3.
15. *The Pentateuch*, vol. 1, Genesis, translated and explained by Samson Raphael Hirsch, rendered into English by Isaac Levy, 2nd edn. (Gateshead, 1989), 643.
16. Ibid. 634.
17. See also G 127.
18. Levi Shalit, 'Joseph in Egypt: The Beginning of Jewish Dualism', *Jewish Affairs* 49/2 (Winter 1994), 6–8.
19. Cited in Kugel, *Potiphar's House*, 141.

CHAPTER 3

❖

The *Mayse-bukh* and the Debut of the Myth

The earliest published version of the Jewish pope myth in Yiddish literature appears in the seventeenth-century 'Book of Stories', the *Mayse-bukh*. This anonymous collection of stories, folk tales, jokes and legends originated from a variety of medieval Jewish oral and written traditions, and included material both from Talmudic *aggadah* and Midrash, as well as Judaized material from non-Jewish traditions after the manner of such medieval Christian collections of moral *exempla* as the *Gesta Romanorum*, originally printed about 1473. The *Mayse-bukh* was first compiled in the late sixteenth century, but not before 1580, the year in which the mystic Jacob Luzzatto published his book *Kaftor va-ferah* in Basle, from which the compiler of the *Mayse-bukh* borrowed several stories to supplement his own collection. Many of the narratives, however, were part of a folk tradition deriving from both Western and Eastern sources and passed down orally from generation to generation before they were written down. Of the 255 narratives collected in the volume, 157 are of Talmudic origin, some 27 have their setting in Regensburg, and a number deal with incidents concerning the city of Worms, demonstrating clearly that the work was the product of Ashkenazi Jewry to whom it spoke in an early form of Yiddish.

While a number of published collections of imaginative narratives had existed previously, the earliest extant edition of the *Mayse-bukh*, as it is now known, appeared in Basle in 1602. The printer of this edition, Jacob Pollak—or, as he styled himself on the book's title page, Jacob ben Abraham of Mezhirech—a compiler of religious textbooks, printer, publisher and bookseller, claimed that this was the first edition of the book and that it included more than 300 tales. The collection, which had certainly existed in manuscript earlier, might also have been printed earlier and been abridged before the production of the Basle edition, which in fact includes only 255 tales. The work, chiefly designed for the masses of scantily educated craftsmen, petty traders, journeymen, peddlers and, above all, women, is written in an undemanding style that employs an easily accessible vernacular. It aimed to provide observant but unscholarly Jews with a pious substitute for the widely circulated popular romance literature of the period, which the compiler of the *Mayse-bukh*, among other didactic writers of the time, regarded with contempt as godless and corrupting. Determined to replace secular with religious reading while at the same time making necessary concessions to the popular taste and its craving for entertainment, he sought to offer a new kind of ethical instruction in the vernacular, permeated with a spirit of piety and intended at all times to strengthen the reader's faith. The book imparted to the Jewish folk tale a devout spiritual character that made it agreeable to religious leaders while at the same time delighting the many men and women who engaged with it. Its two dominant motifs—fear of a hostile environment and a belief in magic—signalled the prevailing superstition and the fraught uncertainty of Jewish life in medieval Europe, to counter both of which the tale's moral is made explicit at its conclusion. Homiletic literature of this type exerted an enormous influence on Jewish daily life, since it simultaneously appealed to the imagination, inculcated ethical and spiritual truths, and offered a source of solace and comfort to Jews in times of trouble and despair.

The stories in the *Mayse-bukh* are of three primary types. The main section comprises tales originating in the Talmud and in Midrash, drawn primarily from the *Ein Ya'akov* (1516), the immensely influential collection of narrative material and interpretation abstracted from the Talmud and its earliest commentators by R. Jacob ben Solomon Ibn Habib (?1445–1516). The second category is made up of a cycle of twenty-seven legends designed to offer moral inspiration from the lives and deeds of R. Samuel and his son R. Judah *he-Hasid*, 'the Pious', two great mystics and the authors of the *Sefer Hasidim* (twelfth century), the major ethical treatise produced by the Jews of medieval Germany. The third category consists of a variety of legends concerning Jewish scholars and saints that are often Judaized versions of Christian moral *exempla*, French *contes* or *fabliaux*, and other entertaining anecdotes derived from a wide variety of secular sources. From its first appearance, the *Mayse-bukh* was hugely popular: by 1763, twelve separate new editions had been published. Like the

Tsene-rene (1618), 'Go forth and see, [O daughters of Zion]' (Song of Solomon 3:11), the paraphrase of the Pentateuch designed for unlearned women by Jacob ben Isaac Ashkenazi (1550–1628), the simple, easily identifiable emotions and honest didactic piety of the *Mayse-bukh* were quickly taken to heart by every Jewish person able to read or absorb its contents orally. The *Mayse-bukh* soon proved to be more than a literary text—it established an entire literary school. Up until the end of the eighteenth century, it formed the primary narrative tradition for the whole of Ashkenazi culture, and offered immeasurable inspiration to generations of Yiddish storytellers.[1]

By the end of the sixteenth century, when the *Mayse-bukh* first appeared, the Protestant Reformation had diminished the international dominance of the Catholic Church, but the lot of Jews in Christian Europe had scarcely improved. On the contrary, the ideological thrust of the Church's Counter-Reformation resulted in the determination of the papacy to confine Jews, wherever in Catholic Europe they were permitted to dwell at all, in ghettos, for the privilege of which they had to pay exorbitant taxes while being denied any of the rights of citizens. In the very year in which the *Mayse-bukh* was published, the ghetto was enforced in both Padua and Mantua.[2] The metonymic myth of the Jewish pope consequently waxed vivid in the Jewish consciousness in proportion as the myth of the Wandering Jew grew more grotesque in the Christian mind. At the time the *Mayse-bukh* appeared, this sinister figure, named Ahasuerus, harbinger of calamity, was reportedly sighted in Lübeck (1603) and Paris (1604).[3] Simply by contemplating the conditions of their perilous day-to-day existence, ordinary seventeenth-century Jews had no need of great learning to know either that their lives and property lay at the mercy of violent mobs, or that their right of domicile anywhere in Europe could be withdrawn in a moment; they did not have to be scholars to know that Christians regarded their obduracy as a deadly insult, and that Jewish apostates were their most dangerous foes. They were constantly reminded by their rabbis that chief among their persecutors during the medieval time of terror had been such betrayers of Israel as Pablo Christiani, who had disputed with Nahmanides and had organized public burnings of the Jews' holy books.[4] Thus the appearance of a version of the Jewish pope myth in the *Mayse-bukh* is a matter of more complexity than is covered by the generally accepted view that it is simply a Judaization of one tale from the *Gesta Romanorum*.[5]

Apart from the fact that to locate in the *Gesta* the provenance of every tale in the *Mayse-bukh* is unwaveringly to insist upon Jewish subjectification to Christian interpellation in every dimension of Jewish life, the tale in the *Gesta* which is generally cited as the Jewish model, Number 81, 'Of the birth, life, and death of Pope Gregory',[6] is remarkable chiefly for the fact that its central concerns have nothing whatever to do with the putative Jewish 'reworking'. The two tales emanate from diametrically opposed psychological terrors. In *Gesta* 81, the prodigy ultimately chosen to become pope is the offspring of an incestuous union between brother and sister. Put out to sea by his guilt-stricken mother, this infant is found by the abbot of a monastery, and is given into the care of impoverished foster parents. Discovering by chance the secret of his birth, he leaves the care of the abbot, becomes a knight errant, frees his mother's kingdom from the oppression of an evil duke, and, all unwittingly, marries his mother to protect her realm from further depredations. When this dreadful double incest is revealed, the son-husband isolates himself on an inaccessible rock for seventeen years until a voice from heaven declares that he must be sought out and crowned pope in Rome. This is done, and he becomes Pope Gregory I. Once installed, he gives his mother absolution, makes her an abbess, and, in full penitence, follows her into death shortly thereafter. In Freudian dream-interpretation terms, behind the manifest content of this story, Oedipal in its primacy, lies that latent wish-fulfilment fantasy, common in Christian folklore, of a sexual consummation that defies the most rigorous of all socio-cultural taboos. This latent content is displaced into an acceptable orthodox Christian parable supposedly demonstrating 'the wonderful dispensations of Providence'. Providential determination is indeed the sole idea common to both tales; in all other respects they are so far apart that it is difficult to see how they could ever have been connected.

One possible reason may lie in the fact that, from the point of view of Jewish history, Gregory I (590–604) was the most important of the earlier popes, for it was he who, in both its positive and negative aspects, formulated the papal policy towards the Jews that was to endure for centuries. In his sermons, Gregory deplored the stubbornness of the Jews, and ensured that all existing canonical restrictions on them were fully and severely enforced. He objected to the observances of any church ceremonies that showed the influence of Judaism or that blurred the boundaries between Church and

Synagogue. Though he condemned forced baptisms, he did not oppose rewarding Jewish converts financially for their apostasy, believing that though the parents might be insincere in their conversion, their children would be brought up as believing Christians. Nevertheless, he also censured the burning of synagogues and the desecration of Jewish cemeteries, and insisted that the Jews should be treated with humanity. He attempted to have those legal rights permitted them from pagan times confirmed and respected. In June 598, to Victor, Bishop of Palermo, Gregory wrote: 'Just as one ought not to grant any freedom to the Jews in their synagogues beyond that permitted by law, so should the Jews in no way suffer in those things already conceded to them.' This dictum, which began in Latin with the words *Sicut Judaeis*, was subsequently invoked and repeated in the bulls of later popes.[7]

By striking contrast with the *Gesta* tale, the story in the *Mayse-bukh* grapples with Judaism's ideological demand that incomprehensible providential designs be accepted with perfect faith as ultimately beneficent, despite the fact that their ambiguity continually undercuts such acceptance. Each element of that ambiguity, repeated in every reworking of the myth, is worth reviewing here in relation to its origin in the Joseph paradigm. Pharaoh's Egypt is transformed into Christian Europe, Jacob's son is once more raised to its rulership, but the seed of Jacob must still come as humble petitioners to their own brother. Jacob reappears in the figure of the rabbi-patriarch of his generation with an only son of exceptional intellectual and physical gifts. Abducted in childhood and baptized, this son grows up to govern the lives of those from whom he sprang. Aware of his Jewish origins, yet unwilling to surrender his Gentile power, this son, too, brings his father to an alien land through a trick that forces the parent to kneel in supplication to the child. Hiding his identity throughout this interview with the old rabbi, the young pope confounds him in religious disputation and checkmates him at chess, thus using the learning he acquired in childhood to destroy the parent who bestowed it. In this stark personification of the struggle for Jewish survival, the father (Synagogue) is manifestly no match for the son (Church). Jewish claims of spiritual chosenness, made from a condition of pitiable temporal dependency, are laughed to scorn by Christian counter-claims flourishing unchallengeable worldly dominion as proof.

The central problems inherent in this Joseph-pope tale are hinted at in the master-narrative itself. Some resolutions that have been suggested demonstrate more the desiderata of ideology than the dictates of reality. One germane example can be found in the rabbinical commentaries on Genesis 42:8, *va'yaker yosef et ehav v'heym lo hikiru'hu*, 'And Joseph knew his brethren, but they knew not him.' Unspoken possibilities are pregnant here. Now that Joseph has his brothers at his mercy, there is nothing to stop him from wreaking a terrible vengeance on them. Jewish exegetes, however, content themselves with observing that his siblings knew him not because he was bearded, and was in dress, name, language and bearing an Egyptian. Joseph's singular gifts have enabled him easily to disidentify himself from his brothers and their world. Why does he not punish them? RaShI, quoting from Midrash, deflects the revenge possibility by drawing a contrast between Joseph's values and those of his brothers that implies a correlation between moral and social superiority: 'When they were in his power, he knew them as brothers and was merciful to them, but when he was in their power, they knew him not.'[8] Because the biblical narrative is concerned to illustrate the moral regeneration of wrongdoers through trials of increasing severity, it includes only *exempla* of morally virtuous persons. Hence rabbinical literature consistently designates Joseph as *yosef ha-tzadik*, 'Joseph the Righteous'. Joseph has chosen the morally better way—but he might just as easily not have done so. This is where the pope-tale derivative comes terrifyingly into its own. It raises and contemplates the alternative possibility. When the Jewish pope first sees his rabbi father after a separation of many years, the *Mayse-bukh* relates, *den er kent glaykh zayn foter vi voyl doz im der foter nit kent*, 'then he immediately recognized his father, although his father knew him not'. Having become a Christian Pharaoh, there is, in material terms, absolutely no logical reason why this Joseph should become a Jewish slave once more.

The Yiddish text of the *Mayse-bukh* that I examine here is that of the original edition, enlarged and republished in Amsterdam in 1723.[9] I have also chosen to refer where germane to a modernized Yiddish text of this tale prepared by Jacob Maitlis and published in Buenos Aires in 1969.[10] Although in his introduction to this personal selection from the original *Mayse-bukh* of 1602, Maitlis claims that his modernization involves only 'a minimum of editorial changes and those mainly to do with chronology', comparison with the original text reveals this assertion to be inaccurate in a way interesting for the present study. While his modernization follows the plot of the pope story accurately enough, in search of what he takes to be stylistic elegance Maitlis enlarges and adorns the spare narrative with a number of Talmudic phrases largely absent from the original, which is composed in the Germanized Yiddish known as *taytsh*, the language most readily accessible to the unlearned. In so doing, Maitlis reveals through his 'modernization' an understanding of the extent to which the discourse of Judaism subjectifies its adherents to a depth even more explicit than is present in the original. In significant places, I shall call attention to these textual variants in an attempt to show what they reveal. I have preferred to make my own translations of the quotations I use, although two published English translations are readily available.[11]

The author of the *Mayse-bukh* is the first to recognize that the attraction of the Christian call to convert lies not in its demonstration of superior spiritual capacity but rather in its seductive offers of temporal supremacy. Rendered powerless in body, the Jews attempt to make themselves powerful in spirit, but when the boy, here named with multi-layered irony Elkhanan ('the Lord was gracious'), is raised to the papacy, he is fully prepared to sacrifice the spiritual for the material, and boldly admits as much:

> *mayn libe foter, di vayl ikh bin azoy lang unter goyim gevezn un mikh hob es gevisht dos ikh ayn yehudi bin geborn un di gute teg glaykh du zikhsht di hobn mir derbay gehaltn dos ikh bin nit oys gekumen.*

> My dear father, the reason I have remained this long among Gentiles even though I knew I was born a Jew is because the good days, exactly as you see, retained their hold on me and thus I did not extricate myself from them.

Maitlis's modernized expansion of this passage is even more explicit:

> *ikh bin dokh azoy lang farblibn tvishn goyim, hagam ikh hob gevust az ikh bin a yid, un hob nisht khoyzer betshuve geven. es iz mir gegangen tsu gut, vi du zest, un di gute yorn zaynen geven a gvaldike menie, vos derfar bin ikh nisht frier tsurikgekumen tsu mayn yidishkeyt.*

> I continued to linger indefinitely among Gentiles, for although I knew that I was a Jew, I had no real desire to repent. All went far too well with me, as you see, and the good years were an enormous obstacle, because of which I did not return sooner to my Jewishness.

The *Mayse-bukh*'s narrative voice is also fully aware that Christian claims to have superseded the Jews as possessors of the Covenant demand the elimination of Jews *qua* Jews. Thus he shows the motives of the zealous *shabes-goye* in abducting the child Elkhanan to spring from complete conviction that, given the truth of her faith against the speciousness of the Jewish faith, she has a holy duty to baptize the faithless:

also nam di goye dos kind un tsug mit im avek un tsit dos kind shmadn. do meynt zi nun zi het eyn kurbm gibrakht den fartsaytn hobn zih gor fil oyf dos shmadn gihaltn.

Thus the Gentile woman took the child and carried him away to be converted. In this way she believed she had now brought a sacrifice, for in those days they dearly loved the act of conversion.

Embedded in the *Mayse-bukh* narrative are two interdependent ideological assumptions about Jewish identity that manifest the effect of Christian subjectification from without, and Jewish subjectification from within. Once the talented Jewish boy has been snatched away from Jews, *es ging im azoy gor voyl doz er unter goyim blib glaykh men voyl gedenken kon*, 'it went so well with him in consequence of his remaining among Gentiles, as one can easily imagine'. From this 'easily imagined' supposition follows the conviction in the minds of Jewish readers that the world known to Christians must obviously be more attractive than that known to Jews. Their faith indoctrinates Jews to accept as unalterably normative all the misfortunes that befall them in this world, for they are sinners not only in Christian eyes, but—more importantly—in their own. R. Shimen's serving-maid announces that his son has been abducted *bavoyneseynu-horabim*, 'on account of our many sins'. In immediate response, *r. shimen fastet tog un nakht*, 'fasted day and night' in the manner prescribed by centuries of rabbinic law, since the tragedy appears to him self-evidently the punishment of a just God. In catering to its readers' demands for thrilling supernatural adventures, the *Mayse-bukh* measures R. Shimen's great saintliness in proportion to his possession of great magical powers, and hangs three legendary mirrors in his house: *do hot er als drinen gezehn vos geshehn iz un vos geshehn zol*, 'there he was able to see everything that had come to pass and that would still come to pass.' These magic mirrors, however, are now useless to assist him, for *hakadosh borukh hu hot es far im farhalt vu dos kind iz hinkumen*, 'the Holy One, Blessed be He, withheld from him where his son had disappeared to.' Never in this tale is a question posed to challenge the justice of this, never does a moment of anger flash out that the only reward for scrupulous piety seems to be pointless affliction. On the contrary, when the discriminatory papal edict forbidding Jews to practise the central rites of their faith arrives, R. Shimen is foremost in leading his community along the well-worn path: *fil meshtadl zayn bay dem hegemon*, 'to plead greatly for intercession from the bishop', and then *geyn nokh rom doz er bay den afifyor mekht meshtadl zayn*, 'to go to Rome that he might plead for intercession from the pope'. Significantly, the *Mayse-bukh* employs Talmudic words of Greek derivation to designate these Christian notables, *hegemon* for 'bishop' and *afifyor* for 'pope', in this way placing them firmly in the realm of the foreign and the hostile. Maitlis, by contrast, by employing the Germanisms *bishof* and *poyps*, tends to naturalize these offices through discourse, and thus removes the alienating menace implied in the older language of the *Mayse-bukh*.

In preparation for their only-to-be-expected degradation, the Jews again respond in the only way their ideology permits, with fasting, prayer and the giving of alms to the poor, as the best means of averting the evil decree. The response of the Roman Jews to the plight of their Mainz brethren is informed by the same self-censuring principle: *dos muz ayn far zinde zakh bay aykh in taytshland zayn*, 'this must be as a result of some sinful doing among you Jews in Germany'. Their conditioned response is to confront brutal reality with wishful thinking: *filaykht vert inen hakadosh borukh hu eyn neys ton*, 'perhaps the Holy One, Blessed be He, would perform a miracle'. Diaspora Jews are shown to have been rendered incapable of conceiving themselves as other than twofold subjects, their identity determined for them by the discourses of both Christianity and Judaism.

Consciously or not, the *Mayse-bukh* narrator understands this perfectly, as his depiction of the malevolent behaviour of the Jewish pope demonstrates. This apostate, fully conversant with Judaism's central ideological underpinnings, strikes the Jews mortally by forbidding the performance of those primary commandments by which they identify what a Jew is:

do shraybt er eyn briv nokh ments an den hegemon [...] doz er zolt den yuden farbitn keyn shabes tsu haltn nokh keyn kind yudshn tsu lozn un keyn froy nit tvile tsu geyn.

The pope wrote a letter to the bishop in Mainz [...] instructing him to forbid the Jews from observing any Sabbath or from circumcising any child or permitting any woman to go to a ritual bath.

The Old Law is replaced with the New by a fiat from a Jewish apostate who then confronts the Mainz delegation, led by his father, with the time-honoured accusation of all Jew-haters: sinister accusations against the Jews have reached him from Mainz, leaving him no alternative but to ban the practice of Judaism. No reports about Jews can be too bad either for Christians to believe or for Jews to accept. They are ever ready to suffer any injustice wrought against them by man in the belief that this must be the just visitation of God.

Because the Jewish narrator of this tale has been constituted in the same self-negating way, the discourse of his narrative persists in sustaining this ideology despite the fact that it simultaneously dramatizes its appalling consequences. The supremely gifted Elkhanan, marked out from early youth as a natural leader, is shown to be ruthlessly capable of turning blessed means to cursed ends. The matter-of-fact description of the proselyte pope in learned disputation with the pious rabbi nakedly expresses that anxiety most deeply embedded in the legend:

der afifyor hab mit dem r. shimen on tsu reydn eyn pilpul dos er den r. shimen hagodl khas vesholem shier hot menatseyekh gevezn dos im zelbst vunder nom doz ayn zelkhn leyb unter goyim zol zayn.

The pope began a debate on a point of [Talmudic] law with R. Shimen in which he almost, God forbid, vanquished R. Shimen, and the rabbi himself was amazed that such a living being should exist among Gentiles.

The narrative also tellingly transforms a game of chess into a metaphor for spiritual battle. This game of chess, and the narrative's emphasis on one secret move known only between father and son, is the most significant of the motifs added to the developing Jewish pope myth. This secret move is a secular substitute for that Midrashic interpolation that establishes a secret code between Joseph and his father, enabling the aged Jacob to know for certain that his long-lost son is indeed alive. Joseph sends his brothers back to Jacob with a message regarding 'the heifer whose neck must be broken in the valley'. This is a reference to the last section of the Torah that Joseph was supposedly studying with Jacob before he disappeared, and is known only to the two of them. In the pope myth, we meet this motif for the first time at the very end of the *Mayse-bukh*'s narrative, when we learn that:

der r. shimen hagodl hot den zun gekent an shakh tsovl den er hot im eyn tsug gelernt do er nokh kleyn var un den zelbign tsug hot er in mit dem foter geton. do hot er gemerkt das dos zayn zun iz gevezn.

R. Shimen the Great recognized his son in the game of chess for he had taught him a move when he was still a small boy, and now he [the son] made the same move with his father. Through this he [the father] recognized that this was his son.

Since chess and its moves continue to be used in a number of literal and metaphorical ways throughout the Jewish pope myth, it is worth glancing at the way the game achieved high regard among Jews.

Originating in Persia, chess first became known to Jews in tenth-century Spain when the Arab conquerors introduced it into Europe. While the specific names of chess pieces vary from language to language, the designation of their functions, and the symbolic forces they represent, have remained constant. The designation given to the King always bore the title given to the local ruler; the Queen was named the 'consort' or 'mistress', while the Knight was always a horseman, and the Pawns always foot-soldiers. The Rook ('rock') always represented a fortress, and only the Bishop, as the piece became known in the West, was clearly a Christian appellation designed to find a place in battle for the Church; in its Persian origin, the piece was designated according to its function, as a fast mover, an elephant in Persian or a 'runner' (*Läufer*) in German.[12] In Spain, the great scholar Abraham Ibn Ezra (1092–1167) learnt and enjoyed chess, even describing the game in a poem, but his gratification was not initially approved by other rabbis. Maimonides (R. Moses ben Maimon, Spain/Egypt, 1135–1204), in his commentary on the Mishnah for example, condemned it when played for money, and the *Halakhah* censured it for being a profitless waste of time, scorning it as fit only for women and invalids. By the eighteenth century, however, the game had grown in status; earlier, R. Moshe Isserles (Poland, c.1520–72) held that, as long as it was not played for money, it was a fitting pastime for observant Jews and could even be played on the Sabbath. A long tradition subsequently grew up of intellectual and pious Jews studying the Torah and seeking their recreation in playing chess, among them devout rabbis of the greatest learning, like R. Elijah ben Solomon, the Vilna Gaon (Lithuania, 1720–97). Apart from the intellectual skill required to play the game properly, Jews might well have found it attractive because by metonymically representing the engagement of two armies that were potentially equally powerful, it fed a consolatory fantasy that they might one day triumph in real life as they so often triumphed on the game board.

In accordance with an established Jewish tradition, therefore, R. Shimen is presented as a chess-player of unsurpassed ability, *doz men zayn glakhn nit fond in gatntsn oylem*, 'whose equal could not be found in the whole world', *nokh matet im der afifyor*, 'yet the pope checkmated him'. Shock, *shrok*, and amazement, *vunder*, is the rabbi's ongoing response. To the spare use of these two words in the *Maysebukh*'s original text, Maitlis adds emphasis in his modernization: there the pope's learning leaves R. Shimen *zitsn a farbliepter*, 'stunned'; the pope's skill at chess *hot dos r. shimen gvaldik gekhidusht*, 'violently astounded [him]'; *er hot poshet geshtoynt*, 'he was left starkly agape' by the pope's profound theology. The effect of this shock is profoundly destabilizing, rooted as it is in terror that Christianity may be as intellectually more powerful than Judaism as it is temporally, and that consequently the sibling religion may be possessed of greater truth than its parent.

In discussing these victories of pope over rabbi, David Lerner holds that 'to the medieval Jewish audience, which knew his true identity, the pope's victory over his father—like the amazing intellect demonstrated by the pope in his discussions with the rabbi—merely reinforced a message of Jewish superiority'.[13] While this may perhaps be the narrator's overt intention, however, it seems to me that fear of the contrary possibility represents the tale's effective subtext and unconscious impetus. Moreover, nowhere in the Yiddish text of the *Mayse-bukh* version is there any evidence to support Lerner's contention that 'the second discussion between R. Shim'on and the pope [...] is an intellectually exciting exchange in which each party learns from the other and enjoys the experience'.[14] On the contrary, its repeated narrative assertions of stupefaction and pious expostulations deny this reading.

The *Mayse-bukh* presents R. Shimen as a folk-hero whose moral credentials and daily doings are the stuff from which midrashic legends are made. He is throughout described with the cognomen *hagodl*, 'the Great' in learning and piety, and right from the beginning of the tale we are told that, apart from his magic mirrors, *okh hot er gehat tsu koppn oys zayn keyver oyf dem bes-khayim eyn kval brunen aroys gin*, 'he also had at the head of his grave on the cemetery a spring of fresh water bubbling forth'. To these bare details in the original, Maitlis, in his modernization, adds some stylistic additions that are revealing of his understanding of the tale's import. His repeated introduction of Hebrew or *loshn-koydesh* phrases of Talmudic origin, almost wholly absent from the original, permits Maitlis—in the mid-twentieth century—to buttress the dominant discourse of orthodoxy. He adds to the original's enumeration of R. Shimen's gifts asides like *keyedue*, 'as it is known', *yesh omrim*, 'there are those who say'; events befall the rabbi-father *beshas*, 'in the [divinely appointed] hour [in which they are meant to happen]'; R. Shimen sees clearly from the way the pope plays chess that this Christian springs *mizera ha-yehudim*, 'from the seed of Jews'. In Maitlis's version, the arrival of the injurious papal decree is introduced with the portentous biblical phrase, *va'yehi hayoym*, 'and the day came to pass [in accordance with the Will of the Almighty]'. The intellectual gifts of the Jewish pope make him a *melumed*, one learned in secular (Gentile) matters, as opposed to a *lamdn*, one learned in holy (Jewish) matters. Maitlis goes beyond the *Mayse-bukh* in his narrative embellishments, but the effect of both original and modernization is the same—both are meant to fortify the reader's faith that everything happens with God's foreknowledge for the ultimate good of the Jewish people. How good ends can best be achieved by evil means remains a mystery submitted to with unquestioning faith. No real questions dare to be asked, because—of course—no real answers can be provided.

The hope to which religious ideology has always directed Jews is the coming of the Messiah, of whom a Jewish pope may well be the legendary precursor. Hence the narrative introduces the wishful fantasy that when the pope quits Rome to return to his people, he uses his power to better their earthly lot:

alzo makht der afifyor eyn seyfer virot di emune un shlist es in eyn gevelb un makht velkher der afifyor zolt vern der muz drinen leynen. es iz nun fil derfun tsu shraybn vos in dem zelbige seyfer shteyt.

Thus the pope composed a [holy] book concerning faith and locked it in a chamber and decreed that whoever would become pope was obliged to read in it. There is now much to write about what is contained in that book.

Since the apostate returns to Judaism, he can write a *seyfer* rather than a *bukh*, now made especially holy since, we are meant to understand, it deplores Christianity and exalts Judaism. While this fiction satisfies the tale's overtly homiletic purpose, it does nothing to dispel the fearful dangers implicit in the actual events. What might have happened had the son used his talents to destroy Jewry, as his menacing decree gave every indication of doing? In what way does a reacceptance of degraded exile dispel the temptation to flee it? There is unintentional mordancy in the narrative's assurance that when the pope resumes the faith of his fathers, he comes provided not only with greater spiritual, but also material, means to live it. If he must return to Jewish slavery, let it at least be with some of the benefits of Egyptian kingship:

un nit lang dernokh heybt er zikh oyf mit groysn mammon un tsit nokh ments un vird vider eyn khoshever yehudi un tsu rom hot men nit gevisht vu er iz hin kumen.

A short while later he [the pope] rose up with a great treasure of money and returned to Mainz and became again an important Jew and in Rome it was not known what had become of him.

Why he chooses to do this is of course never explained, since for Jews a spiritual virtue must always be made out of a temporal necessity. Thus the pope, led falsely astray, must as a matter of ideological course recognize the error of his ways and make the only-to-be-expected penitential return to the true faith. Nevertheless, disquieting questions continue to lurk within both text and subtext. The tale's conjunction of events unconsciously bespeaks a dread that if divine intentionality exists at all, it need not necessarily be favourably disposed towards the Jews. The exact moment at which the boy is handed over to priests is distressingly recorded as when *ider vird even in der shul gevezn*, 'every [Jewish] person was even then at prayer in the synagogue'. Jewish piety is shown to provide no protection against Gentile menace. Elkhanan's first observation after he has revealed himself to his father sounds the possible absence of divine favour too closely for comfort:

ikh bin dayn zun elkhonen der dir farloren iz gevordn durkh di shabes-goye. dos ikh nun zol zogn vos di aveyre iz, oder vi es iz, dos kon ikh nit visn. ikh denk hashem yisborakh hot es azoy veln hobn.

I am your son Elkhanan who was lost to you on account of the Gentile woman who came to light the Sabbath fire. I cannot now say what the sin was, or how it is; that I cannot know. I think the Holy One, Blessed be He, wanted it to be this way.

The *Mayse-bukh* narrator spares no effort to quiet these menacing incomprehensibilities by setting them within a framework of readily identifiable orthodox signifiers. By the end of the tale it is clear why in the opening few sentences we have been told that after R. Shimen's death, at the head of his grave in the cemetery in Mainz, a fresh spring of water gushed forth. Directly invoking the imagery of Psalm 1:3, which is used in the Ashkenazi burial service, this detail literally manifests the figurative Waters of Life that flow from the Torah, from which R. Shimen *hagodl*, great in knowledge of the Law, drank abundantly during his life.

As a parallel, the tale's closing sentences hasten to inform us that, with his son's return,

oyf dos mayse hot r. shimen hagodl gemakht eyn yoytser fun rosheshone (el hanan nahlato be'noam le'hashper) derhalbn zolt ir nit meynen dos es shlekhste zakhn zunder; es iz gevis geshehn vi es do shteyt.

in respect of this story, R. Shimen the Great composed an intercessionary prayer for the New Year, 'The Lord was gracious to his inheritance, he gave them a goodly portion', so that you should not think that the worst things happen randomly; everything transpired exactly as it is related here.

By adroitly linking the meaning of the returned apostate's name, Elkhanan, to the opening words of one of the oldest *piyyutim*, liturgical poems, in the Ashkenazi liturgy for *Rosh ha-Shanah*, 'the Lord was gracious',[15] the *Mayse-bukh* narrator is able piously to justify the ways of God to Jews, concluding with the only hope that can make exiled subjection endurable: *hakadosh barukh hu zol unz unzer aveyres fargebn durkh r. shimen zayn zkhus omeyn selah*, 'May the Holy One, Blessed be He, forgive us our sins through the merit of R. Shimen, Amen Selah'. Such an ending, while it may satisfy received rabbinical doctrine, is merely a palliative, soothing the symptoms of unease without ever diagnosing a cause resident in the irreconcilable tensions between the real workings of the world and the way in which conflicting ideologies interpret them.

Notes to Chapter 3

1. Charles A. Madison, *Yiddish Literature: Its Scope and Major Writers* (New York, 1971), 1–9; *Encyclopaedia Judaica*, xi. 649–51; Jacob Maitlis, *The Ma'aseh in the Yiddish Ethical Literature* (London, 1958), 5–11.
2. Paul Johnson, *A History of the Jews* (London, 1987), 244.
3. Ibid. 233.
4. See Jeremy Cohen, 'The Mentality of the Medieval Jewish Apostate: Peter Alfonsi, Hermann of Cologne, and Pablo Christiani', in Todd M. Endelman (ed.), *Jewish Apostasy in the Modern World* (New York and London, 1987), 20–47.
5. This general view has been argued by Moses Gaster (ed. and trans.), *Ma'aseh Book* (Philadelphia, 1934), Introduction, pp. xvii-xliii; and by Maitlis, *Ma'aseh*. Maitlis specifically names Tale 81 of the *Gesta Romanorum* as the source of the Jewish pope myth in the notes to his Yiddish modernization: see Yakov Maitlis (ed.), *Mayse-bukh: 84 dertseylungen*, vol. 36 of Shmuel Rozhansky (gen. ed.), *Musterverk fun der yidisher literatur* (Buenos Aires, 1969), 203–4.
6. *Gesta Romanorum*, translated by Charles Swan, revised and corrected by Wynnard Hoooper (1876; New York, 1959), 141–54.

7. Jacob Marcus (ed.), *The Jew in the Medieval World* (New York, 1974), 113; *Encyclopaedia Judaica*, v. 919; *Encyclopaedia Judaica*, xiii. 853.
8. A. Cohen (ed.), *The Soncino Chumash* (London, 1979), 262.
9. *Ma'ase-bukh*, St. 3902, Opp. 40. 1410, Bodleian, listed Cowley p.406.
10. Yakov Maitlis (trans. and ed.), 'Der yidisher poyps', in *Mayse-bukh: 84 dertseylungen* (Buenos Aires, 1969), 194–204.
11. The first is in Nathan Ausubel (ed.), *A Treasury of Jewish Folklore* (New York, 1948), 576–81, republished from A. Löwy (ed.), *Miscellany of Hebrew Literature*, 2 vols. (London, 1872–7). The second is in Moses Gaster (ed. and trans.), *Ma'aseh Book*, 2 vols. (Philadelphia, 1934), Tale No. 188, 'The Jewish Child who was Stolen by a Servant and Later became Pope', ii. 410–18.
12. *Encyclopaedia Judaica*, v. 401–7.
13. Lerner, 'Enduring Legend', 157.
14. Ibid. 169.
15. The *piyyut* begins *or olam b'otzar hayyim*, 'The Eternal Light in the treasures of everlasting life [...]'. See A. T. Philips (trans. and ed.), *Mahzor l'Rosh ha-Shanah/Prayer Book for the New Year* (New York, 1931), 181–2.

CHAPTER 4

❖

Ayzik-Meir Dik, Reformer through Fiction

Ayzik-Meir Dik (1807–93) or AMaD, as his favourite acronym proclaimed him on the title page of hundreds of story-books, was not only the earliest professional Yiddish writer—he was the first to earn a (meagre) living from his pen—but also the first to write best-sellers.[1] He was born around 1807 in Vilnius, Lithuania, where his father was a cantor who, refusing to take a salary for holy work, earned his living as a grain dealer. The young Ayzik-Meir received the traditional Jewish education of *kheyder* and *yeshive*, proving himself an apt student; later he also helped his father to run his business. He married young, settling in the Lithuanian town of Ziupronys where he lived a comparatively wild life, taking part in the kind of carousing which, while commonplace today, was startlingly at variance with the behaviour expected of a pious *yeshive-bokher* in his age and world. Dik's first wife died early and childless, and he soon remarried. His second wife was the daughter of a well-to-do householder from the important Lithuanian political and cultural centre of Nesvyzius, a town in which Dik and his wife lived as long as his father-in-law supported them. In this marriage, too, there were problems. Dik's in-laws were staunch Hasidim, while Dik himself despised Hasidism, regarding it as almost akin to idolatry.

In Nesvyzius, Dik made the acquaintance of the local Catholic priest who taught him to read in German; he taught himself Polish and Russian. In this town, where Dik was virtually the only *maskil*, he became increasingly convinced of the necessity for making Jews critically aware of the superstition and primitivism that pervaded their traditional way of life. Militantly rationalistic, Dik early became convinced that the twin curses of Jewish life in Eastern Europe were Hasidism and the refusal of Jews to acquire Western education. An excellent Hebraist himself, Dik personally despised Yiddish as a literary medium, believing—like so many of his contemporaries—that while the true language of Jews was Hebrew, they should also make every effort to acquire German, which he regarded as the language of Western culture. He openly proclaimed his own maskilic allegiance in the way he spelled his name: not Yitskhok, as would have been its Ashkenazi Hebrew pronunciation, but Ayzik, as the name would have been pronounced in the West.

At the end of the 1830s Dik and his family returned to his birthplace, Vilnius, where he was to spend the rest of his life. There he enthusiastically pursued his own secular education, sharing wholeheartedly in the work of other Vilnius *maskilim*. They established not only a cultural circle but a maskilic synagogue called *Tohoros hakoydesh* (The Purification of Holiness), the services at which aimed to free the Ashkenazi liturgy from folk usages which had, in their view, gradually debased it. In addition, Dik started publishing scholarly articles in Hebrew, promoting the aims of the *Haskalah*. To the same end, Dik corresponded with the Russian minister of education, Count Sergius Uvarov, urging the necessity for Jewish school reform; when the tsarist government permitted the first Jewish folk school to open in Vilnius in 1841, Dik eagerly accepted a comparatively well-paid teaching position there, and spent the next thirteen years of his life in dedicated service to it.

Passionately determined to reform Jewish life, Dik was one of a group of Vilnius *maskilim* who on 23 July 1843 petitioned the district governors of the Pale of Settlement to prohibit the wearing of traditional Jewish dress.[2] This petition evidently accorded with the views of the Russian government itself, which in 1835 had banned Jews from contracting marriages between girls under sixteen and boys under eighteen,[3] and the clothing decree was accordingly issued in 1844. In 1846, when Sir Moses Montefiore visited Vilnius, Dik was among those who submitted to him a scathing report on 'The State of the City of Vilnius in These Times' which blamed repressive Russian policy for the desperate economic plight of the Jews.[4]

Such high-profile 'modern' activities drove the strictly orthodox Jews of Vilnius to denounce Dik to the authorities; as a result he was imprisoned for a short while. Influential friends interceded on his behalf with the governor of the province, and he was soon released. Like so many other *maskilim*, including the Hebrew poet Y. L. Gordon (1831–92), Dik's faith in *Aufklärung* made him an ardent supporter of the liberal reforms of Tsar Alexander II (1855–81), during whose reign Dik produced his best works, all single-mindedly extolling Westernization. Believing as he did that the best thing that could have happened to Poland was its incorporation into the Russian empire, Dik was also convinced that the new tsar's progressive zeal would bring the Jews into modern European life as equal citizens. He was determined to throw all his energy into assisting this process, so that in 1861 he declared that he would henceforth 'degrade the honour of [his] pen' to write in Yiddish 'for the benefit of our women whose eyes look only into a *taytsh-khumesh* written in a language of stammerers which includes unseemly passages that should never be uttered by the mouths of pious women and maidens'.[5] He wanted to expose the unlearned, especially women, to a practical morality different from the only other kind available to them in medieval books of simplistic piety approved for their reading by the orthodox patriarchy, ancient romances and Hasidic wonder tales—all of which Dik believed inculcated only credulity and eroticism. He dedicated his own work to the service of that political, social and cultural emancipation he believed was being promoted by the tsar's new policies. Consequently, his bitterness at their failure, and at the severe repression which followed Alexander's assassination—most markedly against the Jews themselves—was, like that of all his progressive Jewish contemporaries, concomitantly greater.

Dik was among the earliest of the *maskilim* to understand the tremendous significance of mass Jewish emigration to America, and he urged many of his friends and acquaintances—among them the young Alexander Harkavy (1863–1939), who could later lay claim to having taught English, virtually single-handedly, to the whole of Yiddish-speaking America through the numerous dictionaries and study manuals he compiled and published—to go, especially in the wake of intensified anti-Jewish persecution following the promulgation of the May Laws of 1882. Dik believed passionately that only in a new world, far from the old, could the Jews grow into a better people. Yet he did not support early Zionism, and—again like Y. L. Gordon—was an opponent of the *Hibat Zion* movement.

Dik lived his whole life in straitened circumstances, emotionally aggravated by the fact that he and his wife were never happy together. Nevertheless, his modest apartment was always spotlessly clean. Dik took upon himself all the most burdensome household chores, and went in person to shop in the market, holding that it was not a proper

Jewish attitude for men to regard such work as beneath them. Despite his advanced views, though, Dik gradually came to be held in great esteem and affection by the larger Jewish world of Vilnius because of his honesty, integrity and affability. His aphorisms and witticisms, both in daily speech and in his writing, become widely celebrated. No doubt the fact that he himself remained strictly observant all his life contributed greatly to the respect he earned among the great majority of Vilnius Jews who did not share his ideals. When he found that the 'reformed' synagogue he had helped to found began attracting ignorant boors seeking a lax form of observance, he resigned from it; visitors to his home regularly found him wearing a skullcap and poring over Midrash. Surprisingly to a modern eye, Dik did not see any contradiction in simultaneously holding what were, for the time, almost blasphemously heretical views on the course modern Jewry should follow, and organizing his personal life strictly in accordance with orthodox observance. When the school in which he taught was closed in 1864, Dik suffered still greater material hardship. Much as he despised what such work involved, he was compelled to try to make ends meet by relying on the pawn brokerage his wife ran from their own apartment, and even on some money-lending on a minor scale.[6] His dire financial position drove him to seek additional income from his pen, and he attempted to survive by writing stories that he initially sold to Warsaw publishers for a pittance.

The problems faced by the earliest nineteenth-century writers of Yiddish fiction were compounded by the fact that the pitifully few Jewish publishers licensed by the tsarist government generally refused to take secular writing. Jewish printing, like every other aspect of Jewish life under Russian rule, was severely harassed. It had been permitted under Catherine II in 1783, was forbidden under Alexander I after 1815, but was allowed again, subject to stringent censorship, under Nicholas I at the beginning of 1837. *Maskilim* who wanted to publish books had either to send them to Germany at great expense, or to rely on all manner of subterfuge to disguise them as *sforim*, books of rabbinical piety. This disguise—all too often penetrated, and resulting in the wholesale destruction by outraged Jewish conservatives of the *bikhlekh* thus unmasked—was chiefly assumed in the use of traditional typography, extensive employment of Hebrew on title page and preamble, and fulsome stylistic parades of the formulas of rabbinical discourse.

One of the great Jewish publishing houses of Eastern Europe was that of Borukh Romm, which had been founded in Vilnius in 1799, and remained under Romm family control until the outbreak of the Second World War. Until late in the nineteenth century, the house of Romm remained a stronghold of orthodoxy, and normally rejected maskilic works outright. Dik was the first reformer whose writing they decided to take. Yet even after Dik had signed a contract with this eminent firm, his financial position remained uncertain because the production of much of his work was delayed for up to seven years in consequence of a quarrel between Romm's widow and her sons. Eventually, however, when these difficulties had been sorted out, Dik gained a scanty competence and Romm proved to have made a publishing decision of exceptional shrewdness: Dik's work immediately became, and for decades remained, its major source of income. Such was the demand for Dik's story-books that in 1865 Romm enticed the author into a contract to provide a story every week. Among the specifications of this contract was a clause that gave the publishers exclusive rights 'even to a single page which he might write in Yiddish'. Although this agreement lapsed after a year and was never renewed, Dik was content to leave everything he wrote in the hands of Romm for the rest of his life. For every one of the over four hundred books he produced, they paid him the flat rate of four roubles each, without any royalties, even though these publications subsequently sold hundreds of thousands of copies. Each book was issued first in an edition of between four and six thousand, and book peddlers disposed of them in the market-place on Fridays. Housewives preparing for the Sabbath soon came to include a copy of Dik's latest book among their purchases.

In the last years of his long life—one that covered almost the whole of the nineteenth century and made him a contemporary of all the founders of what may justly be called modern Jewish literature—Dik was seriously ill and virtually indigent, since his only son could not afford to support him and no public money could be raised on his behalf. Before he died, Dik made his son promise not to permit any public recognition of his passing. So strictly did his son observe this wish that when the old man died in 1893, his funeral was not announced, and he was privately buried in the new Jewish cemetery in Vilnius. Only a tombstone erected later testified to the gigantic literary contribution he had made.

Between 1860 and 1870, Dik produced his most influential stories. Eager to reach the widest possible audience, Dik, despite his contempt for the literary capacity of the language, wrote in Yiddish; careful not to alienate pious traditionalists, he deliberately cultivated a style characterized by the moralizing strain that typified the earliest Yiddish chapbooks, writing a somewhat archaic but homely prose laced with German and Russian expressions. 'To demolish an old building,' he remarked in explanation, 'one must use a heavy pickaxe, not a golden needle.'[7] In this choice of both language and style, forced upon him by the exigencies of traditional orthodoxy and the ever-watchful eye of its rabbinical censors, Dik—as David Roskies has shown—developed narrative strategies and modes of discourse that employ traditional forms only in order to subvert them. One of Dik's favourite modes inevitably became parody; the genre he unavoidably found most congenial was satire. His determination to 'uplift' his readers by enlarging their vocabulary and raising their general literacy, and his urge to drag them head-first into enlightenment, led him to employ German and Russian words and phrases which he elaborately explained in Yiddish parentheses throughout his texts. These innovations pleased neither his readers nor his publishers—consumers of popular fiction have never taken kindly to having 'improvement' thrust upon them when they are only seeking entertainment—but Dik's unquestioned gifts as a storyteller ensured that he remained popular in spite of his intentions.

In almost all his work in Yiddish, Dik's plain purpose was to show Jewish people ways of equipping themselves to play a productive role in the modern world. In his lengthy introductions, and sometimes even in the middle of his stories, he offered thought-provoking opinions about contemporary Jewish educational, cultural, social and moral life. He relentlessly attacked those traditional institutions he abhorred: child marriages, for example, the suppression of which he wholeheartedly supported in 1835. He vehemently rejected that *altheymish* value system which esteemed as meritorious the practice of sending wives out into the market-place to become the family breadwinners while their husbands split Talmudic hairs in the study-house. He justly recognized that, by abetting this inverse dependency, normative Eastern European orthodoxy made itself complicit with tsarist discrimination against the Jews. Such a system of economic degradation and systematic impoverishment intensified the curse of Jewish unemployment because it denied both opportunity and demand for skilled vocational training. For Dik, true rabbinical Judaism demanded that a man should combine Torah study with business acumen, should develop vocational or entrepreneurial skills alongside and in equal proportion to the skills of scholarship, and should become, in short, economically independent and concomitantly socially dignified.

Yet Dik was too much of a craftsman either to let moralizing subsume the narrative tension essential to a good tale, or to disregard the techniques necessary for spinning it as suspensefully as possible. His yarns crackle with intrigue, villainy and charlatanism, and, though virtue always wins out in the end, his evocation of vice is disturbingly true to life. Intimately familiar with the daily lives of ordinary folk, possessed of an exhaustive knowledge of Ashkenazi folk customs, with a sharp eye and an exceptionally retentive memory, Dik greatly assisted the cultural awakening of Lithuanian Jewry, faithfully holding a mirror up to traditional Jewish life, while urgently pointing the way in which it ought to be improved.

The greater majority of Dik's tales are addressed to his 'dear lady reader'. The reasons for this apostrophe have been variously interpreted. Unquestionably, Dik did primarily address himself to women, in hopes of weaning them away from their well-thumbed fantasy fables to a diet of reading matter which, through entertainment, might simultaneously provide serious educational and moral advancement. But at the same time, Dik was too shrewd not to be aware that new books lying about a house, printed in the latest square block typeface called *ivre-taytsh* and vocalized to boot, would be readily accessible to men of limited learning as well. And if to them, why not also to learned men of a maskilic bent? These latter would immediately identify not only the propagandistic purpose of the books' contents, but also—more importantly—the materials from which they had been shaped, and the degree to which these traditional materials had been subverted. Establishment-approved reading matter long available in *sforim* (holy books) could in this way be made to serve a radically alternative purpose: a mere *bikhl* (story book) might be transformed into a new kind of *sefer*, and those among the learned who might be discovered glancing into one need not be compromised, since it could always be discountenanced as contemptibly fit only for women. Thus there is something too ingenuous in Zalmen Reyzen's claim that the '*tayere lezerin*' became Dik's chosen addressee because the author, in his modesty, believed that his work was too lightweight to command a serious readership. Proof to the contrary lies in the fact that his stories were indeed highly popular among learned *maskilim* who delightedly unearthed in them not only 'rich mines of ethnography and folklore', as Reyzen has it, but their calculated subversiveness. The areas these story-books demarcated opened up vast fields for further creative exploration. The literary games in which they engaged, the narrative strategies derived from a cunning exploitation of intertextuality that they developed, were so innovative that they challenged all who read them: Dik's influence is writ large all over subsequent Yiddish fiction from Mendele Moykher Sforim to Isaac Bashevis Singer. Dik's Yiddish style, too, despite its intrusive Germanisms and Russianisms, is replete with folk wisdom, proverbs and wisecracks on which Sholem Aleykhem, who mined the same vein, placed the highest value, describing Dik as 'the richest belletrist' in Yiddish. Later, the authoritative Yiddish critic Shmuel Niger perceptively noted that Dik 'sometimes forgot that he was a reformer and told a story for its own sake'.[8] What that 'sake' was, of course, is a matter that engages the fascinated attention of every student of Yiddish literature today.

Dik's version of the Jewish pope myth, a product of his best period, was first published in Vilnius in 1874. On the title page, reprinted as this book's frontispiece, the following information is given in both Yiddish and Russian:

> Rabbi Shimon Barbun,
> the Rabbi of Mainz
> or The Tripartite Dream
>
> In addition there are presented here two other small true narratives:
> one concerning the MaHaRaM of Rothenberg;
> the second concerning two young folk, good friends.
> All three moreover true and rare;
> moving, and for a moral purpose:
> by AMaD.
>
> VILNA
> Published by the Widow
> and the Brothers Romm,
>
> Shmutsky Lane,
> in the Houses Nos. 327–328.
>
> Permitted by the censorship
> 13 March 1874, Vilnius.

Dik's concern in the two concluding *mayselekh*, as it is in the major story which precedes them, is to challenge the widespread belief that dreams are to be dreaded because they have prophetic power.[9] For the purveyor of maskilic ideals, who happens also to be a believing Jew, such a task presents serious difficulties, because the sacred truth contained in dreams, and the divine purposes they serve, are vigorously attested to in Scripture, notably in the cases of Joseph (Genesis 37:5–7; 40:5–23; 41:1–37) and Solomon (I Kings 3:5–15). Dik would in no way have wished—nor indeed would he have found it possible—to challenge the authority of Scripture. A full frontal attack on beliefs which were so deeply ingrained in popular lore and which had, moreover, the highest sacred authority, would have been totally counterproductive to his didactic purpose. Nevertheless, he is determined to find a way to eliminate contemporary superstition in favour of an understanding consonant with reason. To start with, throughout his work, Dik was at pains to portray KHaZaL, 'Our Sages of Blessed Memory' as the medieval commentators on the Scriptures are known to orthodoxy, as precursors of the Enlightenment, a transparent but highly successful strategy to lend unchallengeable authority to the work of the *maskilim*. As Roskies reminds us, the first generation of Eastern European *maskilim*, all the products of traditional orthodox educations, were not at all freethinkers. They wanted not the abolition of the Law, but a return to what they perceived to be the pristine practice of Judaism, freed of the mystical accretions of Hasidism, and the primitive superstitions licensed by 'folk custom'. They desired a return to decorum, rationality and practical good conduct, seeing the spiritual purpose of Judaism as inculcating faith in a true God rather than breeding fear of imaginary demons; of building a Jewish moral character that expressed itself in productive daily life and virtuous communal intercourse. To give authority to this essential distinction between 'custom' and the core of Torah observance, Dik assumed the time-honoured Jewish storytelling *persona* of the *maggid* or travelling preacher who went from town to town delivering practical homilies in everyday terms. In this role, Dik could continue the pious practice of drawing a wholesome contemporary moral from reading the past in the light of the present. He could follow illustrious precedent in using history and hagiography to show how much progress Jews had mercifully made since the arrival of Emancipation.

Dik distinguishes sharply between 'earlier times' and 'our more enlightened age'. In 'earlier times', all kinds of wonders were possible because people then were closer to God than we are today. Dreams of divination were quite possible *then*, in the same way that the commentaries of the earliest Sages, the *Rishonim* and the *Aharonim*, according to rabbinical judgement carried more authority than the commentaries of those who came after them. For this reason, Dik insists on qualifying his reports of prophetic dreams and miraculous visitations with comments like this:

> In the like accounts, former generations trusted mightily: whoever wishes to pin his faith in such, takes them for moral lessons. Even for that person who does not credit such doings, there is at least some value in knowing how the world appeared to previous generations beset with their great terrors.[10]

Today, of course, Dik argues, in our 'new enlightened age', we are governed by reason and so free of these 'great terrors'.

When Dik's version of the Jewish pope myth was published in Vilnius in 1874, Russian Jewry, benefiting from nearly two decades of tsarist reform, was confronting the belated arrival from the West of the *Haskalah*, the Jewish Enlightenment. As was only to be expected from so ardent a supporter, Dik shared the *Haskalah*'s conviction that only secular education could make Jews productive members of society and restore their human dignity. Dik re-tells this tale of the Jewish pope so that his 'lady readers' may learn from it their *glik vos du lebst in dize gliklikhe epokhe (tsayt rekhenung) un grade in der tsivilizirte eyropa* (Y 3–4), 'good fortune that you live in this happy epoch (period of time) and stage in civilized Europe [...] and not in previous centuries'. Dik's faith in the future of European Jewry becomes a consolatory assurance that in the modern present, by contrast with the medieval past, gifted Jewish boys need no longer seek conversion to Christianity in order to realize their talents. Dik can hardly be blamed for sharing an enthusiasm for contemporary European socio-political life that for nearly half a century held out so much hope for the Jewish people, but he seems entirely unconscious of numerous more deeply rooted ironies he exposes in faithfully reshaping his materials. His reworking shifts the parameters of the problems inherent in the myth to pose, if not to resolve, the burning contemporary question of how Jews can fulfil the aims of the *Haskalah* while at the same time remaining faithful to the ideological teachings of traditional Judaism.

Dik's maskilic bias leads him to overstate those ghetto conditions, enforced upon Jews for centuries by the Catholic Church, that Raul Hilberg has identified as chief among the precedents so savagely imitated in the Nazis' 'Final Solution'.[11] Concomitantly, however, this detailed description (Y 4–5)[12] accentuates the degree to which Jews internalize the role in which Christians cast them. Forced to survive by stealth, they assume the outward appearance of *betler*, 'beggars', in accordance with the expectations of their oppressors. This creation of Jews as hopeless subjects is unconsciously reinforced by Dik's maskilic habit of deliberately peppering his Yiddish with Germanisms. The result of this sustained use of Gentile language, quite contrary to its user's high-minded reforming intentions, comes steadily to connote acceptance of Gentile attitudes. Given its context as a piece designed to promote the aims of the *Haskalah*, Dik's pope tale tries to free Jews from the inferior condition imposed upon them through centuries of Christian enmity. So the narrator takes pains to show Jews as possessed of gifts that would enrich the world, were they but given an opportunity to exercise them. The problem with this seemingly laudable aim is that it is promoted, however unconsciously, from the weak position of apologetics by rooting itself not in Jewish self-esteem, but in Christian denigration.

While Dik ostensibly makes a pointed contrast between the bad old days and the good new ones, his reconstruction simply confirms Jews as stereotypes created both by Christians and by themselves. Their uncomplaining acceptance of their inferior and subordinate construction bolsters them as subjects of an illusion which, they insist, is an irreversible condition of reality. Thus the narrative evokes the contradictory and disturbing interrelationship between history, discourse and identity. 'History' tries to record what happens to people within the social formation, but as soon as it attempts to work out reasons for what happens, it must employ one or another kind of discourse which, existing extra-textually and continually shifting, succeeds only in classifying the subjects it is investigating according to one or another ideology. At the same time, inevitably, that discourse is part of the meaning of what is being recorded. Hence the Germanism Dik puts into the mouth of his Jewish pope to describe the condition of being a Jew, *verachteter Jude*, takes on a terrifyingly proleptic quality. That phrase will become in time the justification for driving such people directly into Auschwitz. Additional evidence for the truth of this can be found beyond Dik's unconscious use of loaded language in his conscious selection of historical facts to illustrate the degree to which Jews were literally reduced to a condition of abject subordination to their Christian overlords. All such examples that Dik meticulously records in the nineteenth century are also adduced in the twentieth century by Raul Hilberg in the aftermath of the Holocaust.

The frequency with which it is possible to cite the correspondences between Dik's illustrations and those of Hilberg make this point tragically clear.

On one level, the narrative's depiction of the Jews' skill at chess represents what Hilberg has identified as 'alleviation attempts [that] are typical and instantaneous responses by the Jewish community [of the Diaspora]'—what is called in Yiddish *shtadlones*, in other words, through the effectiveness of which, the narrator takes pride in recording,

> [...] *flegn zey tsu hobn imer gute gelegnheyt tsu ton a toyve—amol zikh, amol eynem andern, un amol dem klal. den durkh dem hobn zey bakumen groyse bakantshaft mit groyse layt vos zey flegn oys tsu virkn durkh zey vos nor miglekh* (Y 5).

> [...] they gained excellent opportunities to perform good works—sometimes for themselves, sometimes for one another, and sometimes for the community as a whole. By this means they established firm acquaintanceships with persons of influence through whom they were able to accomplish whatever could be accomplished.

In narrating this sequence of events, Dik presents as a self-evidently correct Jewish response—gratitude for the chance to beg favours—a reaction that makes the Jews of his Mainz ghetto complicit with the persecutions visited upon them. As Dik presents it, the immediate reaction of R. Shimen and his community—automatically to assume that they are indeed guilty of some (unspecified) sin or crime and to hasten their efforts to atone for it—epitomizes what Hilberg has identified as 'alleviation attempts' on the part of Diaspora Jewry against threatened Christian persecution that were continually repeated for nearly two thousand years of ghetto existence. As Hilberg defines them,

> [...] alleviation attempts are typical and instantaneous responses by the Jewish community. Under the heading of alleviation are included petitions, protection payments, ransom arrangements, anticipatory compliance, relief, rescue, salvage, reconstruction—in short, all those activities which are designed to avert danger, or, in the event that force has already been used, to diminish its effects [...]. One of the most sagacious alleviation reactions in the Jewish arsenal is anticipatory compliance. In this type of alleviation attempt, the victim foresees the danger and combats it by doing the very thing demanded of him. But he does so before he is confronted by ultimatums. He is, therefore, giving in on his own terms. In a sense, this is the action of a man who—sensing a fatal blow—wounds himself. With this wound he seeks to demonstrate that the blow is unnecessary.[13]

Moreover, an unconscious and ambiguous metaphor intrudes itself in Dik's presentation. While the narrator insists that chess opponents respect each other's prowess (Y 5–6), he implies that behind the sedate moves of tokens across a board lies an intricate struggle for survival with hostile powers. Extending beyond Christian civil laws and their effects on unwanted Jewish communities, the metaphor—as the whole story goes on to demonstrate—can even more validly be applied to the ongoing ideological struggle between Judaism and Christianity, which can be resolved not by equality of opportunity, but by the complete surrender of one of the parties. The fictional insistence that Jews are always victorious to the extent that *fil yunge layt fun di kristlekhe hershaften veln kumen zikh tsu lernen es bay zey* (Y 6), 'many young Christian princelings would come to learn it [the game] from them', unconsciously tries to invert the age-old Christian representation of Jews as monsters who 'eat' children. Thus in the very act of reconstructing Jewish skills at survival under the most unfavourable circumstances of the old social formation, to imply how much more they will be able to accomplish in the glowing promise of the new emancipated world, Dik's fiction deconstructs itself into a positive reinforcement of Christian prejudice.

In the same way, the narrator attempts to use the partially internalized stereotype of the hard-bargaining Jewish money-grubber against itself by making his R. Shimen a specialist dealer in old coins (Y 6). Because this device is grounded in a subject model established by Christian subordination, however, it fails to counter the ugly stereotype it invokes. Rather than raising R. Shimen in status, as the writer consciously intends, it reduces him merely to a high-class version of every stock Christian prejudice. Crucial in identifying Dik's unconscious maskilic problem with ghetto Jews is his presentation of R. Shimen's response to repeated entreaties to assume the rabbinical chair. Despite his exceptional qualifications, he consistently refuses for two reasons:

[...] *mayne tsayt vos blaybt mir iberik fun mayne gesheftn vil ikh nit farkoyfn far gor di gelt. tsveytns, ven ikh vel vern eyn rov, past dokh shoyn nit far mir tsu geyn tsu mankhn groyse gaystlikhn (dukhavnes) tsu shpiln in shakh, un mit dizer shpil ken ikh fil mer tsu nits kumen tsu unzer gemeynde als mit mayne rabones.* (Y 7)

[...] the leisure I enjoy after my business affairs I do not wish to sell for any amount of money. Secondly, were I to become a rabbi, it would no longer be seemly for me to visit various high-ranking clergymen to play chess, and through these games I can benefit members of our community far more than through my rabbinical function.

R. Shimen not only values the social prestige that money made through 'business affairs' can buy; his expressed concern for his community also implies an immutably fixed value difference, established by Gentiles and accepted by Jews, between the degraded condition of a rabbi and the influential status of a man of affairs. Only this premise can explain the startling narrative observation that, as a consequence of their grief at their son's disappearance, R. Shimen and his wife *zaynen durkh dem oykh arop fun maymed un der r. shimon hot shoyn gemuzt nit vilndik vern a rov dortn in der ghetto* (Y 8), 'also came down in the world and R. Shimen was unwillingly forced to become a rabbi there in the ghetto'. In the act of fictionally constructing the bright new future the Emancipation will create for Jews, the tale radically undermines traditional orthodox Jewish values—inevitably the risk courted by every attempt, however partial, at assimilation.

This process is extended in the narrative's presentation of the boy Joseph. A genius scholar, he receives rabbinical *smikhe*, licensing, in the year of his *barmitsve*, making him the most eligible of traditional Jewish sons-in-law (Y 15). The prospective father-in-law who is chosen to take this Joseph, a precious only son, into his family *var a groyser sar un tsu glaykh a groyser gaon, eyn geviser don menakhem fun orleans* (Y 17), 'was one who was alike a great prince and a great scholar [...] a certain Don Menachem of Orleans'.

So impressive a personage embodies the highest ideal of *maskilim* who, prefigured in the desire of Joseph's upper-crust parents for the best of two mutually exclusive worlds, hoped *tsu zehen in ihrem hoyz toyre un gdule tsuzamen*, 'to see Torah and worldly grandeur joined in their home'. Dik's unconscious awareness that, in the social formation imposed upon Diaspora Jewry by their Christian overlords, such a conjunction is impossible, leads him precisely at this moment to transfer his *Wunderkind* into the bosom of the Catholic Church. Christianity, not Judaism, is alone capable of joining spiritual and temporal glory in this world.

This awareness informs the confrontation between the degraded rabbi father and the exalted pope son, and the more the narrative voice attempts to rationalize in orthodox theological terms the meaning of this calamity, the more the ambiguities multiply. On the surface, their meeting appears to be a contest between the greatest of the Jews with the greatest of the Christians. The outcome, from a Jewish point of view, should be a foregone conclusion, yet the dispute is disturbingly unevenly matched, for the learned R. Shimen has the ground cut from under his feet by a pope who adds to a comprehensive knowledge of Judaism an equally comprehensive knowledge of Christianity (Y 24–5). This disputation is the figurative precursor of the chess game which literally follows, and in both the pope leaves R. Shimen outmanoeuvred. Consequently the narrative's presentation of the conclusion of this dispute in one flat sentence is utterly unconvincing:

dizer disput hot gedoyert mehr als dray shtunden un hot zikh ge'endet mit der nitsokhn fun dem r. shimon barbun den er hot dem papst goyber geven. (Y 25)

This disquisition lasted more than three hours and ended with the victory of R. Shimen Barbun, when he finally gained mastery over the Pope.

This is a stock construct whose credibility has been eroded by the fictional context in which it has been placed. So powerfully does the narrator create the contrary probability that the formulaic ending to which he is bound by his own cultural allegiances becomes self-exploding. Who, after all, is the final judge of this victory? Knowing nothing of the pope's secret theological moves in the religious game, R. Shimen cannot possibly be a winner, a point shatteringly reinforced by the chess game that follows. Here we have two players of unsurpassed ability, the younger the pupil of the older and possessed by him of all his secret moves. Add to this the personal gifts of the younger player, and the older player has no chance at all of victory. The pope's subsequent taunt is thoroughly invested with all the terrors of the complete victory of Christianity and the utter destruction of Judaism:

'und vos bevunderst du mikh der bay?' hot im der papst gefregt. *'ist den der shakh shpil oykh nor eyn eygentum (yerushe) fun aykh juden vi ayer religyon dos du khidesht zikh oyf mikh dos ikh fershteye im azoy vayt?'* (Y 25)

'Why are you so astonished?' asked the Pope. 'Is chess playing, like your religion, the exclusive property of you Jews as well, that my good understanding of the game so startles you?'

Significantly, the conclusion of this game of chess is never disclosed. Play is interrupted by the pope's revelation of himself as the rabbi's son. An ellipsis like this marks every place where the contradictions constructing the text break down and render the discourse articulating it powerless to repair the damage. The narrative cannot impose meaning on what is happening, not because language itself is lacking, but because the significance of the 'historical' experience being recorded defies resolution. It is simply not possible for any rabbi to find an adequate response in his cultural and spiritual armoury to deal with the conversion of a beloved only son; still less for a rabbi in reality to come to terms with a son who has risen to the papacy, given the significance attached by Catholic Christians to the incumbent of Peter's Throne.

Those scriptural references that are intended to set the restoration of the lost one to faith and family firmly within the orthodox exegetical tradition end up as ambiguous as everything else. All of them focus on fathers who, having lost sons, recognize the impossibility of being reunited with them either in this life, or in a normal parent–child relationship. The most important of these is Jacob, upon whose quoted words at Genesis 46:3 the narrator feels obliged to offer his own exegesis in *loshn-koydesh* (Y 26). This interpolation exposes the inherent fragility of the master-text model, which is the primary source of the contradictions with which Dik is grappling. His chief problem is that his own literary text, offered as a resolution of these contradictions, sits uneasily between the traditional orthodox refusal of Christian norms, and the pressures of history, manifested in the emancipation and the *Haskalah*, towards counter-identification. Dik cannot bridge this gap in his fiction any more than he could in his life, as two biographical details supplied by Zalmen Reyzen illustrate:

tsugebndik a groyse badaytung di yidishe reformen fun der tsarisher regirung, hot [Dik] zikh bataylikt in tsunoyfshteln dem gevisn geheymen memorandum (fun 23/VII/1843) fun di vilner oyfgeklerte yidn [...] vegn farvern di alte yidishe malbushim. [...] nit kukndik oyf zayn maskilishn radikalizm, iz er gegangen lang geklaydt un hot oykh nit lib gehat di naymodishe oyfgeklerte on khokhme un on toyre [...][14]

Attaching great significance to the Jewish reforms of the tsarist government, [Dik] participated in compiling that secret memorandum dated 23 July 1843 from the enlightened Jews of Vilnius [...] regarding the prohibition of traditional old Jewish modes of dress. [...] Despite his maskilic radicalism, he himself went about in a long gabardine and moreover disliked the new-fangled enlightened people ignorant of traditional Jewish learning and law [...]

In Scripture, Jacob's initial response, *ered el b'ni avel she'olah*, 'I will go down to the grave to my son mourning' (Genesis 37:35), is later followed by his remark, *amutah ha'pa'am aharei r'oti et panekhah ki odekhah hai*, 'Now let me die, since I have seen thy face that thou art yet alive' (Genesis 46:30). The narrator of Dik's tale interprets these words with reference to David's lament for his child by Bathsheba (2 Samuel 12:23) and Terah's loss of his son Haran, the brother of Abraham (Genesis 11:27–8). The cumulative emphasis is consequently placed upon the finality of death—or assimilation, which in orthodox Jewish terms is the same thing—rather than upon the possibility of restoration. For the devoutly orthodox, a child's slightest approach to assimilation, in however minor a way, was cause for the mourning that normally accompanies a bereavement. It was traditional for devoutly orthodox Jewish parents in nineteenth-century Eastern Europe, for instance, to curse their sons when these exchanged the long capote for the short hacking jacket of modern fashion with the chilling death-wish, *zol im farkirtst dos lebn vern*, 'May his life be shortened [like his coat]'. About what the parents of Jewish children who converted were to do, the *Halakhah* was explicit—they were obliged to mourn these converts as though they had died, and were never afterwards to refer to them again.

Dik's narrative places its stress first on R. Shimen's anguished outcry on learning of his son's initial disappearance (Y 17–18) and later, confronting his pope son, on his own desire for extinction, manifested in his reluctance to regain consciousness from repeated swooning (Y 27–8). His first words hereafter echo not Jacob, but the doomed King Hezekiah: *hinei l'shalom mar li mar* (Y 27–8), 'Behold, for my peace I had great bitterness' (Isaiah 38:17). None of this is, in homiletic terms, the slightest bit reassuring.

What follows in the pope's confession to his father is a description of motives which, springing from fear of persecution and love of glory, make it impossible to credit his penitential return to Judaism. Dik's descriptions of the papacy are redolent with fascination at the awesome power, the vast riches, and the exalted honour that a gifted Jewish son enjoyed when he ruled the world. That son himself is given lengthy lamentations about the great deprivation he must endure in sacrificing the magnificence of Christendom for the abjection of Jewry, in language that startlingly conflates and confuses material and spiritual values:

mayn raykhtum, mayne groyse ehre, un mayne groyse fargenign hobn mikh azoy vayt ayngenumen, azoy vayt beroysht, dos es var mir shoyn zeyer shver aroys tsu raysn zikh fun maynem gaystlikhn shtand um tsu vern vider ein verachteter jude […] *nokh hot keyner azo eyn opfer (korbm) gebrakht tsu got far zaynem das vi ikh hob gebrakht. dermon zikh vos far a gdule, vos far akhires, vos far a koved ikh hob avek gekayklt unter mayne fis, um nur ein jude tsu blaybn. toyznter hobn far mir nider geknit. kenige zaynen in shtoyb gelegn far mir. ikh hob es mit blut oys maynem hartsen oys gerisn, um nur zikh mit maynem gevisn (kharakter) oys tsu zehen (gut fraynd vern)* [...] (Y 30–1/35)

My riches, my great eminence, and my enormous gratification seduced me so thoroughly, impressed me so deeply, that it soon became very difficult for me to tear myself from my spiritual height to become a despised Jew again. [...] No one has ever made such a sacrifice to God for his faith as I have made. Remember what sort of glory, what sort of riches, what sort of honour I have allowed to roll away from under my feet, only to remain a Jew. Thousands have knelt before me. Kings have prostrated themselves in the dust before me. With blood have I torn all this from my heart, only to make peace with my conscience [...]

Pope Joseph here carries to a logical extreme the ambivalences present in both the figure of R. Shimen and the narrator himself. There is the utmost fascination in this picture of the great ones of the world abjectly abasing themselves before an all-powerful Jew, and the most piercing sense of loss that all this has to be given up only to become once more *ein verachteter Jude*. Thrilled indulgence in the fantasy of a Jew reversing that role to which for centuries the Christian world has relegated him is finally the subtext of this maskilic version of the pope myth, reflecting as it does a total Jewish subordination to the value system upheld by Christian ideology. Dik's Jewish pope is a powerful spokesman for a value system that presents the power of the temporal not only as stronger but as more attractive than the power of the spiritual.

Doubtless the narrator intends Jewish faithful to applaud as entirely proper the pope's surrender, but the language in which this surrender is expressed speaks more strongly of loss than of gain. We never hear him discuss the theological issues that he has supposedly explored so profoundly. What we do hear him speak about, often and at length, are the opulence of the material, and the dominion of the temporal, Christian world. About Jewishness, we hear only of squalor, subterfuge and *shtadlones*.

The unconscious subtext of Dik's tale—which its opening paean of praise for the opportunities supposedly offered to Jews by the promises of Emancipation reinforces—is that Jews should take a full share of the riches and authority of the world, even at the cost of their unendurable and self-created role as 'God's suffering servants'. Consciously, of course, Dik would like them to continue being devout Jews at the same time, but his Jewish pope is a powerful spokesman for a value system that presents the power of the temporal not only as stronger, but also as more attractive than the power of the spiritual, for as things have stood for centuries, to be a Jew is to be powerless and despised, while to be a Christian is to be powerful and honoured. R. Shimen himself is given a remarkably ambiguous sentiment in this context. Reasoning his way to the meaning of the mysterious tripartite dream by which he was visited, he stresses:

... *du vos du host geblibn frum zayendik zelbst a papst hob ikh nur tsu fardanken dem troym, den nur tsuliḥ dem troym aleyn hob ikh gezen ayn tsu flantsn in dir mit ale meglekhkeyt in der velt eyne yore ta'are damit du zoltst nit nikhshal vern in azelkhe avoynes vos du zoltst darfn vern durkh dem a groyser baltshuve.* (Y 37)

[...] I have only the dream to thank for your having remained piously observant even as a pope. For solely as a result of that dream did I ensure that I implanted in you, through all available means, a reverence for purity so absolute that you might not be led astray into sins such as would later force you into massive repentance.

Why 'solely as a result of that dream'? Does not the Covenant lay upon all Jewish parents the solemn obligation to consecrate their sons to the total service of the Torah? This, after all, is what R. Shimen's wife does, *vi amol khane*, 'as Hannah did of old', while the prayers of R. Shimen himself during his wife's pregnancy are largely informed by a foreboding that [*fun*] *dize matone fun got* [...] *er vet hobn mer tsar als nekome derfun* (Y 14), 'this gift from God [...] would bring him more sorrow than consolation'. Pious and ignorant women, personified by R. Shimen's wife, seem to be presented here as more reliable custodians of the Jewish tradition. Learned and skilful men, like R. Shimen himself, through their contact with, or potential contamination by, worldliness, appear to be more greatly exposed to temptation and more likely to succumb the greater they perceive their gifts to be. The word 'solely', as R. Shimen uses it, tends to suggest, however unconsciously on the narrator's part, that—by painful contrast with his dutifully observant father—the only place in which the enormous gifts of this brilliant Jewish child might receive their full scope and encouragement is in the world of Christians, to whom indeed appears to have been given the kingdom, the power and the glory. To the Jews, in the visible world at least, appears to have been granted only discouragement, denigration and defeat.

The narrative's attempt to make the pope explain why it was necessary for him to terrorize an entire Jewish community in order to see his father presents us with further evidence of the power of this temptation in an unconscious metaphor of a divided self, simultaneously needing to embrace its Jewishness and to banish it entirely:

> [...] *ikh hob mikh bashlosn dos ikh zol zikh zehen mit dir. un vayl ikh hob es nit gekent ton oyf graden veg, dos heyst shraybn tsu dir dos du zolst kumen tsu mir—vayl es volt di zakh gevis noyde gevorn un dos hob ikh nit gevolt, vayl es ken shodn ton mir un dir—hob ikh daher aroys gegebn dizn bafel dos men zol aykh juden aroys traybn fun maynts.* (Y 31–2)

> [...] I resolved that I would meet with you. Since I could not do so in the normal way, by writing asking you to come to me—for the matter would certainly have become common knowledge and I could not afford this, since it would have done great harm both to you and to me—I consequently issued the command that all Jews should be expelled from Mainz.

So far from setting fears to rest or solving problems, all this explanation does is to identify it as *eyne bashtimung fun got un vayter nit* (Y 32), 'simply a determination of Providence and nothing more'. In the pious hope that this will resolve all ambiguities and bring the whole thing into line with orthodox teachings, this 'determination' is again linked directly to the biblical Joseph. Theoretically, the biblical narrative resolves all contradictions in other texts deriving from it. Unwittingly here, the narrator not only undermines his own text, but the master-narrative as well. The Jewish pope calls attention to the extent of Joseph's assimilation into Egypt by reminding his father (and us) that Joseph *hot zaynem a zun a nomen gegebn manasseh vayl got hot im gemakht fargesn zayn elnt un tsu glaykh oykh dos hoyz fun zayne eltern* (Y 32), 'named his son "Manasseh", for God caused him to forget as one both his loneliness and the house of his parents'. In response, the archetypal ghetto rabbi reminds his son of the rabbinical exegesis of Joseph's remark in Genesis 41:51, *ki nasa'ni kol amali: zogn daroyf unzere khakhomim dos iz gemeynt ikh hob fargesn gor di toyre vos ikh hob erlernt mit groys mi* (Y 36), '"for God hath made me forget all my toil", which our Sages interpret to mean, "I have entirely forgotten the Torah which I studied with great effort" '. Now Dik's narrative demands that we believe, despite every suggestion to the contrary, that Joseph Barbun has forgotten neither the house of his parents nor the Torah, which is why he gives up being *ongetonerheyt in zayner papstlikhe ornate (formaylnost) mit der heylike kroyn oyf den kop un mit shkipeter (sharbit ha'zahav) in der hant* (Y 23), 'clad in his papal vestments, with the holy crown on his head and the golden sceptre in his hand' in order to appear *gants farvaksn, ongeton in a zak, dos hoypt bashotn mit ash* (Y 35), 'heavily bearded, dressed in sackcloth, his head scattered with ashes'.

The moment of truth has now arrived in Dik's tale, and predictably the attempt at *éclaircissement* dissolves behind a screen of mystical assertions regarding the ineffability of God's purposes drawn from the stock responses of orthodoxy. To the fundamental question of why God permitted the only son of a saintly rabbi to become a Christian pope in the first place, the narrative can only offer the standard rabbinical doctrine regarding the suffering of the innocent:

un itsund farshtey ikh shoyn oykh dem varen zinen fun dem posek vos got hot gezogt tsu moyshe rabeyne als er hot zikh gebeten bay im, 'hodieni na et d'rakhekhah', dos heyst vayz mir dayn hanhoge. hot er im daroyf geentfert, 'v'raita et ahorai u'fanai lo ye'ra'u', dos heyst du kenst nor farshteyn dem sof vos dos heyst okhor fun yeder hanhoge mayne ober nit dem tkhiles vos heyst ponim fun mayner hanhoge. (Y 37)

Now, too, do I understand [R. Shimen tells his now penitent son] the true meaning of that passage in Scripture [Exodus 33:13, 23] which recounts the answer God gave to Moses our Teacher when Moses asked, 'Show me now Thy ways.' God replied, 'Thou shalt see My back, but My face shall not be seen.' In other words, mortal men can only understand the meaning of God's purposes in their conclusions, but not in their inceptions.

This answer supposedly explains everything, despite the fact that the meaning of God's reply is imponderable. As J. H. Hertz, a modern commentator, evasively notes, for example: 'It is, of course, quite impossible to penetrate the full mystery of these words, conveying sublime truths concerning the Divine nature in the ordinary language of man.'[15]

In the daily experience of ghetto Jews, it ceases to have any practical meaning at all, since all it instructs them is to go on observing the *mitsves*, commandments, and bearing persecution and degradation; to go on praying for the coming of the Messiah and seeing Christian oppressors set in mocking power over them; to go on believing in God's justice in the teeth of every earthly demonstration of man's injustice.

Since—however much his actual achievement may subvert it—Dik's overt purpose is didactic, he tries to cover all possibilities in his explanation of the Jewish pope phenomenon. The son assures his father, on the authority of Genesis 45:5, 7, that he has fulfilled the role of Joseph again in his own time:

ikh var a papst nor tsum shayn. in hertsn ober var ikh eyn hekhster juden. un hob gegloybt dos ikh bin gevorn a papst um nor gutes tsu ton mit unzere brider [...] den ikh hob mevatl geven kame vekame gzeyres koshes fun yidn beyoyter ober in di letste tsvey yor vos zaynen iber gegangen nokh daynem erkenen zikh mit mir. (Y 36)

I was a pope only in appearance. In my heart, however, I was a Jew in the highest degree and believed that I had become a pope only in order to benefit our brothers. [...] I have annulled countless harsh decrees against Jews, the majority, however, in the last two years which have passed since your recognition of me.

The final qualifying clause is of course the complete give-away. The pope is recalled to his crypto-messianic role only by the reappearance of his father; prior to that, as far as the Jews of Mainz are concerned, his influence has been felt only as a malign tyranny that in a stroke deprives them of life and livelihood. That earthly rather than spiritual power is wholly operative is reinforced by the tale's deployment of the phrase 'holy father'. In the discourse of traditional Judaism, such an appellation is properly applicable only to the Creator; Christian discourse applies it to what their ideology insists is the Messiah's Vicar on Earth. True to its strategy of disidentification, the *Mayse-bukh* never employs it; its R. Shimen addresses the pope as *ayer kiniglekhe genodn*, 'your royal grace'. But having thoroughly adopted the interpellatory discourse of the Christian world as part of the price of *Haskalah*, both the narrative voice and R. Shimen in Dik's version servilely apply the title to human creatures, first to the ruler of Mainz (Y 20), and several times thereafter to the accoutrements and person of the ruler of Christendom (Y 23, 25, 26). Then, in what the narrative evidently intends as a masterful stroke of irony, the title is applied by the pope to his natural father at the end of his confession:

nun heyliger foter blaybt mir nokh dos eyntsige iberik mit vos dikh tsu traysten dos ikh vel zehen tsu erfilen oykh daynen letsten troym. (Y 32)

Now, holy father, all that remains for me to comfort you is to set about fulfilling your last dream as well.

The pope's 'holiness' is assigned only by the values of the Christian world; the rabbi's 'holiness' is assigned only by filial guilt. The holiness of the Father of the Children of Israel is fabricated as an ideological ineffability to be accepted with total resignation. All the tale's attempts to justify the ways of God to man resolve themselves only into the traditional formula, *tzadik ha'shem be-hol dera'khav ve-hasid be-hol ma'asav* (Y 37), 'The Lord is righteous in all His ways, and gracious in all His deeds'. *Alzo mayn kind iz shoyn di ehre fun got geretet*, 'Thus, my child, is the honour of God preserved', says R. Shimen to his son by way of complete explication; believe this despite everything else I have related to you, dear lady readers, says Dik in effect to us. But these are the pat answers of an ideology which, however unconsciously, the discourse employed by the narrator has thoroughly deconstructed.

Notes to Chapter 4

1. See Zalmen Reyzen, *Leksikon fun der yidisher literature, prese un filologie*, 4 vols. (Vilnius, 1929), i, cols. 711–34; David G. Roskies, 'Isaac Meir Dik: The Master of Lore', in Roskies, D. G., *A Bridge of Longing: The Lost Art of Yiddish Storytelling* (Cambridge, MA, and London, 1995), ch. 4.
2. The text of this memorandum was first published in Russian in *Voskhod* Library Pamphlet, no. 5 (1901), 4–5. It appears in full English translation in Mendes-Flohr, Paul R. and Reinharz, Jehuda (eds.), *The Jew in the Modern World: A Documentary History* (New York and Oxford, 1980), 314.
3. This custom of marrying off mere children had ironically enough been devised by Jews as a desperate means of trying to circumvent the cantonist decrees of 1827 promulgated by Tsar Nicholas I (1825–55), which demanded a compulsory period of twenty-five years' conscription into the Russian army of a percentage of all Jewish boys in every town and village. Newly married men were exempted from this decree. Dik himself idealistically believed that conscription was a duty owed by Jews to the state, which thereby recognized them as equal citizens.
4. Roskies, 'Isaac Meir Dik', 67.
5. Quoted by Roskies, ibid. The *taytsh-khumesh* or 'Yiddish Bible' was not a translation but a loose paraphrase of the Pentateuch interspersed with simple homilies and moral aphorisms for easy memorizing.
6. Roskies, 'Isaac Meir Dik', 68.
7. Quoted in Charles Madison, *Yiddish Literature: Its Scope and Major Writers* (New York, 1971), 23.
8. Ibid. 25.
9. I have published an annotated translation of these other two tales. See Joseph Sherman, 'Reforming through Fiction: An Appreciation of Ayzik-Meyr Dik', *Jewish Affairs* 53/3, (Summer 1993), 27–33. My complete translation of Dik's Jewish pope tale, which has never before appeared in English, is published in this volume as Appendix A.
10. Quoted in Sherman, 'Reforming through Fiction', 32.
11. Raul Hilberg, *The Destruction of the European Jews* (New York, 1961), 5–7.
12. All quotations from the original Yiddish text of Dik's tale appear after the letter Y, followed by the relevant page number. Page references are to the original 1874 edition. All translations into English are my own.
13. Hilberg, *Destruction*, 14–15.
14. Reyzen, *Leksikon*, i, cols. 713–14.
15. See J. H. Hertz (trans. and ed.), *The Pentateuch and Haftorahs* (London, 1958), 363.

CHAPTER 5

❖

Y. Y. Trunk and the Myth after the Holocaust

Yehiel Yeshaya Trunk (1887–1961) was born into a wealthy Hasidic family in the village of Osmólsk Górny near Łowicz in Poland. In youth he received a traditional Jewish education in addition to studying secular subjects with private tutors. He was able to travel abroad a good deal: he lived in Palestine for twelve months between 1913 and 1914, and spent the years of the First World War in Switzerland. He returned to Poland in 1919, and settled in Łodz, where he was active in the manufacturing industry. Six years later, in 1925, he moved to Warsaw where he played a leading role in Yiddish cultural affairs, and during the 1930s he ran the Warsaw Yiddish PEN Club. At the outbreak of the Second World War, he was fortunate to be able to flee Warsaw and make his way eastwards, crossing the Soviet Union and the Pacific Ocean to arrive in the United States in 1941. There he remained for the rest of his life.[1]

Trunk possessed a philosophical turn of mind and was a gifted literary critic. Like so many of his contemporaries, he first started writing in Hebrew, but fell early under the influence of the prominent Yiddish belletrist and polemicist Yitskhok Leibush Peretz (1852–1915), whom he came to know through his father, and under Peretz's influence he turned to writing in Yiddish. His earliest essays appeared in Peretz's journal *Yidisher vokhnshrift* in 1908. In his earliest years, Trunk was especially interested in the relationship between art and realism, and he published extensively on this subject. His early work, all published in Poland, included historical and critical essays on Sholem Aleykhem, Y. L. Peretz, Knut Hamsun and Oscar Wilde, on whose novel *The Picture of Dorian Grey* he published a perceptive analysis. In the United States, Trunk published his major work, *Poylin*, a personalized history of the Jews in Poland in seven volumes (1946–53), which he described as 'a portrait of my life in the frame of, and in relation to, the portrait of Jewish life in Poland'.[2] Subsequent works included a volume of 'poems in old age', two novels, and several volumes of short stories including *Kvaln un beymer* (New York, 1958), a collection that includes Trunk's own reworking of the Jewish pope myth, 'Der yidisher poypst: historishe dertseylung', 'The Jewish Pope: A Historical Tale'.[3]

Trunk shared the view of Jewish national identity held by the influential Jewish historian Shimen Dubnov (1860–1941). Dubnov shifted from his original belief that Jews were a religious rather than a national entity to the view that they continued to exist as a nation whether or not they possessed their own independent state. He argued that a shared history and common language were more important than territory in preserving Jewish peoplehood; civic rights, Dubnov held, were not sufficient to ensure Jewish survival, so he advocated the Jews' right to cultural autonomy even as a people dispersed among other nations. Trunk's reworking of the Jewish pope myth is in part a dramatization and a defence of Dubnov's views. He employs the standard motifs and materials of the Jewish pope myth to define the Jewish present in the light of the Jewish past, employing the raw materials of folklore and legend to examine secular values through Jewish eyes, and the way the Christian world intrudes into Jewish self-definition.[4] Rewriting the tale in latter-day America, in the aftermath of the Nazi destruction of European Jewry, Trunk shows how far he is aware of the ambiguities in Dik's version by closely modelling his own on its essential structure; his extensions highlight the dilemma of continued Jewish existence in a world in which Jewish necessities are supplied neither by God nor by Gentiles.

Starting out in Dik's familiar *tayere lezerin/libe leyener*, 'dear reader', style, the chatty mock-didactic tone slips suddenly into a wry acceptance of Jewish sufferings as givens in an unalterable equation of history:

yidishe tsores zenen eybik vi di velt. [...] *oykh dos hayntike dor yidn zenen nisht keyn bney-yekhidimlekh fun unzer geshikhte. benegeye tsores hobn mir, di hayntike yidn, nisht andekt amerike.* (Y 127)

Jewish troubles are as eternal as the world. [...] Even the present generation of Jews are not the chosen little favourites of our history. With regard to troubles we, the Jews of today, have not discovered America. (my translation)

This assertion dismisses the belief in progress so cherished by the *maskilim* and their heirs, the materialists and rationalists of the nineteenth and twentieth centuries. For Jews, their identity permanently constructed for them by the ideological imperatives of both Judaism and Christianity, nothing changes. Scholars who preach progress *viln unz aynvign in an onreydenish* (Y 127), 'want to lull us asleep with a fantasy'; the world, so far from galloping forward, leaves Jews *nokh tif in di blotes fun mayse-bereyshis* [...] *nokh keseyder bay 'ma tovu'*, *dos heyst, gor gor fun forent* (Y 127), 'still knee deep in the mud of the story of Creation [...] still constantly attached to [ideas of] "How goodly" [Balaam's blessing, Numbers 34:5], that is to say, very far indeed from the front'. Implied in these ironic reflections is a rejection of the doctrines of orthodoxy. But the narrator's presentation of the materials of the tale also suggests that it is not simply their own ideology that makes Jews the victims of eternal tribulation; their lot is also one defined for the weaker by the stronger. The narrative voice suggests that forces of history, controlled by Christians, maintain Jews as perpetual victims of suffering as long as they demand their right to an identity separate and different from that of the majority among whom they dwell. Hence an examination of the old parchments reveals only an *eybikn itst in velkhn ale zeygers hobn zikh opgeshtelt* (Y 127), 'an eternal present in which all clocks have stopped' (E 128–9). The medieval Christians of Frankfurt am Main live in *shtrenger un farbiker shefe*, 'austere and colourful plenty'; their Jewish counterparts in an *ayngetsoymte un opgeshlosene khashkhes*, 'an enclosed and secluded darkness' (Y 128/E 129). The consolations of a putative *oylem-habe*, World to Come, are thin by contrast with the deprivations Jews endure in *oylem-hoze*, the world of the present, the earthly world.

As Trunk's narrative presents the situation, since they share the same human ambitions and desires as Christians, Jews denied these ambitions in the flesh must seek them in the spirit. Their quest for the 'higher' world becomes a compensation for being unable to possess the 'lower', exactly as their skill at chess substitutes figurative for literal conquest:

fun alter derfarung veysn ober yidn vi men kon altsding oysnutsn far a moshl. di gantse velt iz nisht mer vi a moshl. (Y 129)

their age-old experience teaches Jews how to use everything as a parable. The whole world is nothing but a parable. (E 130)

What such a parable teaches, however, depends upon who interprets it. To powerless Jews, victory at the chessboard is an illusion in the battle for survival in a world where the weapons are not antique curiosities, nor the opponents wooden figures. The past and the present are *di eygene yente nor andersh geshleyert* (Y 127), 'the same harridan in a different getup', rendering concepts of good and evil relative to the human desires in which they are rooted:

der yetser-hore un der yetser-tov zenen minastam der eyner un der zelbiker malekh. es iz a malekh a purim-shpiler. a shkots un a genarnik, vos tut zikh nor on di kapote in velkher mir viln im zen. (Y 129)

The Good Spirit and the Evil Spirit are most likely one and the same angel. An angel who acts in Purim skits. A rascal and a rogue, who merely dons the cape in which we wish to see him. (E 130)

If the relation of Jews to Christians is one in which good and evil are measured only in terms of what works or fails to work, then it epitomizes a condition of existence which Sartre has called *le mauvais foi*, 'bad faith' or the refusal of freedom, in which individuals make themselves entities as rigidly determined as the objects that surround them. They deny that they are free to choose the nature of their existence, and so evade the responsibility of having to do anything to change it. They remain safe in the belief that they are what they are because they have always been so.[5] In response to a senseless world, they create illusions of freedom for themselves in their own fantasies. So the Jews of Frankfurt am Main, as Trunk presents them, acquiescing in the lot imposed upon them by *zeyere mekhtike shkheynim un badriker* (Y 130), 'their mighty neighbours and oppressors', or by a malign destiny interpreted as the will of God, find substitute equivalents within the ghetto for everything enjoyed by the Christians outside it (Y 130, E 131).

In Sartre's terms, these Jews—like all who come before or after them—are guilty of living a totally 'inauthentic' life by attaching importance to the banality of everyday subsistence: existing according to the dictates of the past, defining their being according to the image others have created of them and fulfilling the expectations of these others, and by pretending to give meaning to existence in theoretical systems.[6] This tale's narrator may understand and identify all these falsifications, but he acquiesces in and so remains complicit with them, for he is trapped into identifying with all the Jews of the Diaspora, and is unable—perhaps unwilling—to envision, let alone to enact, a method of change. Orthodox Jews living in what they regard as exile, bound by faith and choice to the tenets of their religion and rejecting all forms and modes of assimilation, are obliged to accept the subaltern status imposed upon them by the powerful because their ideology rejects moral relativity. Locked as they are into a conception of history that does not change, the Jews presented in Trunk's tale believe that it is no affirmation of existence to cease being oneself in order to become another. Other varieties of Diaspora experience, where different conditions may have produced different attitudes in Jews, are of no interest to the narrator of this tale; in the aftermath of the Holocaust, Trunk, the tale's author, sees the lot of Jews throughout the world as eternally the same.

So, like his predecessors, Trunk's use of *loshn-koydesh* fixes his rabbi-leader R. Shimen within the framework of orthodox Jewish values. In his daily doings and dealings, he is the Sages' embodiment of *torah v'gedulah be-makom ehad*, 'Torah and worldly glory in one place'; he is possessed of a *shem tov*, 'a good name' (Y 131), which Scripture asserts to be *mishemen tov*, 'better than precious ointment' (Ecclesiastes 7:1); his childlessness is described not with the pejorative Russian term *bezdetnik* used by Dik (Y 10) but with the pious Talmudic phrase *hashukh-banim* (Y 131). All these stylistic signifiers seek to place R. Shimen in the highest ranks of what orthodox Judaism regards as the ranks of the saints. However, in a world governed by Gentiles, for whom Jewish sainthood is valueless, the narrative moves towards simultaneously posing and answering the question, *iz es nisht keyn meshugene akshones aroystsurufn naye yidishe doyres fun di kumendike tsukunftn?* (Y 131), 'Isn't it a stubborn madness to call forth new Jewish generations for the future?' (E 132). The narrative doggedly takes a stand for 'stubbornness', a determination to choose to be a Jew despite all worldly reasons to the contrary. Because of the conflicting ways in which Jews have been made subjects of the hegemony of others, they are compelled to choose both to be chosen and to be outcast. They are condemned to justify themselves by the choices they make, not only for themselves, but for all the generations of Jews that will follow them. Such an act of choice imposes the heavy duty of making them at once subjects of the past and authors of the future in an unending quest to resolve the dilemma of their existence. They are knowable only by actions that reinforce the ideology by which they have been interpellated, and by accepting its subjectification they give meaning both to themselves and to that ideology. Hence Trunk's tale is not a movement of counter-identification, but a courageous reassertion, in its very resignation, of the necessity to be 'stubborn', to behave authentically, in Sartre's phrase, with full reference to the past in order to ensure the continuity of the future, however troubled and difficult the present may be.

To make his presentation of this choice and its reasons convincing, the tale's narrator plays the devil's advocate, pressing the demands of *dem fremdn, vos volt in yene fartsaytns arayngekumen in der yidn-geto fun frankfort baym mayn* (Y 131), 'the stranger who might in those days of old have entered the Jewish ghetto of Frankfurt am Main'. The reader soon becomes aware that the words most often repeated in this tale are *tunklenishn* and *khashkhes*, synonyms for darkness in different degrees. In these terms, the Jewish ghetto is contrasted with the Christian metropolis (Y 128, E 129), becoming a paradigm for the exiled condition of all Jews. Balaam's reassurance, 'How goodly are thy tents, O Jacob' (Numbers 34:5), daily repeated as the opening invocation of the Ashkenazi liturgy on entering the synagogue, is belied by everyday experience, so that the apostate pope Joseph's observation when it is made simply becomes a statement of the obvious: *vos zenen yidn? an eybikn tunklenish* (Y 152), 'What are Jews? An everlasting darkness' (E 153). The *goyisher amolikayt*, 'Gentile bygones', which in the Frankfurt ghetto, as this tale presents it, provide Jews with their livings, become metonyms for a Jewish existence predicated on the discarded glories of a Christian world which moves unstoppably forward while the Jewish world remains immovably rooted in the past. Continued Jewish survival becomes increasingly dependent upon chance, and not—as far as they or we are permitted by this narrative to see—on the unfolding of a divinely beneficent plan. Jews are shown to live entirely at the mercy of Christians: a sudden decree from the pope expels them from Frankfurt, only for that same decree to be exposed later as a cruel ruse. Why does the son punish a whole Jewish community only to make contact with his father? The narrative answers this by inverting the biblical story of Joseph, and turning this inversion into a centrally binding motif. In Genesis, Joseph uses successive tricks to test his brothers' capacity for repentance, and Joseph himself, though he recognizes the moral necessity for this trial, acts out his deception with pain—at several points in his encounter with his confounded siblings he even turns aside to weep (Genesis 43:30). Trunk transforms his biblical master-text into a trial of Jacob by Joseph for a purpose designed more to demonstrate temporal power than to instruct by moral example. For R. Shimen Barbun, choosing as he does the way of Jewish 'stubbornness', there is no choice but to keep silent and return to Jewish obscurity. For his son, Pope Joseph, the alternative lies between the dazzle of the world and the darkness of the ghetto. His eventual commitment to the gloom of Jewishness takes place in Trunk's narrative amidst external circumstances—a fiercely uncontrollable storm—which imply that Joseph is exchanging assurance for doubt, power for impotence. As a renegade from Jews, Joseph rises to the greatest power in Christendom; as one returned to them, he sinks back into *fintsternishn* [...] *tseshnitn* [...] *mit sharfe likhtike blitsn* (Y 155), 'darknesses [...] shredded [...] by bright jagged lightning' (E 156). To reinforce this ambiguity, two other words recur almost chorically to particularize R. Shimen's responses to the events which befall him: *geziftst* and *getsitert*, repeated sighing and trembling at Jewish misfortune and Jewish impotence to amend it. In Trunk's tale, language itself becomes a metaphor for power. The priests, bishops, cardinals, the pope himself, are rich in speech of all kinds; the Jews are reduced by Christian decree to communicating among themselves in *shtum-loshn*, the language of deaf mutes. In response to Joseph's confession, *r. shimens leftsn zenen geven farshlosn mit toyznt shleser* (Y 153), 'R. Shimen's lips were sealed with a thousand locks' (E 154). In the degree to which the Jews are rendered powerless, they are wholly unable to respond to the overwhelming odds against them in any discourse other than the fixed formulations of liturgical utterance.

Trunk's manipulation of scriptural quotation, in striking contrast to the use made of it by Dik, becomes his chief means of challenging orthodox responses to exile while resignedly accepting that to preserve their identity in this world, Jews have no alternative. Almost the first words of this tale are those of Jeremiah 50:17, *seh fzurah yisrael*, 'Israel is a scattered flock'. When Shimen Barbun hears that his son Joseph is no more, he responds with Jacob's anguished cry, *tarof toraf yosef*, 'Joseph has been torn to pieces' (Genesis 37:33); the chapter in which the pope makes himself known to his own father is specifically entitled *yoysef in mitsraim*, 'Joseph in Egypt' (Y 149, E 150). Yet where God also promises, through Jeremiah, *v'shovavti et yisrael el naveyhu*, 'I will bring Israel back to his pasture' (Jeremiah 50:19), in the world governed by the Roman Church they remain scattered. Again the ambiguities of the master-text narrative are exposed in Trunk's retelling of the pope myth. Where in the Bible Joseph is honoured for being a Hebrew, and his father Jacob is invited into Egypt by Pharaoh himself, in the Egypt that is Rome Joseph must deny his Hebrew origins, and his father must come as an unwelcome petitioner to the anguished recognition that *yoysef iz an optriniker* [...] *er hot farlozn di alte getseltn fun yakov* (Y 150), 'Joseph is a renegade [...] He has deserted the old tents of Israel' (E 151). There can be no joyous accommodation of the Jewish way of life to the Christian—Rome is not the land of Goshen. To the Christians remain the kingdom, the power and the glory; to the Jews only the repetition of Psalm 102, *tfilah l'ani ki ya'atof*, 'the prayer of an afflicted man when he is overwhelmed'.

In Trunk's version, Jews are marked out as unalterably alien, not only in dress but also in modes of perception, through which we are given a judgement of the Gentile world, most evident in the detailed descriptions of Rome which mark Trunk's most significant extension of Dik's model. This city is literally and figuratively not simply the antithesis but the destruction of Jewishness. Merged in one are pagan Rome, the seat of Titus the Destroyer and Hadrian the Evil who burned the Temple and dispersed the Jews, and Christian Rome, the seat of the Church Triumphant that outlawed and pauperized them. The Jewish ghetto in Rome is not only *der troyer-flek oyfn nitskhoynesdikn velt-toyer* (Y 141), 'the mournful spot on the victorious Gateway of the World [*capita/porta mundi*]'; it is also situated where it can bear perpetual witness to the fact that nearby, in the Circus Maximus, *flegn gvaldike hamoynem roymer tsukukn tsu [...] di kamfn fun mentshn mit khayes* (Y 140), 'huge mobs of Romans came here to watch [...] the fights between men and beasts' (E 141). The same struggle for dominance between the human and the bestial seems to the bemused gaze of the Jews to be terrifyingly bodied forth in the Renaissance sculptures which adorn the fountains of Christian Rome:

tayl fun di figuren hobn gehat kep fun mentshn—ober leyber hobn zey gehat fun alerley tsehirzshete ferd un vilde bufel-oksn. [...] [es] hobn fun zeyere piskes gegosn un geshpritst mit vaser glaykh vi zey voltn geven geshrien un gevoyet mit vaser-koyles. (Y 147)

Some of the figures had human heads—but the bodies of all manner of whinnying horses and wild buffalo. [...] water gushed and spewed from their chaps as though they were howling and bellowing with watery uproar. (my translation)

Through Jewish eyes, the art treasures of the Vatican reflect a sybaritic and idolatrous worldliness which has its inevitable concomitant in a desolate World to Come:

yeder zal hot mamesh oysgekukt vi an ander velt. tayl zaln zenen geven shefedik un raykh vi di gemekher fun di shtarkste malkey-arets—un tayl—tunkel un naket vi a kristlekhe 'yene velt'. [...] alerley eyl-lompen hobn gebrent iber hiltserne un goldene tsloymim—un baloykhtn di penimer fun alerley yoyzls. (Y 148)

Some of the rooms were opulent and luxurious like the chambers of the most powerful kings on earth. And some were dark and bare—like the Christian afterlife. [...] all sorts of oil lamps were burning over wooden and golden crosses—illuminating the faces of all kinds of Jesuses. (my translation)

Everything they see, from wanton women to architectural ornamentation, bespeaks the carnal: *afilo di shteyner lakhn un freyen zikh in a tayvediker un brunstiker freyd* (Y 147), 'even the stones were laughing and enjoying themselves with a lusty and rutting pleasure' (E 148). Their very access to the papal presence is procured for them by the most desired courtesan in Rome. Her name, Imperia, connotes the nature of the rule exercised in this world just as her concupiscence defines the source of its power (Y 145, E 146).

This presentation of the Christian world through Jewish eyes gives R. Shimen's response to the platitudinous comfort offered him by the electoral bishop of Frankfurt its full ironic import: *vos veysn di umeshooylem fun bitokhn?* (Y 138), 'What do the Gentiles know about faith?' (E 139). Unlike the Christian bishop, R. Shimen is forced to measure the clichés of ideology against the pain of personal suffering, and there is no bridging the gap. In theory,

> r. shimen barbun iz zikher geven vi der tog, az yidn vern getrogn fun a groyse rakhmim. ay zayn eygene vund, vos hot zikh nokh nisht farshlosn? vu hot got bavizn rakhmim tsu im aleyn, tsu r. shimen barbunen? (Y 146)

> R. Shimen Barbun was as certain as the day that Jews were borne by a great mercy. But what about his own wound, which had never healed? When had God shown mercy personally to him, to R. Shimen Barbun? (my translation)

In this last question, any incipient rebellion against the precepts of Judaism and the sorry lot into which these have led observant Jews under Christian domination is aborted by an admiration of *yene vunderlekhe akshones*, 'that wondrous stubbornness', so reviled by Christians, but which in this tale becomes the Jews' chief claim to self-assertion, an existential choice which has its own value and confers its own meaning. It unhesitatingly leads the father to reject his apostate son:

> di shtim fun foterlekhn blut iz kimat vi ibergeshrien gevorn fun der shtim fun altn folk yisroel. a shtim fun velkher es hobn aroysgeredt ale nisyoynes un yene vunderlekhe akshones, vos ruft zikh yidishe geshikhte in der velt. (Y 150)

> The call of paternal blood was drowned by the voice of the ancient people of Israel. A voice pronouncing all the temptations and that wondrous stubbornness that is Jewish history in the world. (E 151)

At the very moment that R. Shimen rashly condemns the spiritual weakness of the Roman Jews who appear unprotestingly to obey Christian commands to hear a conversionist sermon every month (Y 143), he is brought up short by conduct which asserts their kinship with what Hebrew Scripture describes as *am kshey oref*, 'a stiff-necked people' (Exodus 32:9; 33:3–5). They cunningly turn Christian denial of their right to exist into an act of self-affirmation by stopping up their ears with wads of cloth, deafening themselves to both threats and temptations, a survival strategy that claims R. Shimen's esteem of them as *a tayer am-kshey-oref*, 'a dear stiff-necked people' (Y 144). This same 'stubbornness' converts the public badge of shame forced on them by Christian decree—the wearing of pointed hats—into a proud emblem of disidentification from an impure world, emphasized in the narrative by the quasi-choric enumeration of the occasions on which they do so. When R. Shimen leads the Frankfurt delegation to the bishop, he puts on *dem shpitsikn yidnhut*, his 'pointed Jew-hat', not because Christian law but because Jewish self-identification demands it. This is possibly the most moving moment in Trunk's tale, for though the narrative nowhere refers directly to the Holocaust, no reader, either when this story first appeared or since, can encounter without emotion this deliberate strategy of disidentification from the age-old Jewish 'badge of shame', in our times transformed into the Yellow Star by the Nazis. R. Shimen assumes the 'Jew-hat' with pride, not with shame, and in that moment converts the insult into an accolade and an assertion.

From the beginning of Trunk's tale, Jewish existence in the Christian world is likened to that of *shtoybelekh in shturm-vintn* (Y 127), 'specks of dust in a hurricane' (E 128), blown about by forces over which they exercise no control. Caught up in the maelstrom of worldliness that is Rome, *di fir yidn in di shpitsike yidnhit hobn zikh gefilt vi shtoybelekh in tsepentete vintn* (Y 140), 'the four Jews in their pointed Jew-hats felt like specks of dust in raging winds' (E 141). Only by adopting clearly marked identifiers, imposed upon them by the hatred of Christians, can these specks of dust lay claim to their own unique identity. Overwhelmed by manifestations of Christian worldliness, *di blase yidn in di shpitsike yidnhit hobn oysgekukt vi opgeshrokene fremde in der velt fun palatsn, tifles un marmorne shprung-brunemer* (Y 147), 'the pale Jews in the pointed Jew-hats looked like terrified strangers in the world of palaces, churches, and marble fountains' (E 148). But once they are back in the Roman ghetto they are themselves again: *zey hobn ersht opgeotemet ven zey hobn zikh vider gefunen tsvishn yidn* (E 140), 'they only breathed freely when they found themselves among Jews once more' (my translation). There they receive and confer identity on one another, there they are safe from the temptations of the world which threatens to obliterate them. In making this emphasis, Trunk's tale overtly challenges the possibility of any Jew *qua* Jew ever being able to survive in a Christian/Gentile world, for as the tale presents it, Jewish identity is not simply a matter of religious observance or of adherence to doctrines. It is dependent upon a sense of identification with the oppressed and persecuted, and to disregard any empathy with such a condition is to join the oppressors and persecutors. The apostate son will have to choose between remaining in the Christian light, which for Jews is the glare of subjugation and self-effacement, or returning to the Jewish darkness which is the shade of Jewish independence and self-expression.

This is why R. Shimen, torn between being a father and being a Jew, must reject his pope-son. His response to the alien and threatening figure clad in all the signifiers of Christian anti-Jewishness is absolute certainty that to succumb is to be effaced: *farshtop dir di oyern, shimen, vi di yidn, vos du host gezen in der roymishe geto* (Y 153), 'Stop up your ears, Shimen, like the Jews you saw in the Roman ghetto' (E 153–4). Any tendency the tale may evince towards counter-identification is restrained by this ideological acceptance. While in itself his conduct may perhaps have no absolute meaning, R. Shimen remains deaf to the surrogate call of the world so enticingly sounded by his apostate child (Y 152/E 153). The strength of his existential assertion resides in his silence—he utters not a single word after his son has revealed himself. There is nothing to say—words are deceivers, as his son's incredible experience and elaborate self-justification both demonstrate. Hence, for the same reason, the narrative rejects pat explanations for the apostate's return to Judaism. The pope-son simply reappears, at midnight, to a father who *iz gezesn oyf der erd mit ash oyfn kop. opgerikht khtsos* (Y 154–5), 'was sitting on the ground with ashes on his head. Reciting the midnight prayers in memory of the destruction of Jerusalem and for the restoration of Israel' (E 155). He joins his father keening upon the floor; his father acknowledges his return only with silent resignation: [*er hot*] *dem fremdn orkheporkhe, zayn tsurikgekumenem zun yosef, geglet ibern kop* (Y 155), 'he stroked the head of the strange vagabond, his returned son, Joseph' (my translation). Joseph has left the brightness of Egypt for the darkness of

Israel, a condition to be embraced in the silence of that old 'stubbornness' which alone defends Jewish identity.

This seeming closure of the tale does not preclude the narrative from investigating its painful ironies, however. At several points, a specific correspondence is drawn between the intellectual effort expended by Jews on both chess and Talmudic dialectics to point up the incapacity of either meaningfully to engage with the actual conditions of Jewish existence in the real world. Great victories on chessboards are illusions in cloud-cuckoo land where *in di tifste tifenishn kon men zikh shpiln mit volkns* (Y 129), '[i]n the bottomless depths one can play with clouds' (E 130). In cold truth, the Jews are *shvakh fun der eybiker tunklenish un alt fun an eybikn ol* (Y 129), 'weak from the eternal darkness and old from the eternal burden' (E 130) of their Covenant. When Trunk uses the prophet's description of the Children of Israel as *tola'at ya'akov*, 'thou worm, Jacob!' (Isaiah 41:14), it is sadly to call attention to the abjectness through which his people accept as their own a negative Christian assessment of their worth. Where Isaiah bids Israel, likened to a worm in meekness, to fear nothing since God is their supporter and redeemer, Trunk highlights the contemptuous application of this phrase to a people reduced to crawling under trampling Gentile feet and consoling themselves with delusory games, among which is *pilpl*, hair-splitting Talmudic dialectic, itself presented in metaphors drawn from chess (Y 142/ E 143). When the rabbis of Frankfurt and Rome meet, *es hot zikh farviklt a sharf riter-gefekht tsvishn tsvey gedoley-toyre*, 'a keen joust ensued between these two knights of the Torah', armed with *fayln fun pilpl*, 'arrows of casuistry' and *vurf-shpizn fun svores*, 'spears of speculation' (E 143). They indulge in intellectualizations until *es hot epes vi oysgekukt, az ot di tsvey zikh-amperndike yidn hobn kholile fargesn tsu vos zey zenen zikh do tsuzamengekumen*, '[i]t almost appeared as if the two debating Jews had forgotten, God forbid, the reason why they had come together here' (E 143). Revealed as little more than idle escapism from the brutal reality of the world they inhabit, this debate over the meaning of the Law, for so many centuries held by observant Jews to be the chief reason for their existence, is here exposed as an exercise in impotence and inadequacy. Again the implied subtext of Trunk's tale evokes the shadow of the Holocaust, inviting the recognition that the mainstay of Jewish self-definition through centuries of exile was in the final confrontation with utter annihilation utterly useless to defend them or to ensure their survival.

The self-protective reaction of the rabbis in Trunk's tale after the conversionist sermon they are constrained to attend is to launch into a *sharfer pilpl vegn halokhes 'avoyde-zore'* (Y 145), 'sharp and dazzling casuistry on the laws concerning idol worship' (E 146). Yet all their learned bickering cannot free them from the compulsion of attending this diatribe against them enforced by the Christian power: all they can do is to stop up their ears. The actual Yiddish text of Trunk's sombre presentation of this action belies David Lerner's superficial—not to say inaccurate—description of it as 'a cheerful picture in which R. Shimen and the Roman Jews stuff their ears with cotton before the sermon, and communicate in sign language'.[7] In the same way, when he loses his only son, R. Shimen almost automatically transfers his metaphorical fight against the real world to an equally metaphorical fight against the metaphysical world in the absence from both of any discernible meaning (Y 136/E 137). If, as Trunk's narrative postulates, Talmudic disputations are merely games, like chess, then they radically undermine the benefits purportedly conferred by rigorous adherence to the Law. The divine rebuke from Isaiah (65:2) blazoned across the conversionist chapel throws into the faces of Jews the uncompromising Christian doctrine that Jerusalem was destroyed and the Covenant removed as their exclusive privilege by their stubborn rejection of the warnings of the prophets. Against this assertion, Jews can only cling to their wholly unsupported faith that God also promised through Isaiah (43:2) that *ki telekh b'mo esh, lo tikaveh, v'lehava lo tivar bakh* (Y 146), 'if you go through fire, you shall not be burnt and no flame shall singe you' (E 147). The Gentiles live in self-satisfied possession of *oylem-hoze*, the world of the present; the Jews can only await in gloomy anticipation a putative *oylem-habe*, the world to come.

As a recurring trope in so much post-First World War Yiddish fiction, the figure of the crucified Jesus is revived here in the aftermath of the Second World War yet again to represent the crucifixion of the whole Jewish people.[8] The *oysgedartn faratsvetn yid* 'scrawny, melancholy Jew' who *hot mit zayne halb-fargleyzte oygn epes vi aropgekukt un epes vi biter geshmeykhlt* (Y 144), 'stared vaguely with his glassy eyes and smiled vaguely and bitterly' (E 145) down from his cross at the mute, poverty-stricken Jews forced to attend a regular preachment reviling them for their obduracy, both embodies and mocks the suffering of his fellow-Jews, for it is in his name that Christianity has conquered and possessed the world, and in his name that it has reduced the seed from which he sprang to beggary and contempt. In its contradictory content, the symbol of the Jewish pope, the crucified transmogrified into the crucifier, thus becomes a horrible inversion of Jewish martyrdom, continuing to deny Jews the right to identity in their own terms. The chapel inside the ghetto assumes a strange, symbolic cast. Denuded of the worldly splendour which adorns its fellows outside the ghetto walls, it looks as if

[...] *di mekhtike katoylishe geter hobn zi farlost. zi shteyt umetik un umheymlekh tsvishn yidn. di tifle hot zikh epes vi aher farblondzhet in di tunklenishn fun yidishn goles.* (Y 141)

[...] the powerful Catholic deities had abandoned it. It stood mournful and sinister among the Jews. The temple had somehow strayed here into the darkness of Jewish exile. (E 142)

As the home of the naked, bearded Jew whose sign proclaims him to be *der kinig fun di yidn*, 'the King of the Jews' (Y 144/E 145), it partakes of *goles*, exile, in a disturbingly ambivalent way. As part of the ghetto and akin to it, and part of the Catholic Church yet cut off from it, it is very much like the crucified figure it houses. This Jesus appears to be despised and rejected not only by Jews but also by Christians, since the monk's invective seems directed as much towards the figure of Jesus as towards the coerced congregation (Y 145/E 146). Although the Christian Church professes the triumph of flesh over spirit, Jesus, like his Jewish brethren, is cast out from it. The worship offered in his name is presented as an unashamed blend of pomp and prurience, idolatry and harlotry (Y 140/E 141). Moreover, the narrative ironically places on the highest representatives of the Christian religion vestigial but unmistakable tokens of discarded Jewishness. The crucified Jesus wears on his head a *shtraymele fun derner* (Y 144); the pope wears *a vays yarmlkele* (Y 148). The accepted English renderings 'crown of thorns' and 'skullcap' do not convey the connotations of these Yiddish nouns, which, by specifically denoting head coverings worn for traditional religious observances in a context at the utmost remove from the faith which informs them, invite the speculation that if, in this tale, the pope has for a long time been planning to return to his people, so also may Jesus. The most deep-rooted of Christian terrors is exploited to offer a potential, though highly ambiguous, release from Jewish hopelessness.

Notes to Chapter 5

1. See Charles Madison, *Yiddish Literature: Its Scope and Major Writers* (1968; New York, 1971), 323–4; Zalmen Reyzen, *Leksikon fun der yiddisher literature, prese un philologye* (Vilna, 1928), i, cols. 1193–5.
2. Madison, *Yiddish Literature*, 323.
3. Y. Y. Trunk, 'Der yidisher poypst: historishe dertseylung', *Kvaln un Beymer* (New York, 1958), 127–55. An English translation of this tale is available in Joachim Neugroschel (trans. and ed.), *Great Works of Jewish Fantasy: Yenne Velt* (London, 1976), 128–56. All quotations are taken from these two editions; page references to both Yiddish and English versions are cited parenthetically after the letter Y (Yiddish text) and E (English text). On occasions I make my own translation of individual passages being examined; these are indicated accordingly.
4. See Sol Liptzin, *The Maturing of Yiddish Literature* (New York, 1970), 157–60.
5. Brian Masters, *A Student's Guide to Sartre* (1970; repr. London, 1979). 19.
6. Ibid. 21.
7. David L. Lerner, 'The Enduring Legend of the Jewish Pope', *Judaism* 40/2 (Spring 1991), 148–70, at 167.
8. See David G. Roskies, *Against the Apocalypse: Responses to Catastrophe in Modern Jewish Culture* (Cambridge, MA, and London, 1984), 258–310.

CHAPTER 6

❖

Radical Subversion with Isaac Bashevis Singer

Though the product of a similar Polish-Hasidic upbringing to that of Y. Y. Trunk and, within a decade, his contemporary, Isaac Bashevis Singer (1904–91) turns to folklore and legend for antithetical ideological and artistic ends. So far from seeking a reconciliation of Jews to a secular world, or from reflecting a passive resignation to a Jewish lot that cannot be amended, Singer's reworking of the pope myth militantly disidentifies itself from the assimilationism encouraged by the heirs of the *Haskalah*. In general, Singer tends to refuse any ideological system, since in his perception, none is capable of dealing adequately with the omnipresence of undeserved suffering in the world. In resistance to the punctilious observances of orthodoxy, he posits protest against what rabbinism is prepared to accept as the immutable will of God:

> I myself try to think that I have made peace with human blindness and God's permanent silence, but they give me no rest. I feel a deep resentment against the Almighty. My religion goes hand in hand with a profound feeling of protest. [...] My feeling of religion is a feeling of rebellion. I even play with the idea of creating (for myself) a religion of protest. I often say to myself that God wants us to protest. He has had enough of those who praise Him all the time and bless Him for all his cruelties to man and animals. [...] I may be false and contradictory in many ways, but I am a true protester. If I could, I would picket the Almighty with a sign, 'Unfair to Life'.[1]

Fiercely antagonistic to assimilation and 'enlightenment', Singer insists that material ambitions cut Jews off from any potential sources of validation for life. Singer's work consistently embodies his view that although Revelation, as the Torah defines it, may be uncertain, the moral absolutes of the Ten Commandments are not. While the premises that God created the world, gave the Jews the Torah, and through the Torah pointed them to the way of life may not have been true, 'once people believed in them, there was a way in life for [them]'.[2] By contrast, Singer has argued, 'the worship of reason [is] as idolatrous as bowing down to a graven image'.[3] For Singer, too, the materials of the Jewish pope myth provide the opportunity to make a central statement about the nature of Jewish identity and the possibilities for its continued viability.

In its Yiddish version, 'Zeydlus der ershter', the story was first published in the inaugural issue of the New York journal *Svive* (1943), under the subtitle, *fun a serie dertseylungen oyfn nomen fun 'dos gedenkbukh fun yetser-hore'*, 'from a series of short stories entitled "The Memoirs of the Evil Inclination" '. The Yiddish text was republished in book form the same year in Singer's first volume to appear in the United States, *Der shotn in goray un andere dertseylungen* (New York, 1943), with a foreword by Aaron Zeitlin. This edition was photo-mechanically reprinted by the Yiddish Department of the Hebrew University of Jerusalem in 1972, from which edition all the citations that follow are made. The English translation, approved by Singer, was made by Joel Blocker and Elizabeth Pollet for Singer's third anthology to be published in English, *Short Friday and Other Stories* (1964).[4] Where the Yiddish text differs in significant respects from the official English version, I have made my own translation and noted the discrepancies and omissions, which are often of considerable thematic significance. Obvious as it is that any writer's purpose is revealed primarily through his use of language, Singer's case is complicated by the fact that the discourse of his Yiddish texts differs in significant ways from that of the best-selling English translations of them made under his rigorous supervision. An examination of these differences in his version of the pope tale reveals the degree to which his Yiddish insists upon disidentifying itself absolutely from the values of the secular world. For Singer, Jews acquire meaning not in the degree to which they ape Gentiles, but in the degree to which they assert moral superiority. While Singer may choose to address a watered-down version of this statement to readers who know no Yiddish and are predominantly non-Jewish, his Yiddish text boldly addresses a readership whose lot, having been cast in the Diaspora, he demands they confront by rejecting what is alien and clinging resolutely to what is their own.

Through a series of devastating ironies, Singer radically subverts the traditional materials of the Jewish pope myth. This is why, although it was published fifteen years earlier than Trunk's, I have nevertheless chosen to treat Singer's version in thematic rather than in chronological sequence. In his reworking of the pope myth, the Jewish genius hungry for Christian glory that Singer sets up seems at first to have inherited all those distinctions most esteemed by devout Jews. The only son of an *ongeshtopte oysher*, 'an immensely rich man' (Y 274), he traces his descent back through the great medieval sage RaShI to King David himself (Y 274/E 212), a sanctified lineage reflected in his name, Zeydl Cohen. The surname, Cohen, marks out its possessor as a member of the priestly caste, upon whom the *Halakhah* lays mandatory ritual obligations to preserve their purity. The personal name, Zeydl, is amuletic, deriving from the Yiddish word *zeyde*, 'grandfather', and expressing the parents' prayer that the infant boy so named should reap the rewards of an observant Jewish life by living to old age and enjoying many grandchildren.[5] In this way, Zeydl's subsequent defection is made to assume the extremity of transgression. An embodiment of sterility and self-obsession, Zeydl discards all vestiges of Jewish concepts of purity. His acquisition of learning is likened, in a telling comparison, to the acquisitive way in which his father stockpiled his wealth: *glaykh vi zayn foter [...] hot a gants lebn tsunoyfgeleygt a groshn tsu a groshn, a rendl tsu a rendl, azoy hot zeydl ongezamlt visn*, 'just as his father had all his life hoarded penny after penny, coin after coin, so Zeydl accumulated learning' (Y 275, my translation). By equating learning with money, the narrative stresses its transactional rather than its spiritual value, making Zeydl's motivation the direct converse of that which should inform the true Jewish scholar, who studies to approach more closely the will of God, not the will of the world. In time, the narrative's metaphors will intensify this correspondence between material and spiritual gain to drive home its point.

In the first sentence of his reworking, Singer invalidates *ab initio* any potential temptation in the belief that arid book learning will buy Zeydl glory in the Christian world by making his narrator the *yetser-hore*, Evil Inclination, himself. This narrative device, by indicating from the start that Zeydl will succumb, leads naturally to a trenchant examination of the illusory nature of Zeydl's goals. Since for Singer Jewishness is a way of life confined within absolute categories of good and evil, he consistently views the attempts of the *maskilim* and their intellectual heirs to downgrade Judaism into simply another 'religion' as an exercise in moral relativism that deprived Jews of certitude and gave them nothing in return, a point Singer also never tired of emphasizing in numerous press interviews:

I am against the idea that Enlightenment can save us. Enlightenment, no matter how far it goes, will not bring redemption. [...] I would consider myself more of a Jewish writer than most of the Yiddish writers, because I am more a believer in the Jewish truths than they. Most of them believe in progress. Progress has become their idol. They believe that people will progress to such a degree that Jews will be treated well, they will be able to assimilate, mix with the Gentiles, get good jobs, and perhaps be President one day. To me, all these hopes are obsolete and petty. I feel that our real great hope lies in the soul and not in the body. Thus, I consider myself a religious writer.[6]

In using this tale to dramatize these views, Singer makes his tempter-narrator mouth every one of those arguments, grounded in the secular notion that the moral aspiration of Jews is merely an effect of their temporal deprivation, used by the more militant and transgressive of the *maskilim* against what they regarded as obscurantism and backwardness.

Discarding Judaism's moral imperative that man is obliged to acknowledge his insignificance in the face of God's greatness, the *yetser-hore*, playing to the hilt his role as *maskil*, heaps contempt on those persons whom Jewishness elevates to sainthood because they earn their livings as *shusterlekh un vaser-tregers*, 'small-time shoemakers and water-carriers', two of the humblest trades in Jewish folklore (Y 277/E 216–17). He dismisses the whole corpus of Jewish law as hair-splitting over trivialities, and holds the very language in which that law is formulated to have been deliberately corrupted for the incapacitating purpose of keeping ignorant subjects in a perpetual state of ideological abjection (Y 277). Having totally accepted the Christian definition of themselves as inferior beings through centuries of exile, the Evil Inclination goes on to argue, Jews are so far from possessing any sense of self-worth that they are driven to reconstitute King David as he is represented in the Gemara as *a kleynshtetldik rebl, vos paskent shayles-nisim* (Y 277), 'a [petty] provincial rabbi advising women about menstruation [the laws concerning the purity of women]' (E 217), *als kedey tsutsunemen fun im dem koved-hamalkhes*, 'only to deprive him of the majesty of kingship', a condition of exaltation that they have now become incapable of claiming as their own. Citing the Jews' ungrateful treatment of Moses and the Prophets, the *yetser-hore* concludes that, in regard to *groyskayt*, 'greatness', *der amenivkhor hot faynt* (Y 277), 'the Chosen People hate', while Gentiles *hobn lib* (Y 277), 'love'.

Consistent with the materialist pose he is adopting, this demon rejects as nonsensical Judaism's central ideological belief in the Chosenness of Israel, through whose acts of worship alone the knowledge of God's existence is given to the other nations of the earth[7] and hence the concomitantly great responsibility placed upon Jews to keep God's laws minutely (Y 278). He goes on to disallow God's close familial relationship with His people, supported everywhere in Scripture—for example Exodus 4:22–3—in favour of a secular view of a supremely indifferent Almighty. Its logical conclusion is to deny the possibility of *shkar ve-oynesh*, 'reward and punishment' (Y 278) in *mayse filosof*, 'after the manner of philosophers' (Y 278). This latter phrase, a pejorative description always given by the traditionally pious to rationalistic ideas, especially those circulated by the *maskilim*, leads, as Singer repeatedly demonstrates in his other work, to the nihilistic view that the world operates *les din veles dayen*, 'without Judge and without Judgement'. Christianity, and by extension, the whole of 'enlightenment', is presented as nothing but idolatry, in which a solipsistic brand of 'humanism' has replaced a community-oriented, theocentric view of the universe: *oyb zeyer got iz a mentsh, ken bay zey a mentsh zayn a got.* [...] *zey iz alts eyn vos eyner iz,—abi r'iz groys, makhn zey im far a gets* (Y 277–8), 'since their [the Christians'] god is a man, a man can be a god to them. [...] It's a matter of indifference to them what a man is—as long as he's great, they make an idol of him' (my translation). In this *reductio*, *got* and *gets*, divinity and idol, are made synonyms, religious faith is rendered a logical absurdity, and its profession is confirmed as an act of worldly expediency. In short, what this *yetser-hore* offers Zeydl is what tempted Heine to apostasy—a belief that, through conversion, he will be able fully to embrace and wholly to reap the rewards of European culture which, since it is under the control and in the gift of Christians, must be bought through conciliation and only on their own terms.[8] This represents the supreme temptation of the heirs of 'enlightenment' and, as far as Singer is concerned, it is a spiritual nullity.

But of course the *yetser-hore* is not a *maskil*; he is a demon playing a role and, like all Singer's Jewish demons, he can only function within the parameters of halakhic distinctions between good and evil. If these distinctions cease to exist, the demons cease to exist as well.[9] Singer's strategy for reminding us of this is his subtle manipulation of Yiddish discourse. Perfectly clear always that, as Max Weinreich has conclusively demonstrated, Yiddish is a vehicle for Jewishness and inseparable from it,[10] Singer exploits to the full the phenomenon that Weinreich identifies as *lehavdl loshn*,[11] in-built linguistic structures which differentiate categorically between things Jewish (sacred) and things Christian (profane). Since from the Jewish point of view, as Weinreich notes, 'ours' is *a priori* better than 'theirs', every word that designates what is 'theirs' is loaded with connotations of denigration and disparagement to which Zeydl may deaden himself but to which Singer's Yiddish readers are fully alive. Thus in praying, while Jews *davn*, Christians *blekekhtsn* (Y 278); whereas in preaching, a Jewish scholar gives a *droshe* (Y 273), Christian priests deliver *predikts* (Y 282); a Christian priest himself is a *tome*, 'an impure one'; a Gentile is an *orl*, 'an uncircumcised one' (Y 280). Yet, in a crowning irony typical of Singer, the *yetser-hore* amusingly affirms that he only exists because there is an opposite and equal Good Inclination, a *yetser-tov*, through his instinctive use of Yiddish and *loshn-koydesh* pietisms and pejoratives. His first mention of God is to the *reboyne-sheloylem*, 'Master of the Universe' (Y 277); he promises Zeydl he will become pope *im yirtseshem*, 'if God wills it' (Y 279). The demon derides the very idea of divine revelation: *a sheyn ponem volt got gehat, er zol zikh oystaynen mit a yilod ishe*, 'God would've looked a proper fool to argue things out with a creature born of woman', and he crudely dismisses Jesus as *a mamzer fun notsres*, 'a bastard from Nazareth' (Y 278/E 217). Instead of trying to believe such stuff, the blasphemous tempter cynically suggests, Zeydl will reach the pinnacle of worldly glory *az du vest [...] tsunoyfshteln epes a treyf-posl vegn dem yoyzl un zayn muter, di psule* (Y 279), a chunk of Yiddish discourse, of a piece with his earlier dismissal of Jesus, that entrenches a denigration absent from the English version approved by Singer, 'if you throw together some hodge-podge about Jesus and his mother the Virgin' (E 219). In Jewish law, a *mamzer* is not simply a 'bastard', an illegitimate offspring, but, far more gravely, the fruit of an adulterous union, the child of a married woman by a man who is not her husband; a *treyf-posl*, literally 'ritually impure offal', was the term of obloquy applied by the pious to all works of the *Haskalah*, even—often especially—if these were written in Hebrew.[12] The specific use of the Hebrew word *psule*, 'virgin', conspicuously absent from the Hebrew text of Isaiah 7:14, deliberately denies its controversial Christological interpretation, making the conjunction of a *muter* who is simultaneously also a *psule* a self-evident absurdity.

The only motivation that the Evil Inclination offers Zeydl to abandon Judaism for Christianity is *oyb du vilst koved oyf der-velt* (Y 278), 'if you want honour in this world'. The picture of ultimate worldly honour that the demon paints for Zeydl is a savage undercutting of the putative glory of the papacy. Delivered with cynical mockery, the description that so dazzles a *mebulbldiker*, 'befuddled', Zeydl (Y 279) reduces the glory so alluring to the Jewish popes of the earlier Yiddish versions to an empty parade of idolatrous vanity. It heaps mockery on all earthly glories in what might almost be a parody of midrashic interpolations about the pomp with which Joseph was borne aloft in Egypt:

un mirtseshem, az alts vet geyn oyfn glaykhn veg, vestu vern an afifyor, un di goyim veln dikh trogn oyf a gilderner shtul, vi a gets, un m'vet far dir roykhern veyroykh, un m'vet zikh bukn tsu dayn opbild in shpaniye un in kroke un in roym.
—*un vi vel ikh heysn?—hot zeydl gefregt.*
—*zeydlus der ershter.* (Y 278)

And God willing, if everything goes smoothly, you'll become a pope, and the Gentiles will carry you about on a golden chair, like an idol, and incense will be burned in front of you, and they'll bow before your image in Spain and Cracow and Rome.
—And how will I be called? Zeydl asked.
—Zeydlus the First. (my translation)

The crowning absurdity here is the demon's mock-solemn enunciation of the grotesquely Latinized form of Zeydl's name, a jarring malapropism that makes everyone laugh but Zeydl himself. Nothing could be more explicitly condemnatory of the Jewish impulse towards what Singer regards as 'enlightenment', on which his reworking of old materials is, on one level, a biting satire.

Close attention to the register of the demon's discourse should reveal the extent of the ridicule he is heaping on Zeydl's worldly ambitions. Apostasy, as the tempter presents it, is the process of becoming *a zeyrike* (Y 279), 'one of theirs'. To convey the full ironic extent of what this actually means for a believing Jew, the demon narrator wickedly plays with the religious connotations of the Yiddish idiom for 'getting quickly to the point': to broach the subject of conversion with 'them', Zeydl should *a shmues ton vegn akhtsn un draytsn* (Y 280), literally, 'have a chat about eighteen and thirteen'. For a devout Jew, these numbers unequivocally call to mind central elements of his faith: eighteen are the number of blessings uttered in the central prayer of each of the three daily services, the *shimenesre* or Eighteen Benedictions; thirteen are the number of the Principles of the Faith enumerated by Maimonides. This suggestive phrase is rich in even further connotations, all very much to the point here. Added together, the numbers eighteen and thirteen make thirty-one, for which the Hebrew notation in letters is *lamed-alef*, which in turn form the word *lo*, meaning 'no'. In common parlance, the phrase is thus simultaneously used in three ways: to express an outright negation, as a form of dialogue compelling someone to return to a subject he wishes to evade, and—of special relevance here—to introduce a discussion of money matters.[13] Were Zeydl not so blinded by fantasies of worldly glory, he could hardly miss the devastating multiple irony of this mischievous injunction; that he does, simply confirms the extent of his foolish confusion. Moreover, a further witty play with loaded Yiddish euphemisms comically enables the Jewish tempter to fake reluctance at soiling his lips with profanity, while at the same time acutely emphasizing the degree of defilement involved. Both the black comedy and its serious import are amplified in some further ironic punning that underscores what the demon perceives as the materialistic nature of Christianity and the attendant love of worldliness that draws Jews to it. He describes the act of conversion with a series of word-plays on the figurative disgust-idiom, *oysbaytn s'rendl* (Y 279), 'changing coin'. In proportion as Zeydl's disillusionment with this one-sided exchange increases, the figurative becomes literal—*iz dos torbele mit di gilderne rendlekh, vos iz gehangen oyf zayn halz hintern tseylem, gevorn alts shiterer* (Y 283), 'the bag with the gold coins, which hung round his neck behind the cross, grew steadily more empty' (my translation). Barren learning leads to spiritual poverty, whose concomitant is material hardship. As the money on which Zeydl survives—in close proximity to the symbol of the faith he has embraced—dwindles away, *es hot im shoyn bang geton vorem er hot ibergebitn dos rendl* (Y 283), 'he came to feel regret because he had changed his coin' (my translation). Yet he has had ample warning, for the demon consistently presents the Christian attitude to Zeydl's conversion in metaphors of buying and selling. In appropriate response to the *yetser-hore*'s rhetorical question, *vos kon zayn a besere shkhoyre far a galekh vi a yidishe neshome?* (Y 280), 'what could be better merchandise for a priest than a Jewish soul?', the Christians of Janov hasten to wish Zeydl *goldene glikn* (Y 280), 'golden good fortune', on his apostasy, since, as the narrator hastens to assure us, *di galokhim hobn mer in zinen dos gold vi dos opgot* (Y 282), 'the priests had their minds more on gold than on their god' (my translation). But since *opgot* means 'idol', a double irony is intentionally effected, and a deft equation made between two inseparable types of idolatry.

Similarly, the false scholarship in which Zeydl engages in the hope of *gikh oyle legdule zayn* (Y 281), 'to rise rapidly to greatness', is subjected to a series of verbal derogations that laughs his pretensions to scorn. Aping the standard practice of a piously observant Jew, the demon himself insists upon making a distinction between sacred and profane things mentioned successively together. His tart observation that *zeidls khiber hot gezolt vern, lehavdl, a goyisher yod-khazoke* (Y 281), contains a highly amusing but sharply pointed undercutting sadly lost in the published English translation, since the full meaning of the sentence is: 'Zeydl's treatise would be for Christianity what Maimonides' *The Strong Hand* [an alternative Hebrew designation for *The Guide to the Perplexed*]—you should pardon the gross comparison—was for Judaism' (E 221, translation modified). In seeking material for *dem emes groysn ksav-pilaster* (Y 281), 'the truly great libellous tract', Zeydl's researches issue pitifully in *a pashkvil* (Y 281), 'a pasquinade'; in preparation for *a bukh vegn shikuts mishumam* (Y 282), 'a justification of abomination', he must seek *bilbulim* (Y 283), 'slanders'; in the margins of Jewish holy books he writes *mare mekoymes* (Y 283), 'pseudo-commentaries'; and all this to please what are witheringly described as the *reshoim* (Y 282), 'the wicked ones', euphemistically rendered in the English translation Singer himself authorized as 'the Church' (E 222).

The demon-narrator's disidentification from the corruption to which he tempts Zeydl is completed by his habitual use of *talmud loshn*, words and phrases derived from the Talmud which immutably fix Zeydl's pursuit of worldliness and, metonymically, all 'enlightenment', in the category of the profane. Reading the Vulgate precipitates Zeydl's descent into *a gantser kener in sforim khitsonim* (Y 275), 'a total adept in forbidden books'. The Hebrew term *sforim khitsonim* originally designated the Apocrypha, books 'outside' the authorized canon of the Scriptures, but it gradually became a blanket condemnation of all books forbidden to God-fearing Jews. By using the only synonym in Yiddish for pork, the Talmud-derived phrase *dover akher* (Y 278), literally 'alien thing', the demon adds weight to the sin of eating it. In the act of mocking human claims to being *bkhir-hayetsire* (Y 278), 'the paragon of creation', his discourse reminds us that in God's creative determination human beings are indeed so when they obey God's commands, and he implicitly calls an unheeding Zeydl's attention to the fact that a man can never overreach the superior power which created him. He reinforces this admonition by reminding Zeydl that even Moses was *yilod ishe* (Y 278), 'born of woman', in this way ironically undercutting Christian claims that Jesus, also born of woman, was divine. When he is finally carried from his deathbed down to that *sheol takhtiyes* (Y 286), 'lowest hell', so vividly described in the Kabbalah he once knew so well, Zeydl receives an unequivocal answer to the chief question of his life, one significantly omitted from the official English version: *zenen take di apikorsim gerekht?* (Y 286), 'are the unbelievers then really right?' The term *apikoyres*, 'heretic', was applied with rigorous consistency by the piously observant to all *maskilim*, observant or not, who sought to encompass the divine through reason rather than through faith. As a word of Greek derivation (from the word meaning 'Epicurean') and Talmudic usage it performs the same alienating function as the Graecism *afifyor*, 'pope', which Singer, following the *Mayse-bukh*, chooses in preference to the Germanism *poypst/papst* employed in the other pope myth reworkings. Its connotative effect is to thrust the way of life of the so-designated irredeemably into the obliterative area of Jewish life and thought.

In following his folklore source and selecting as the victim of this temptation a genius scholar embodying, in person, ancestry and interests, the highest ideal of orthodox parents throughout generations of exile, Singer is concerned devastatingly to indict all learning divorced from moral responsibility. Because Judaism recognizes no distinction between orthodoxy and orthopraxis, Zeydl begins as he ends, an outcast freak, whose work is narcissistic self-indulgence. With great wit and irony, Singer wholly subverts the received biblical tradition by shaping Zeydl into a glaringly anti-Joseph figure. Where the biblical Joseph is universally admired for his great beauty, Singer's Zeydl is a compound of desiccation and ugliness, from which even the identifying markers of gender are effaced:

> keyn hor zenen im kimat nisht gevaksn, un tsu zibetsn yor iz zayn shaydl geven naket un shpitsik, un s'iz daroyf fir-un-tsvantsik sho in mesles gezesn a yarmlke. dos ponem iz geven lenglekh, roytlekh un epes vi tsugefroyrn. oyf dem oysgeshpitstn kin zaynen gevaksn bloyz etlekhe hor. oyfn hoykhn shtern zenen alemol geshtanen tropns shveys. di krume noz hot oysgezen meshune naket, a shtayger vi bay eynem vos iz gevoynt tsu trogn briln un r'hot zey oyf a vayl oysgetun. unter di ongeroytlte vies hobn gerut a por gele moyre-shkhoyredike oygn. hent un fis hot der zeydl gehat kleyne un vaybershe. er iz nisht gegangen in mikve un m'hot deriber nisht gevust in shtot, tsi iz er a sores, a tumtum, oder an andruginus. (Y274)

Almost no hair grew on his body; by the age of seventeen [the age at which the biblical Joseph was sold into slavery to begin his meteoric rise] his skull was bald and pointed, and a skullcap perched on it twenty-four hours a day. His face was oblong, flushed and somehow frozen stiff. Only a few hairs grew on his protruding chin; drops of sweat always stood on his high forehead. His crooked nose appeared strangely naked, like that of a man who is accustomed to wearing spectacles but has just taken them off for a while. Beneath his inflamed eyelids shifted a pair of yellow, melancholy eyes. This Zeydl had hands and feet that were small and feminine. He did not go to the ritual bath, so it was not known in the town whether he was a eunuch, a *tumtum* [one with underdeveloped organs of generation] or an androgyne. (my translation)

The narrative further implies that his uncertain gender is responsible for his rich, beautiful wife's inability to conceive, while her miserable, childless arranged marriage—in specific contrast to the happy, fertile marriage of the biblical Joseph, to whose wife Asenath Midrash devotes several highly eulogistic commentaries—is presented as a painfully slow living death:

di kale iz geven fun lublin, a raykhe tokhter un a yefies-to'ar. biz tsu der khasene, hot zi dem khosn nisht gezen, un ven zi hot oyf im a kuk getun farn badekns—iz shoyn geven tsu shpet. bekitser, zi hot khasene gehat un iz keynmol nisht trogedik gevorn. zi iz gezesn in di khadorim, vos der shver hot ir opgegebn, geshtrikt zokn, arayngekukt in mayse-bikhelekh, zikh tsugehert vi der groyser vant-zeyger mit di bagildte keytn un shteyner hot oysgeshlogn shoen un halbe shoen, un, aponem, geduldik gevart biz fun di minutn veln vern teg, un fun di teg yorn, bis vanen s'vet kumen di tsayt tsu geyn shlofn oyfn altn yanever bes-oylem. (Y 274)

The bride came from a rich Lublin family and was of great beauty. Until the day of the wedding she had never seen the groom, and when she did set eyes upon him, just before he covered her face with the veil, it was already too late. In short, she married him and was never able to conceive. She spent her time sitting in the rooms her father-in-law had allotted to her, knitting stockings, reading storybooks, listening to the large wall-clock with its gilded chains and weights chime out the hours and half-hours—patiently waiting, it seemed, for the minutes to become days, the days years, until the time should come for her to go to sleep in the old Janov cemetery. (E 213–14)

Severed from any life-promoting engagement with family or community, Zeydl becomes a zombie. An insatiable craving for books finds him every minute of the day 'rummaging, ferreting, sucking into his lungs the dust from ancient pages' (E 213), *er hot gebletert, genishtert, arayngezoygn dem shtoyb fun di bleter* (Y 273); the furniture of his home, from which light and air are rigorously excluded, 'was always covered with dust' (E 214), *oyf dem mebl [iz] alemol gelegn a shtoyb*; when he walks over his carpeted floors, *di trit zenen geven veykh un fartoybt, vi s'voltn dort arumgegangen nisht mentshn, nor rukhes* (Y 275), 'the steps were soft and muffled, as if spirits, not men, were wandering about there' (my translation). Zeydl's total disjunction of erudition from ethics is strikingly conveyed in one notable instance to which the narrative gives specific weight. By the age of seven, we are told, he knew by heart the whole of *Kidushin* and *Gitin*, the two tractates of the Talmud governing marriage and divorce (Y 273/E 212). Apart from the fact that the practical application of these laws must be beyond the grasp of any child, Zeydl's subsequent behaviour as an adult demonstrates his pathetic incapacity to translate book-learnt theory into life-enriching practice. Following the letter rather than the spirit of Jewish law—mere lip-service, as all his observances are shown to be—he enters into an arranged marriage with a woman he has never seen and for whom he feels neither affection nor responsibility (Y 272/E 214).

This disengagement from vivifying human contact finds its correspondence in his miserly refusal to share any kind of hospitality. By contrast with the generosity of the biblical figure of Joseph—and ironically, by contrast with the metaphors of money with which the narrative later invests his conversion to Christianity—Zeydl is shown to be psychopathologically mean, proving Freud's equation of material with emotional parsimony:

oybvoyl zeydl hot keynmol oysgegebn far zikh keyn prute, un rekht nisht gekont dem form fun a matbeye (er hot gekrogn zayn oyshaltenish fun foter), iz er geven a kamtsn un keynmol nisht genumen keyn oyrekh. azoy vi r'hot mit keynem nisht geshlosn keyn frayndshaft, un nisht er, nisht zayn vayb, hobn amol farbetn aheym a gast—hot keyner rekht nisht gevust vi zayn dire zet oys. (Y 275)

Despite the fact that Zeydl never spent a penny on himself, and in truth did not know what a coin looked like (he received the means of his support from his father), he was a miser and never took a poor man home for a Sabbath meal. Since he never established a friendship with anyone, and since neither he nor his wife ever invited a guest home, no one actually knew what his apartment looked like. (E 214, translation modified)

Since Zeydl thus wilfully chooses to cut himself off from the ideological demands of the Covenant which makes all Israel responsible one for another, it is inevitable that the Evil Inclination is able to entrap Zeydl's soul through debate regarding the nature of faith, the validity of revelation, and the existence of truth, since for

Zeydl these things are intellectual questions, not lived experiences. Zeydl's hankering for worldly fame blinds him to the logical conclusion of the Evil Inclination's evaluation of spiritual worth in material terms. For if it is true that Christians simplify the nature of the absolute by conferring divinity upon a man like themselves, Jews surely rightly recognize its mystery in their willing acceptance of the fact that *vos shtoybiker—alts nenter tsu got* (Y 277), 'the closer one is to dust, the nearer one is to God'. But for orthodoxy, this dust is not the self-collected sterility in which Zeydl buries himself; it is the dust into which, by blowing the breath of life, God laid the obligation to fill the interim between cradle and grave with work that, to have any redemptive meaning, must embrace other people. The ideology of Judaism insists that man's arrogant refusal to accept his humble apportioned lot, and his stubborn determination to comprehend the universe through his own unaided intellect, leads an individual wilfully to blind himself to the limitations of mortality. The physical loss of sight that finally overtakes Zeydl is on one level the physical correlative of this spiritual blindness.

If Zeydl were other than the antithesis of the Jewish scholar, pursuing learning to glorify not God but himself, he should be able to see in the Evil Inclination's arguments in favour of conversion to Christianity the strongest reasons for affirming the truth of Judaism. Materialism, which assesses value only in terms of functionality, makes Zeydl totally ignore the ideological reasons that inform the laws governing Jewish conduct, which profoundly assert the existential interdependence of God and the People of Israel: in the Zohar's formulation of this mystical principle, *g'dargin inun mitkashran da b'da, kudsha b'rikh hu v'oraita v'yisrael*, 'Three levels are intertwined: the Holy One, Blessed be He, the Torah, and Israel' (Zohar 3:73). God's command is explicit: 'For I am the Lord your God; sanctify yourselves therefore, and be ye holy; for I am holy' (Leviticus 11:44). To be a holy people imposes enormous responsibility, for if God is invisible, His nature may be made known to other nations only through the behaviour of those whom He chose to be the bearers of His name. Any expression of unholiness on the part of Israel reflects on the divinity of God. Thus orthodoxy locates the importance of the laws of *kashrut*, the dietary laws, for instance, not in their logicality, but in the fact that they are God-given commands. Zeydl's dominating passion, *gayve*, 'pride', makes him wilfully seek counter-identification from Judaism's understanding of revelation. Because of his own determination to deny, Zeydl, always so quick to see faults in the reasoning of others, pathetically fails to recognize the Tempter's argument as a continual assertion through denial of God's direct intervention in human affairs. Zeydl rejoices in receiving *koved*, 'honour', for the first time in his life, foolishly unaware that this 'honour' is bestowed on him by Christians not as an individual but as a living proof that they indeed possess the truth, for as a learned Jew, has he not abandoned his faith, betrayed his ancestors and denied the God of Israel, only in order to become a living witness to the superiority of the Christian faith? All this is emblematized by renaming Zeydl 'Benedictus Janovsky', the 'Blessed One of Janov'.

Psychopathically obsessed with perfection, Zeydl wants to produce a work before whose authority, like that of another revelation, the whole world will bow down. Judging himself a god, he sets standards to which he, as only a man, can never measure up, and his reward is total confusion. His material means and physical strength are dissipated in proportion as his mind rambles, and his degeneration is complete when *yede hofenung tsu vern mefursem bay di umes iz aroysgerungen fun zayn harts* (Y 282), 'every hope of becoming famous among the Gentile nations was wrung from his heart'. From the day he is suddenly deprived of sight, *hot zeydl gelebt in der finsternish* (Y 283), Zeydl lives in darkness as much spiritual as physical. So far from gaining absolute glory, he is reduced to abject humiliation (Y 283/E 223).

Here the narrative takes on an explicitly didactic tone, like a moral tale from the *Mayse-bukh*. Despite Christian offers of help, Zeydl, in a final assertion of his freedom to choose, takes up a beggar's place outside *a groys bes-tume*, a 'great house of impurity', evasively rendered in Singer's officially approved English translation as a 'cathedral'. As the only freedom left to him, its exercise is, in its acceptance under the most negative circumstances, a recognition of the futility of his quest for 'enlightenment' and the beginning of a willing acceptance of the inescapable identity conferred by Judaism. On the steps of the cathedral he mumbles only Jewish learning; he has forgotten *goyishe toyres*, 'Gentile teachings', as quickly as he learnt them. Just as in his days of youthful pride and prosperity he shut out the reality of the world outside, so in his days of beggary and degradation he is both blind and deaf to the life throbbing around him (Y 284–5/E 224–5). This imperviousness to life is what formerly cut him off from that small measure of perception granted to man. He had sought the meaning of life in places where it was lost in rationalization, only to discover at the end that the wages of intellectualism is illusion (Y 285/E 225). On his deathbed, the Christian world whose glory he has sought presents itself to Zeydl, as to Trunk's Frankfurt rabbi, as a vision of savage debauchery:

> *er hot gehert fun gas koyles, geshreyen, a brumenish, a rufenish, a tupenish, a klingen fun glokn un s'hot im tsumol oysgedukht, glaykh in droysn volt a pebl fun heydn gepravt a khoge, mit trumeytn un poykeray, mit shturkatsn un vilde khayes, mit oysgelasene tents un getsndinerishe korbones.* (Y 285)

> Out in the streets he heard voices, screams, stamping hoofs, ringing bells. It seemed to him some pagan multitude was celebrating a holiday with trumpets and drums, torches and wild beasts, lascivious dances, idolatrous sacrifices. (E 225)

The only thing he has learnt after all his travail is simply that man is an effect, not a cause, of Creation and that, the enticements of reason and the world it tries to govern notwithstanding, there is indeed both Judge and Judgment. Even as the *yetser-hore* warns him against any attempt at *tshuve*, 'repentance', or at *vidui*, 'confession of sins', Zeydl receives him *mit freyd*, 'joyously':

> *oyb s'iz do a gehenem, iz dokh do a got oykh!* [...] *oyb a gehenem iz do, iz alts do. un oyb du bist do, iz ER oykh do. itst nem mikh vu du darfst. ikh bin ongebreyt.* (Y 286)

> If there is a Gehenna, there is also a God! [...] If Hell exists, everything exists. If you are real, HE is real. Now take me to where I belong. I am ready. (E 226)

Singer goes much further than any of the versions that precede him. Where these recognize some validity in the temptations held out by Christian worldliness, Singer's tale—equating it with the enticements of the *Haskalah*—unwaveringly condemns it as idolatry, the most wicked of Jewish sins (Y 279/E 219). The contempt of the *leytsim*, 'mockers', who await Zeydl at the gates of Gehenna deliberately contrasts the roles of *yeshive bokher* and *afifyor* to point to the gulf that separates the worship of One God from the adoration of idols, and uncompromisingly vindicates, in blackly comic terms, the Jewish definition of the nature of man. For Singer there is no temptation to resist, since for the Jew of genuine learning, 'enlightenment', metonymically identified with Christianity and rooted in worldly glories, is the exaltation of vanity. Conversion, as the narrator of this tale presents it, is a victory for the powers of evil, because it denies that separation which for Jews must eternally exist between the nature of God and the nature of man. Zeydl's glad acceptance of the torments of hell effectively amounts to Singer's assertion that the powers of evil cannot destroy Israel as long as Israel accepts the subjectification imposed upon it by its ideology.

Notes to Chapter 6

1. Richard Burgin, 'Isaac Bashevis Singer's Universe: The Second of a Two-Part Series', *The New York Times Magazine* (3 Dec. 1978), 52.
2. Richard Burgin, 'A Conversation with Isaac Bashevis Singer', *The Michigan Quarterly Review* 17/1 (Winter 1978), 124.
3. Isaac Bashevis Singer, 'If You Could Ask One Question About Life, What Would The Answer Be? Yes...', *Esquire* (Dec. 1974), 95–6.
4. Quotations from this translation, page references to which are cited parenthetically in my text after the letter E, are made from Isaac Bashevis Singer, *Short Friday and Other Stories* (New York, 1980), 212–26.
5. Shmuel Gorr, *Jewish Personal Names: Their Origin, Derivation and Diminutive Forms* (Teaneck, NJ, 1992), 48.
6. Harold Flender, 'An Interview with Isaac Bashevis Singer', *National Jewish Monthly* 82 (March 1968), republished in Grace Farrell (ed.), *Isaac Bashevis Singer: Conversations* (Jackson and London, 1992), 43–4.
7. See, for instance, Moshe Sharon, *Judaism, Christianity and Islam: Interaction and Conflict* (Johannesburg, 1989), 33.
8. Todd M. Endelman (ed.), *Jewish Apostasy in the Modern World* (New York and London, 1987), 9 109: for Heine's belief in conversion as 'the ticket of admission to European culture' see Mendes-Flohr, Paul R. and Reinharz, Jehudah, *The Jew in the Modern World: A Documentary History* (New York and Oxford, 1980), 223–4.
9. One of the most vivid examples of this positioning of the demon-narrator can be found in Singer's story 'Mayse tishevits' in *Der shpigl un andere dertseylungen* (1975; Jerusalem, 1979), 12–22. The official English translation of this story appears as 'The Last Demon' in Singer, *Short Friday*, 145–58.
10. See for instance Singer's scathing review of the first issue of what was at the time the newly revived *Sovietish Heymland*, July-August 1961, in *Commentary* 33/2 (March 1962), 267–9, where he trenchantly argues this very point.
11. Max Weinreich, *History of the Yiddish Language*, trans. Shlomo Noble, with the assistance of Joshua A. Fishman (Chicago and London, 1980), 193 ff.
12. Ibid. 278.
13. See Lucy Dawidowicz, *The Jewish Presence: Essays on Identity and History* (New York and London, 1978), 161–2; also Maurice Samuel, *In Praise of Yiddish* (New York, 1971), *passim*.

CHAPTER 7

❖

The Case of Israel Zangwill

The central problem of assimilation and dual identity dominating every version of the Jewish pope myth is remarkably dramatized in both the life and the work of the Anglo-Jewish writer Israel Zangwill, who made his own contribution to this myth, through the medium of English, in a story that remarkably anticipates the crises of his own life. The passage of time and the events of modern Jewish history have now made it impossible to review Zangwill's work in isolation from the events of his own life, for rarely has any Jewish writer so explicitly dramatized the conflicts of his own sense of identity in his fiction.

Israel Zangwill (1864–1926) was born to immigrant Russian-Jewish parents in Whitechapel, London, and received his education at the Jews' Free School, a pioneer educational establishment founded well before the Compulsory Education Act and maintained privately, largely by the Rothschild family. It was a school specifically designed by its trustees to ensure the rapid acculturation of the children of Eastern European Jewish immigrants; as Zangwill ironically characterized it later, its bell summoned 'its pupils from the reeking courts and alleys, from the garrets and the cellars [of London's East End], calling them to come and be Anglicised'.[1] A gifted student, Zangwill became a pupil teacher at the same school at the age of eighteen, and in 1884, on a school scholarship, he took an honours degree in English, French and Mental and Moral Science at the University of London. Zangwill worked as a master at the Jews' Free School for six years before he left teaching to become a journalist in 1888. Zangwill's father, an immigrant from Russia who had come to England as a boy, tried a variety of unskilled jobs but never succeeded in making a sound living from any of them. Among the occupations he held for the longest period was that of packman, peddling his wares across the country. This experience of his father's life made a lifelong impression on his son, who recalled it three years before his death in a speech he delivered in New York in 1923: 'My father as he went about the country was subjected to endless sneers and persecutions because he was a Jew. I wanted to end this situation of my people.'[2] Zangwill later portrayed his father's experiences through the character of Moses Ansell in his most famous book, *Children of the Ghetto* (1892):

> To Moses [Ansell or Zangwill] 'travelling' meant straying forlornly in strange towns and villages, given over to the worship of an alien deity and ever ready to avenge his crucifixion; in a land of whose tongue he knew scarce more than the Saracen damsel married by legend to à Becket's father. It meant praying brazenly in crowded railway trains, winding his phylacteries round his left arm and on his forehead to the bewilderment or irritation of unsympathetic fellow-passengers. It meant living chiefly on dry bread and drinking black tea out of his own cup, with meat and fish and the good things of life utterly banned by the traditional law, even if he were flush. [...] It meant carrying the red rag of an obnoxious personality through a land of bulls. [...] It meant putting up at low public houses and common lodging houses, where rowdy disciples of the Prince of Peace often sent him bleeding to bed, or shamelessly despoiled him of his merchandise, or bullied and blustered him out of a fair price, knowing he dared not resent. It meant being chaffed and gibed at in a language of which he only understood that it was cruel. Once when he had been interrogated as to the locality of Moses when the lights went out, he replied in Yiddish that the light could not go out, for 'it stands in the verse that round the head of Moses was a perpetual halo.' A German who happened to be there laughed, and translated the repartee, and the rough drinkers pressed bitter beer upon the temperate Jew. But as a rule, Moses Ansell drank the cup of affliction instead of hospitality. Yet Moses never despaired nor lost faith.[3]

To a contemporary eye, what is most striking about this passage is the attitude of its narrative voice. In the very act of castigating the Christian persecutors of this ineradicably Jewish old peddler, the language chosen also quite clearly implies criticism of this Yiddish-speaking foreigner. Even though the deity of his tormenters is described as 'alien', the old man persists in praying to his own God 'brazenly'; his personality is 'obnoxious' to them so, the tone of the narrative voice suggests, he has only himself to blame that it acts as a 'red rag' on them; his lack of English is insidiously held against him in the unflattering comparison with the outré 'Saracen damsel', and the piety of his response to the crude question about Moses is dismissed by the narrative discourse, as much as by the listeners on the train, as trivial 'repartee'. And most telling of all, the irritable narrative language suggests that the old man's scrupulous observance of

Judaism's dietary laws ensures that 'the good things of life'—reduced here merely to meat and fish—are 'utterly banned' for him through his own stubborn and senseless adherence to a ridiculous convention. In short, the subtext of this passage unmistakably insinuates that most of the afflictions that befall this old Jew are his own fault.

Zangwill's parents, apart from living in materially straitened circumstances, were also sadly ill-matched. His father Moses was far more devout than his mother Ellen, who was an ambitious woman, envious of the greater prosperity of her English relatives, and determined that her children should rise in the Gentile world of England in which they lived. The father withdrew more and more into himself and his pieties, growing more and more estranged from his rapidly acculturating family. The parents' differences in religious outlook deepened with age so that by the early 1890s, to intensify his devotions, the father went to live in Jerusalem where he died in 1908, while the mother, growing ever more lax in her own observance, stayed behind in London.[4]

By the time he was thirteen, the age of *barmitzvah*, Zangwill had rebelled against his father's example, both in piety and in pursuing exclusively Jewish learning. He was irresistibly drawn to the language and literature of England, and like so many Jewish boys eager for assimilation in their adoptive countries, grew to despise his father's inability to speak English properly even after nearly half a century of residence in Britain. Yet at the same time, Zangwill felt bound to the heritage of Judaism and his own Jewish birth, and moved onwards in unresolved and painful dualism, so that all his life he was to remain torn between two conflicting desires—the desire to be integrally part of British culture, and the desire to remain faithful to his people. He was simultaneously attracted to and repelled by his father's faith and culture, as two striking illustrations in his literary work demonstrate. Zangwill made a number of translations from Hebrew into English rhymed verse of the *piyyutim* or liturgical poems included in the liturgy for the Jewish High Holy Days, *Rosh Hashanah* and *Yom Kippur*, which were for many decades included in all new English translations of the *mahzor* or prayer book; at the same time, his English work, especially his most famous book, *Children of the Ghetto*, expressed a deep ambivalence towards the condition of being Jewish, and especially towards Yiddish, a language he despised as a 'the most hopelessly corrupt and hybrid jargon ever evolved'[5] and which he regarded as the hallmark of Jewish illiteracy in Western learning and culture. He seemed often to want to deny that he was a Jew himself, for, he once explained, to say that he was a Jew 'would be to produce a false impression. The conception of the Jew in the mind of the average Christian is a mixture of Fagin, Shylock, Rothschild, and the caricatures of the comic papers. I am certainly not like that, and I am not going to tell a lie and say that I am.'[6] Yet towards the end of his life, more fully aware than he had been in youth of the impossibility of ever being other than a Jew, he could write urgently to the assimilating among the Jewish people: 'Back, back, brethren, back to the Ghetto, to our dream of Messiah, and to our old Sabbath candles.'[7]

Despite his deepening personal ambivalence, Zangwill built his early literary reputation on the publication of sketches and essays chiefly in Jewish newspapers and journals. Above all, it was the appearance in 1889 of his essay 'English Judaism', in the inaugural issue of the *Jewish Quarterly Review* alongside essays by the German historian Heinrich Graetz and the Cambridge Hebrew scholar Solomon Schechter, that brought him to international attention and created the opportunity for him to become world famous. This essay attracted the favourable attention of Judge Meyer Sulzberger, chairman of the newly established Jewish Publication Society of America, then seeking a new book to launch the society's work. What Sulzberger was looking for was, he said, 'a Jewish *Robert Elsmere*', a book that would deal in Jewish terms with the same problems of faith in relation to organized religion raised by Mrs Humphrey Ward in her novel of that title, which had taken the Anglophone world on both sides of the Atlantic by storm in 1888. Zangwill accepted Sulzberger's invitation, and the result was the publication, in 1892, of *Children of the Ghetto*, a novel that was universally received with acclaim, and established Zangwill as both a novelist of international repute, and a major spokesman for British Jewry. The need to fulfil the mandate of the Jewish Publication Society chimed well with Zangwill's deepening ambivalence about Judaism, and in his novel he was able to articulate several aspects of this blurred focus in ways that illuminate well the dilemmas of his own life. Through the character of Esther Ansell, he posed the chief of his own dilemmas:

Esther led a double life, just as she spoke two tongues. The knowledge that she was a Jewish child, whose people had a special history, was always at the back of her consciousness [...]

But far more vividly did she realise that she was an English girl; far keener than her pride in Judas Maccabeus was her pride in Nelson and Wellington

[...] Esther absorbed these ideas from the school reading books. The experience of a month overlay the hereditary bequest of a century.[8]

And through the voice of Joseph Strelitski, the disillusioned minister in the service of the United Synagogue who forsakes his calling, he expressed what he saw as the answer:

How can Judaism—and it alone—escape going through the fire of modern scepticism, from which, if religion emerges at all, it will emerge without its dross? [...] In every age our great men have modified and developed Judaism. Why should it not be trimmed into concordance with the culture of the time? Especially when the alternative is death? [...] Now for the first time in history, is the hour of Judaism. Only it must enlarge itself; its platform must be all inclusive.[9]

Here Zangwill early on articulated the conviction he came to hold with ever greater intensity throughout his life, that Judaism had two stark alternatives before it: either to accommodate itself to the mores of the age, or to die out. These mores were, of course, Christian, and Zangwill increasingly revealed himself as one who had been wholly subjectified by the dominant ideology. He came in time to claim that the teachings of Jesus actually expressed the purest essence of Judaism: 'I regard Jesus as second only to Moses in the long line of Hebrew Prophets who are half revealed and half obscured in the literary masterpieces of my race which begin with Genesis and end arbitrarily with Revelations.'[10] Moses and Jesus, Zangwill maintained, were the two most forceful prophets of a syncretic Judaism comprising both 'Old' and 'New' Testaments, and the pristine teachings of the Jew Jesus should not be confused with centuries of misrepresentation imposed on them by the later Church. There were in fact not two religions but one, Zangwill argued, and the task of modern Judaism was to unify them: 'Israel's [...] only hope of influencing the future hinges on its power to absorb the culture of the day so as to bring its own particular contribution to the solution of the problems of its time, its own moral vision of the world. It must come out of the *débris* of the Ghetto and enrich humanity by its point of view.'[11] Zangwill did not simply rewrite the myth of the Jewish pope as an exercise in fiction; he actually played out a version of the role in his own life, believing as he did that the 'prophetic mission' of his life was to harmonize the teachings, and reconcile the followers, of the Jew Moses and the Jew Jesus.

As one of his first efforts in this direction, on Christmas Day, 1889, in the orthodox Jewish newspaper the *Jewish Standard*, Zangwill published a poem entitled 'The Rencontre' which sought to dramatize the disjunction he hoped to unify:

> ### The Rencontre
>
> In dream I saw two Jews that met by chance,
> One old, stern-eyed, deep-browed, yet garlanded
> With living light of love around his head,
> The other young, with sweet seraphic glance.
> Around went on the Town's satanic dance,
> Hunger a-piping while at heart he bled.
> *Shalom Aleichem*, mournfully each said,
> Nor eyed the other straight but looked askance.
>
> Sudden from Church out rolled an organ hymn,
> From Synagogue a loudly chaunted air,
> Each with its Prophet's high acclaim instinct.
> Then for the first time met their eyes, swift-linked
> In one strange, silent, piteous gaze, and dim
> With bitter tears of agonized despair.

His sense of mission led Zangwill to the radical claim that only heretics were capable of contributing significantly to the civilization of the world, and to prove his point, as well as to extend his analysis of what he regarded as 'essential Judaism', he set out to dramatize the lives of those he took to be the most noteworthy heretics in Jewish history, a list of persons that inevitably included a sizeable number of converts. This project issued in his book *Dreamers of the Ghetto*, first published in 1898.

Even more than *Children*, *Dreamers of the Ghetto* was born of Zangwill's overwrought sense of oppression and confusion in consequence of his inability to reconcile his own competing dual identities: his sense of being British and his ineradicable awareness of also being a Jew. In this book, Zangwill strove to show that the experience of Jews through history expressed a universal philosophy of life equally relevant for both Jews and Gentiles, and he intended to convey through it a religious message to all civilized humanity, one grounded in the ancient wisdom of the Jewish people. Through its creative exploration of the intellectual and psychological dynamics of Jews trying to live authentic lives in a non-Jewish world, *Dreamers of the Ghetto* seeks to find a way in which Jews and Christians might live together in harmony, each with their integrity intact. The difficulty with the way Zangwill sought to address this problem, however, is that he was writing from the weak position of apologetics, from a profound subjectification to Christian values. As his most recent biographer has pointed out, the bearers of his 'universal' message in this book were all Jewish apostates, the real hero of his book was Jesus, and the religious message it preached was Christianity.[12] In his self-created role as a kind of Jewish pope in his own professional and public life, Zangwill was finally unable to distinguish between Christianity and what was authentically Jewish, since a major part of him longed to be integrally part of the Christian culture that dominated the British world into which he was born. From this subjectification developed his highly ambivalent personal attitude to the 'Ghetto', the metaphor he employs for traditionally observant Jewish life in the Diaspora. As an 'Anglo-Jew', Zangwill was simultaneously moved by Jewish fidelity, and repulsed by the fact that this fidelity manifests itself in punctilious observance of the Law enshrined in the Talmud. Throughout *Dreamers of the Ghetto*, the narrative voice repeatedly derogates the Talmud with such pejoratives as 'a Rabbinic manufacture' and 'a parasitic growth insinuating itself with infinite ramifications into the most intimate recesses of life'.

As an epigraph to his new book, Zangwill appended his poem 'The Rencontre' under the new title 'Moses and Jesus'; the main content of the volume was a series of some fifteen fictionalized biographies of historical figures including Uriel Acosta, Spinoza, the false messiah Sabbetai Zevi, and the Baal Shem Tov, the founder of Hasidism, as well as vignettes of the careers of more contemporary figures such as the social reformer Ferdinand Lasalle, the poet Heinrich Heine, the statesman Benjamin Disraeli, and the founder of the Zionist movement, Theodor Herzl. In addition, Zangwill offered three completely fictional stories that, since they are free from the constraints of recorded historical fact, most clearly carry the chief message of the book.[13] The fullest exposition of Zangwill's desire for reconciliation between Jew and Christian—inevitably, on exclusively Christian terms—is found in the second of these stories, Zangwill's version of the Jewish pope myth entitled 'Joseph the Dreamer'.[14] Here Zangwill elaborates the old tale of a gifted and beautiful Jewish boy who leaves the ghetto of Rome one Chanukah evening to attend midnight mass at St Peter's, and there he is overwhelmed by the desire to embrace the religion of Jesus himself, and to convert his Jewish brethren to the beauty of the Christian faith.

In Zangwill's narration, however, several unconscious ambiguities intrude. As always, the squalor of the ghetto—which Zangwill, like Trunk, drew from the pages of Graetz's *History of the Jews* (1853–76)— is overdetermined: unlike the ghetto of Frankfurt, ' the comparative poverty of the Ghetto [of Rome] [...] made its tragedy one of steady degradation rather than of fitful massacre' (p. 24); it is a place of 'marshy alleys where every overflow of the Tiber left deposits of malarious mud, where families harboured, ten in a house, where stunted men and wrinkled women slouched through the streets, and a sickly spawn of half naked babies swarmed under the feet' (p. 25); where 'room was more and more precious in the Ghetto, which was a fixed space for an ever-expanding population' (p. 26). Jews are restricted in the trades they can follow: 'Numerous shops encumbered the approaches [to the Piazza Giudea], mainly devoted to the sale of cast-off raiment, the traffic in new things being prohibited to Jews by Papal Bull, but anything second-hand might be had here' (p. 26); they are denied books by the Christians (p. 31). The persecutory conditions under which the Jews are forced live, coupled with the 'austere simplicity' of life demanded by their own ruling 'Council of Sixty' which forbids Jews 'to vie with *signori* in luxury' (p. 23), makes an escape to the unfettered beauties outside the Ghetto inevitable for aesthetically minded young men like Joseph.

Zangwill presents his Joseph as a visionary whose intellectual brilliance leads him to ask troublesome questions of his teachers, and so makes his flight from the Ghetto inevitable:

> They had had trouble enough, but never such a trouble as this, Manasseh and Rachel, with this queer offspring of theirs, this Joseph the Dreamer, as he had been nicknamed, this handsome, reckless black-eyed son of theirs, with his fine oval face, his delicate olive features; this young man, who could not settle down to the restricted forms of commerce possible in the Ghetto, who was to be Rabbi of the community one day, albeit his brilliance was occasionally dazzling to the sober tutors upon whom he flashed his sudden thought, which stirred up that which had better been left asleep. Why was he not as other sons? (p. 25)

There is calculated irony, as well as a clear striving after typology, in Zangwill's choice of onomastics. The unbendingly stern and devout Jewish father who sits out the Seven Days of Mourning when his son converts, and openly celebrates his physical death at the stake, is ironically named Manasseh, the name that the biblical Joseph gives his first-born, meaning 'making to forget'; the boy's mother is called after the only wife that Jacob truly loved; the young Jewish woman he is meant to marry is named Miriam, after the sister of Moses. All these personal names fix the Jewish characters firmly within the Jewish tradition, while the name given to the chief character recalls not only the prophetic power of his biblical namesake, but also—consciously or not—the extent of his assimilation into Egypt.

Zangwill's Joseph is seduced in the first instance by the opulence of Christianity's external ceremonies: 'the midnight mass—incense and lights and the figures of saints and wonderful painted windows and a great multitude of weeping worshippers and music that wept with them. [...] I was caught up in a mighty wave of organ-music that surged from this low earth heavenward to break against the footstool of God in the crystal firmament' (pp. 28–9). The seductive power of Christian church music was something Zangwill felt keenly in his own life; in one of the essays in *My Religion* (1925), one of his last published books, Zangwill recalled his bachelor days when he lived in London's Inner Temple: 'It is Sunday morning in the Temple. The church bells are ringing, and though I was born a Jew and know that the original Templars on the day they recaptured Jerusalem and the tomb of Christ slew every Jew, man, woman and child—I would willingly quit the work of writing this to sit in the Temple Church.'[15] In the boy Joseph, this aestheticism is disturbingly coupled to an intense masochism that yearns for an orgasmic death in order to bring about the eradication of Jewry:

And suddenly I knew what my soul was pining for. I knew the meaning of that restless craving that has always devoured me [...] in a flash I understood the secret of peace [...] Sacrifice [...] To suffer, to give one's self freely to the world; to die myself in delicious pain, like the last tremulous notes of the sweet boy-voice that had soared to God in the Magnificat [...] Let us pray for faith. When we are Christians the gates of the Ghetto will fall. (p. 29)

This is a strange way indeed to reconcile Judaism and Christianity, by flatly insisting that the one that is weaker is wrong, and should therefore surrender to and be swallowed up by the stronger. In this tale, Zangwill seems to reiterate the demand the Christians had made in vain on the Jews for so many centuries—to hear their message, confess their fault, and convert. Zangwill gives his Joseph a pat answer to Miriam's robust assurance that his missionary preaching will be in vain:

'Cut thyself into little pieces and we would not believe in thee or in thy gospel. [...] Thou wilt no more move them [the Jews] than the seven hills of Rome. They have stood too long.'

'Ay they have stood like stones. I will melt them. I will save them.' (pp. 44–5)

For Joseph—and so for Zangwill—Judaism has dwindled into nothing but empty form, impotent to protect Jews from their life of degradation under Christians, or to offer them anything but dry rabbinical proscriptions to loosen the curbs on their existence. 'Our creed is naught but prayer-mumbling and pious mummeries. The Christian Apostles went through the world testifying. Better a brief heroism than this long ignominy' (p. 30). A peculiar mixture of motives drives this boy Joseph to convert: part self-indulgence, part romantic illusion, part a genuine reaching out for the divine—or so Zangwill tries to persuade his readers. What emerges from his narrative and the language in which he conveys it, however, is an increasingly futile argument in favour of a nebulous spirituality that nowhere makes itself manifest in the conduct or interiority of any of the characters, and in Joseph least of all. The only language to which Zangwill appears to have access in trying to delineate these none too comprehensible vapourings is that of the King James Bible, in words which are not only Christological in the highest degree, but which, through dint of sheer repetition, have become little more than trite phrases devoid of impact. 'By faith are mountains moved', Joseph announces when he is told that the Jews have ritually pronounced the *herem* on him, that anathema that cuts him off from the living community, 'my spirit embraces theirs. We shall yet rejoice together in the light of the Saviour, for weeping may endure for a night, but joy cometh in the morning' (p. 35).

Competing against the pious Jewish Miriam for the love of the handsome Joseph is Helena, the beautiful pagan daughter of his benefactor, whose carefully selected name defines her devotion to Hellenistic culture: 'I am no Christian at heart', she tells Joseph, dismissing Christianity in the same language with which Joseph has dismissed Judaism: 'Rome counts her beads and mumbles her paternosters, but she has outgrown the primitive faith in Renunciation [...] Ah, we have rediscovered the secret of Greece [...] Apollo is Lord, not Christ' (pp. 36–8). For Helena, the 'cowl and gown [of the priesthood]' represent 'that unlovely costume which, to speak after thine own pattern, symbolises all that is unlovely' (pp. 40–1). And the Christian Church is a mass of venality and worldliness, defined by the conduct of the pope, 'a scholar and a gentleman, a great patron of letters and the arts' who is preoccupied not with matters of faith but with political gossip and costly jewellery (pp. 45–6).

Zangwill tries hard not to stack the cards in presenting his fictionalized plea for the unity of faith among all mankind. He weighs the (sadly hackneyed) protestations of the apostate Joseph against the equally predictable rigidity of his Jewish father, Helena's pagan abandonment to humanism, and the corruption of the sybaritic Church, in what he hopes will be read as a carefully even-handed debate, but which simply issues in a series of clichés. The morbidly sensitive Joseph alone is made to speak of disinterested faith, yet it is difficult to believe that he is the bearer of the kind of message Zangwill is trying to send, for this dreamer is a Jewish apostate whose vision of 'universal religion' is of the entire world professing Catholic Christianity and practising unproductive self-immolation: 'What is it I feel is the highest, divinest in me? Sacrifice! Wherefore He who was all sacrifice, all martyrdom, must be divine' (p. 30). It becomes difficult to understand the meaning of Joseph's increasingly empty rhetoric:

Love, love, that is all; the surrender of one's will to the love that moves the sun and all the stars, as your Dante says. And sun and stars do but move to this end, Signora—that human souls may be born and die to live, in oneness with Love. [...] This, this is the true ecstasy, to give yourself up to God, all in all, to ask only to be the channel of His holy will. (pp. 38–9)

This stock construct of what Zangwill takes Christian piety to be rings considerably less true than that area of Joseph's inner life that most closely resembles Zangwill's own:

[Joseph] went about among the people and they grew to love him. [...] But there was one sinner he could not absolve [...] and that was himself. And there was one demon he could not exorcise—that in his own breast, the tribulation of his own soul, bruising itself perpetually against the realities of life and as torn now by the shortcomings of Christendom as formerly by those of the Ghetto. (p. 49)

The only way Zangwill can find in which to resolve this dualistic conflict is by giving his hero a martyr's death, a solution wholly unsatisfactory in both intellectual and literary terms, for it is contrived through a stagey presentation of the traditional 'Jews' race' during the pre-Lenten carnival of Rome, in which Joseph, now a newly minted Dominican friar, takes the place of one of the Jews, suffers the degradation of the people to whom he was born, and at the end, over the corpse of a 'fat old Jew' who has dropped dead from the strain, he flashes out his crucifix and denounces both the carnival and the pope who has permitted it:

In the name of Christ, I denounce this devil's mockery of the Lord's chosen people. [...] I have sinned against my brethren. I have aggravated their griefs. Therefore would I be of them at the moment of their extremest humiliation. [...] But penance is not all my motive. [...] Ye who know me, faithful sons and daughters of Holy Church [...] join with me now in ending the long martyrdom of the Jews, your brethren. [...] It is by love, not hate, that Christ rules the world. [...] Go home, go home from this Pagan mirth, and sit on the ground in sackcloth and ashes, and pray God He make you better Christians. (pp. 53–4)

Predictably, this appeal falls on deaf ears, and Joseph is condemned to be burned at the stake by an outraged Church. About to die, he looks out over the crowd:

his wild, despairing eyes lighted on many a merry face that but a few hours before had followed him to testify to righteousness; and, mixed with theirs, the faces of his fellow-Jews, sinister with malicious glee. [...] Not a face that showed sympathy; those who [...] had followed his crucifix and *pallio* now exaggerated their jocosity lest they should be recognised; the Jews were joyous at the heavenly vengeance which had overtaken the renegade. (p. 59)

Joseph dies with the problem he has wrestled with all his short life even more intensely unresolved that it was before he started:

I do but confess my sins and my deserved punishment. I set out to walk in the footsteps of the Master—to win by love, to resist not evil. And lo, I have used force against my old brethren, the Jews, and force against my new brethren, the Christians. I have urged the Pope against the Jews, I have urged the Christians against the Pope. I have provoked bloodshed and outrage. It were better I had never been born. Christ receive me into His infinite mercy. May he forgive me as I forgive you! (pp. 59–60)

This is no solution, and a prayer for forgiveness—echoing Christ's plea on the cross—is helpless to resolve the big issue Zangwill seeks to treat.

The ending of the tale itself brings symbolic puppets together in a forced tableau that makes a pretty stage picture but is equally devoid of either meaning or hope. This cloying ending is of special interest for the present discussion, for it explicitly manifests the extent of Zangwill's personal subordination to Gentile hegemony. The two female stereotypes who have loved this self-deluded Jewish malcontent—Miriam the humble Jewess, and Helena the militant pagan—meet over the fresh grave of their shared but unavailable beloved where, in the conventionally melodramatic manner of Victorian theatrics, they recognize that they are sisters under the skin:

Helena's tears flowed unrestrainedly. 'Alas! Alas! the Dreamer. He should have been happy—happy with me, happy in the fullness of human love, in the light of the sun, in the beauty of this fair world, in the joy of art, in the sweetness of music.'

'Nay, Signora, he was a Jew. He should have been happy with me, in the light of the Law, in the calm household life of prayer and study, of charity, and pity, and all good offices. I would have lit the Sabbath candles for him and set our children on his knee that he might bless them. Alas! Alas! the Dreamer.'

'Neither of these fates was to be his, Miriam. Kiss me, let us comfort each other.'

Their lips met and their tears mingled.

'Henceforth, Miriam, we are sisters.'

'Sisters,' sobbed Miriam.

They clung to each other—the noble Pagan soul and the warm Jewish heart at one over the Christian's grave. (p. 61)

This crude symbolism underlines in red Zangwill's regret at what he regards as the unnecessary separation of Jew from Christian, and his tale's ending is the warning answer he gives to the question the whole of *Dreamers of the Ghetto* sets out to probe. Where is to be found that healing synthesis whereby Jews, having left the ghetto, can find accommodation within Western society, while at the same time preserving the integrity of their own identities? Jews, Zangwill urged, must retain their distinctiveness while simultaneously living as unobtrusive equals among others; only in this way, he believed, could the great heretics be produced who would ensure the progress of the world. Without this hope, there can only be the obliteration of death for the Jews and their faith. The problem with this story, though, is that this Joseph the Dreamer is no heretic—he is a convinced and believing Christian who wants to convert the Jews and reform the Church, a twofold exercise in futility. The life we are offered in this model is decisively wasted, for it leaves not a single one of those it touches changed in any way. Could Zangwill have known that his own life would be expended with the same degree of futility?

When he was nearly forty years old, Zangwill married Edith Chaplin Ayrton (1875–1945), the daughter of the prominent electrical engineer William E. Ayrton and his first wife, Matilda Chaplin, a pioneering woman doctor in Britain, at a civil ceremony at the London Registry Office on 26 November 1903. From the reception afterwards, most of the groom's Jewish associates were absent. In Udelson's view, this marriage, to a woman who was not Jewish, was Zangwill's unconscious desire to signal to the world that he was now prepared fully to live out his universalist and assimilationist philosophy in both his private and his public-professional life too, but this decision also severed him finally from his closest Jewish teachers, Solomon Schechter, the Cambridge Hebrew scholar, and Moses Gaster, the *Hakham* or spiritual leader of London's Sephardi Jewish community. As Zangwill ceased associating with these eminent Jewish men of learning, he turned instead to his wife's uncle, the Christian religious scholar A. Chaplin,[16] but he remained tormented by his inability to find peace between the binary opposites of his 'double consciousness'. In 1900 he repeated his understanding of this dilemma in a piece for the *Jewish Chronicle*:

> Either let the next generation be trained to consider themselves Englishmen or let them be taught to consider themselves as noble exiles, provisionally doing their duty in the country in which their lot is cast. But let not their brains be muddled and tampered with, as mine was, by two contradictory teachings, nor their natural absorption of English ideas, ideals, and traditions checked and confused by tales of what happened two thousand miles away two thousand years before they were born.[17]

Although Zangwill urged in defence of his wife that 'she is a far better Jewess than I am a Jew', and others claimed, throughout her life, that 'Mrs Zangwill had classified herself as "ethically Jewish"',[18] there were nevertheless those in Jewish circles who resented this marriage, and said so both openly and furtively. In so doing, they proved how far they were from any possibility of embracing, even tentatively, the synthesis of faith and custom on which Zangwill had built his philosophic hopes. In 1904, when Zangwill visited America, the American correspondent of the *Jewish Chronicle* saw fit to note that 'Mr Zangwill's matrimonial venture will surely damage his usefulness as a Zionist propagandist',[19] and Chaim Weizmann, in a letter to Menachem Ussishkin in December 1903, also commented that 'this marriage and the couple's appearance at a Zionist meeting, where Zangwill had been received with applause, has contributed to the decline of the prestige of Zionism in England.'[20] Yet this was a marriage of true ideologues: Edith Zangwill was a woman herself more devoted to high principles than to homemaking, and as a wedding present her husband gave her 'three large cheques for her favourite causes, the Charity Organisation, Women's Suffrage and Zionism'.[21]

Zangwill himself had struck up a friendship with Herzl in Vienna in 1893, shortly after the publication of *Children of the Ghetto*, and simultaneously with his engagement, Zangwill adopted the Zionist cause, and abandoned his hitherto neutral stance towards Jewish nationalism. This commitment, it has been suggested, was yet another quixotic attempt on Zangwill's part to reconcile the dualistic impulses in his life, in which his inability to integrate his identities as both Jew and Englishman was paralleled by an equal inability to choose definitely between them: 'Precisely at the time he decided to cast in his lot with the apparent historical destiny of Western Jewry to have its identity absorbed ineluctably into the majority population [through his marriage to a Gentile woman], he joined actively with those determined to rescue and preserve the Jewish people from just such absorption'.[22] What he could not achieve as a 'pope' in the sphere of religion he now hoped he could achieve in the sphere of politics.

Though Zangwill admired Herzl, and was excited by the First Zionist Congress of 1897, which he attended in Basle as an observer, he remained sceptical about whether the chief goal of political Zionism—to re-establish a Jewish homeland in Palestine—could ever be practically realized. Yet his religious sensibility was moved by the spiritual potential of Herzl's programme, another area in which the dichotomy of his thinking became glaringly manifest. He believed that the emancipated Jews of the West, enjoying conditions of freedom, were destined to assimilate into the majority populations among whom they lived unless they could either revitalize the spiritual content of contemporary Judaism, while the oppressed Jews of Eastern Europe, chiefly those in the tsarist empire, were to preserve their traditional customs and beliefs in a socially and politically autonomous territory of their own. To justify his dual—and essentially contradictory—roles as the simultaneous advocate of assimilationism and as the champion of Jewish nationalism, he formulated a programme, itself the product of severe interpellation by British imperialism, which split the Jewish people into a Kiplingesque East and West in which, it seemed, never the twain would meet. For those in the West, he argued, assimilation into a 'universal Hebraic culture' was the only intellectually acceptable destiny, while those in the East could avoid assimilation if they could be sheltered in an autonomous Jewish state. This view, of course, suggested that some

Jews were more equal than others, and was rightly doomed to disaster.

Zangwill devoted the rest of his life to these dual and genuinely conflicting causes, and for the first two decades of the twentieth century he became the most eloquent spokesman and most energetic activist in the campaign for a politically established Jewish homeland. In 1901 he served as an official representative to the Fifth Zionist Congress and enthusiastically embraced Herzl's 'political' approach. But he continued to see the Jewish homeland as a refuge for the oppressed and persecuted of Eastern Europe, not as a home for all the Jews of the world. It was to be established for primitive *Ostjuden*, not for sophisticated acculturates of the civilized West. Moreover, Zangwill refused to be committed exclusively to Palestine *per se* as the site of the future Jewish homeland, but was prepared rather to accept any place in the world where Jewish nationalists might concentrate their efforts. In justifying this radically utilitarian and colonialist policy, Zangwill argued that his vision was practical, whereas that of the Zionists, which took full cognizance of the religious-historical paramountcy of the Holy Land for world Jewry, was an anachronistic dream. As a result, he strongly favoured first Argentina, and then, in 1903, vigorously supported the Uganda Scheme by which Joseph Chamberlain, the British Colonial Secretary, offered a plateau in British East Africa for Jewish colonization, even though the Sixth Zionist Congress had rejected this offer out of hand. Despite Zangwill's passionate pleas, at the Seventh Zionist Congress those very Eastern Europeans Zangwill imagined he was doing his best to save again unanimously rejected the scheme.

Zangwill's imperialist inclination, coupled with his inability to recognize the centrality of *Eretz Yisrael*, the Holy Land, to the faith of Judaism and to the politico-cultural aspirations of the Zionist movement, led in 1905 to a major schism, as a result of which Zangwill virtually single-handedly created a new Jewish Territorial Organisation (ITO) which split from, and became a chief rival to, the World Zionist Organisation (WZO). Under Zangwill's fervent direction, Territorialism came to birth as a movement originally formed to implement the British offer of land for a self-governing Jewish settlement in East Africa, but which came to articulate the dualistic and mutually exclusive fantasies that haunted Zangwill personally. In the entire twenty years of its existence, Zangwill's Territorial movement strove on the one hand to achieve a separate and autonomous homeland for Eastern European Jewish refugees in which, as Zangwill patronizingly hoped, they could preserve their traditional Jewish heritage and, on the other hand, worked tirelessly to promote the successful cultural assimilation of exactly the same emigrants into the heartland of the United States, the 'melting pot' as Zangwill himself famously designated it. When the British offer of East Africa was withdrawn, Zangwill enthusiastically embraced the 'Galveston Plan', that scheme of the American financiers Jacob Schiff and Oscar Straus to settle Jews in Galveston, Texas, which chimed perfectly with Zangwill's long-argued 'ethnic sociology' which held that for the Jewish people as a whole, the future offered only two categorical alternatives—either total assimilation or territorial separation.[23]

Ironically, when the First World War broke out in 1914, Zangwill, who had spent so much of his life agonizing about whether he was British or Jewish, had an answer forced upon him by a group of Catholic anti-Semites who took vigorous part in the heated jingoistic debates of the day about who was or was not entitled to call himself an Englishman. Despite his British birth, Zangwill was repeatedly accused of being an 'alien'. Such militant Catholic propagandists as G. K. Chesterton, his brother Cecil Chesterton, and Hilaire Belloc argued—for reasons bitterly and ironically akin to those advanced by the Zionists—that the Jews should have a Jewish State to which all Jews should go, a most beneficial move for everyone concerned in that 'the Zionist experiment will relax the strain created by the presence of the Jews in the midst of a non-Jewish world.' Cecil Chesterton said openly at a meeting during the war years that 'he did not look upon Mr Zangwill as an Englishman, but as a Jew. [He] disavowed on his honour being an antisemite. He thought the Jews a different nation and wished them to return to Palestine. Being a separate nation they had no claim to enjoy equal rights in other countries.'[24] These were views often repeated to English Jews during and after the First World War, notably by men of letters. To take only one random example, D. H. Lawrence wrote to Zangwill's cousin, David Eder, 'Cease to be a Jew and let Jewry disappear—much best.'[25] All they proved was the futility of Zangwill's philosophy, which he nevertheless steadfastly maintained, even in defending his right to be a British Jew: 'For my own part, I hold that the highest patriotic service a writer can render to the country of his birth is to offer it his truest thinking and his deepest race-heritage, and to try and make it worthier of his love.'[26]

The fact that the Ottoman empire fought on the German side in the First World War drastically changed Zangwill's estimation of the practical possibilities of settling Jews in Palestine, and he worked hard to make the most of the opportunities offered by the hostilities. By the spring of 1915, he was enthusiastically co-operating with Jabotinsky (1880–1940), the founder of Revisionism, in encouraging the establishment of the Zion Mule Corps, the precursor of the 'Jewish Legion', a battalion of Royal Fusiliers finally set up in August 1917. The Balfour declaration on 2 November 1917, announcing that the British government would support the creation of a Jewish national home in Palestine, elated Zangwill, but he now stridently insisted on the forcible resettlement of the Arab population in a still-to-be-created Kingdom of Arabia, believing that without this, 'Palestine is neither Jewish nor National nor a Home'.[27] Neither the Great Powers nor the WZO were prepared to support Zangwill's radical insistence, however, despite his increasingly shrill speeches and writings on the question, so by January 1920 Zangwill was a bitterly disappointed man, physically exhausted and mentally despairing.

With the failure of his hopes in the post-war arrangements for the Palestine Mandate, Zangwill now began inveighing bitterly, through the medium of essays and stage plays, against those who had spurned his vision for the future of the Jewish people and the preservation of their culture. He now maintained that only ethnic assimilation in the great cauldron of what he termed the American 'melting pot' would ensure the civilized future of the Jewish people. From the New World, this eccentric visionary proclaimed, would emerge the multi-ethnic, multiracial 'new Hebraic man', a biological and cultural synthesis of the Jewish with the Gentile. Zangwill now maintained that only America remained as humankind's true land of 'hopes and dreams', and it was to the American people that he now earnestly set about teaching what he believed were the universal truths about that amalgam of Jewish and Christian culture which he called 'Hebraism'. Through the medium of the stage—and with more than half an eye on hopes of emulating the popularity of Noël Coward at the box office—he also tried preaching his gospel to the unconverted. As always, Zangwill badly misjudged the feasibility of his message, his potential command of the new medium he had chosen, and indeed his own ideas, which were high Victorian in a world that had left Victorianism far behind.

Zangwill's five post-war plays, written and produced largely at his own expense,[28] were a succession of disastrous failures that ruined him both financially and physically, while his mental equilibrium became increasingly disturbed. During his last lecture tour of America, on 14 October 1923 he delivered an acrimonious lecture in New York's Carnegie Hall entitled 'Watchman, What of the Night?' in which he violently deplored the fact that the Arabs in Palestine had not been forcibly shifted out during the war, and dogmatically insisted that 'Political Zionism is dead.' This lecture only served to provoke a storm of widespread and bitter recrimination against him, which in turn goaded him into lashing out even more intemperately at the increasingly hostile audiences in America which he subsequently addressed.[29] He returned to England in 1924 broken in health, and having suffered a severe nervous breakdown, he died on 1 August 1926 at the age of sixty-two.

It would be difficult to find any modern Jewish life that more ironically or more tragically mirrors the central thematic concerns of the Jewish pope myth than that of Israel Zangwill. In every area of his busy and committed existence, he thrashed about desperately, seeking some way to reconcile the inherent dualism of his identity, and the twin yearnings of his soul. He wanted at one and the same time sincerely to profess both Judaism and Christianity, to lay claim legitimately to the heritage of both Israel and England, to define himself in his own mind as much as to the outside world as a single integrated being at peace with itself, not as a divided creature whose two mutually contradictory halves were constantly warring with each other. Yet all the ways in which he tried to create this fusion within himself were predictably doomed, chiefly because they were always grounded in a sense of inferiority before the more powerful hegemonic culture with which he sought accommodation. As Sander Gilman has noted, this abasement of self before the culture of the powerful is what informed Ludwig Börne's contempt for the first emancipated Jews of early nineteenth-century Frankfurt: 'in the acceptance of standards of the beautiful promulgated by the Christian Enlightenment, the Jews' claim for a new manner of seeing the world is but the acceptance of new lenses ground by a Christian lens grinder. They were not refractions of their inner beings.'[30] Try as he might, Zangwill was never able to view the world or his place in it except through the prism of just such lenses as these, and the sad story of his life—like the cheerless message of his stories about those Dreamers of the Ghetto whom he called into fictional life—bear testimony only to the impossibility of wedding two cultures. The concept of a Jewish pope remains, in life as in fiction, an irreducible oxymoron.

Notes to Chapter 7

1. Israel Zangwill, *Children of the Ghetto*, 3rd edn. (New York, 1895), 32.
2. Joseph Leftwich, *Israel Zangwill* (New York and London, 1957), 72.
3. Cited in Zangwill, *Children of the Ghetto*, 66–7.
4. Joseph H. Udelson, *Dreamer of the Ghetto: The Life and Works of Israel Zangwill* (Tuscaloosa, 1990), 61.
5. Cited in Leftwich, *Israel Zangwill*, 44.
6. Ibid. 47.
7. Ibid.
8. Zangwill, *Children of the Ghetto*, 103–4.
9. Ibid. 510–13, *passim*.
10. Cited in Udelson, *Dreamer*, 133.
11. Cited in ibid. 134.
12. Ibid. 5–6.
13. See ibid. 138–40.
14. Israel Zangwill, *Dreamers of the Ghetto* (London, 1925), 23–62. Page references to all subsequent quotations are to this edition and are cited parenthetically in the text.
15. Cited in Leftwich. *Israel Zangwill*, 285.
16. Udelson, *Dreamer*, 149–50.
17. Israel Zangwill, 'Singer vs. Schechter', *Jewish Chronicle* (26 Oct. 1900), 7, cited in Udelson, *Dreamer*, 151.
18. Leftwich, *Israel Zangwill*, 102.
19. Ibid. 103.
20. Udelson, *Dreamer*, 152.
21. Leftwich, *Israel Zangwill*, 102.
22. Udelson, *Dreamer*, 152.
23. My outline here owes much to the detailed account of Zangwill's Zionist beliefs and activities given in Udelson, *Dreamer*, 152–89.
24. All citations from Leftwich, *Israel Zangwill*, 139.
25. Cited in ibid. 81.
26. Cited in ibid. 140.
27. Udelson, *Dreamer*, 188.
28. These were: *The Cockpit* (1921), *The Forcing House or The Cockpit Continued* (1922), *Merely Mary Ann* (1923), *Too Much Money* (1924), and *We Moderns* (1924).
29. Udelson, *Dreamer*, 214–20.
30. Sander L. Gilman, *Jewish Self-Hatred: Anti-Semitism and the Hidden Language of the Jews* (Baltimore and London, 1986), 151.

CHAPTER 8

❖

A Kind of Closure

The recurrence of the pope myth in Yiddish literature strikingly delineates not only the changing socio-political circumstances under which Jews have pursued their quest for self-identity, but also the constraints of the discourse the Yiddish language is obliged to use in order to define this quest. Inevitably, change and stasis are apparent in both. As long as questions of Jewish survival and self-definition remain problematic, and continue to be addressed in an unalterably Jewish language, both problem and resolution can differ only in emphasis, not in formulation. Evidence for this can be adduced as much extra-textually as from within the texts themselves. The degree to which each of the authors of the myth under discussion here has been interpellated both from within and from without by historical circumstances can be measured with reference to the recurrent centrality of Germany as the locality in which the tales are set. Inferences already drawn from discourse can be confirmed by reference to political geography. Why, it may reasonably be asked, do the first three versions of the tale choose to place the events and the rabbi who suffers them squarely in the German cities of Mainz or Frankfurt am Main rather than anywhere else? Equally validly, why, by contrast, does Singer elect to place his papal aspirant in the inconsequential Polish *shtetl* of Janov, a place distinguished only by the fact that in the sixteenth century R. Jacob ben Isaac Ashkenazi, the author of the *Tsene-Rene*, the Yiddish adaptation of the Pentateuch, lived there? Some historical investigation may provide extra-textual support for the extent of Jewish diasporic consciousness in Yiddish thus far advanced from the texts themselves.

Jewish existence in Germany may be seen as prototypical of Jewish existence everywhere in the Diaspora. There, more prosperously than elsewhere, Jews built up successful communities unwanted and barely tolerated; there they survived and flourished; there they were repeatedly turned upon; and thence they were expelled—ultimately, from existence itself. It was in Germany that the Yiddish language came to birth; it was from Germany that the most violent contempt was heaped upon it by Moses Mendelssohn (1729–86) and his disciples; it was from Germany that extermination was decreed for those who spoke it. By the sixteenth century, when the Yiddish language had already established a significant body of literature, the Jewish community in Frankfurt had become so prosperous that general rabbinical synods were held there in 1562, 1582 and 1603[1]— this last only one year after the publication of the *Mayse-bukh*.

The chief character of the *Mayse-bukh* version is introduced as *r. shimen hagodl der hot gevoynt in ments*, 'R. Shimen the Great who lived in Mainz'. Now it is highly significant that Max Weinreich, seeking to identify historical-geographic determinants in the development of the Yiddish language, identifies the character of R. Shimon the Great from a sixteenth-century *responsum* as a prominent historical figure who was a liturgical poet, a scholar, a *shtadlan* or community intercessor, and a wonder-working rabbi. But Weinreich's source insists that he lived and worked in Mans (today Le Mans), a town in central France some two hundred kilometres south-west of Paris.[2] Since the materials from which the *Mayse-bukh* was compiled at the end of the sixteenth century were to some extent drawn from the folklore of four centuries earlier, it becomes a matter of considerable relevance to the present examination to ask why the compiler of the *Mayse-bukh* transplanted this already legendary figure from France to Germany. Unlike Mans in France, Mainz in Germany was one of the oldest settlements of Jews in Europe, dating from the time of the Roman conquests of Germania. Resuming its importance in the tenth century, it came to occupy a central position in the geographical area known by Jews as 'the kingdom of Loter', that area of the Rhineland which Weinreich has identified as the birthplace of the Yiddish language. Until the massacres of the First Crusade, Mainz was, in population, one of the two largest Jewish communities in Loter, steadily establishing itself as the leading business centre, and producing some of the most eminent scholars of the time. This commercial and cultural supremacy meant that for Jews the centre of gravity of the emergent language that came to be known as Yiddish shifted to Mainz. Given that the political structure of medieval Germany placed the actual power of government in the hands of the Church episcopate, the bishops of Speyer and Worms, the only cities of comparable size and influence in the Christian world, were both subordinate to the archbishop of Mainz.[3] In both Jewish and Christian terms, therefore, since Mainz was the pre-eminent city-state of the German Middle Ages, it became the perfect locale, both literally and symbolically, on which to centre that *angst*-ridden contest for spiritual supremacy between Church and Synagogue on which the *Mayse-bukh* focuses. By moving R. Shimen from provincial France to metropolitan Germany, a vital dimension is added to the mythological status of the debate which this earliest version of the pope tale initiates.

The same considerations obtain in respect of Frankfurt am Main as the setting for two of the three reworkings of the pope tale which follow the *Mayse-bukh*. In post-medieval times, Frankfurt succeeded Mainz as the Jewish mother-city in Germany, and Jews came steadily to assume an unrivalled position of eminence there. They staunchly supported the emergent Habsburg dynasty, which was in consequence not unwilling to show the Jews some favour in return, so that under Habsburg protection and patronage, Frankfurt Jewry grew famous all over Europe for wealth and influence. Historically speaking, Frankfurt inevitably took the place of Mainz as the place from which Jews might contemplate entering the mainstream of enlightened European life. So, two and three centuries respectively after the appearance of the *Mayse-bukh*, Frankfurt is chosen as the indisputably appropriate setting for the continuing struggle that the pope myth is recreated to probe. Neither Dik nor Trunk could have been unaware, at the different times at which they wrote, that in exclusively Jewish terms Frankfurt had steadily developed into a centre of orthodoxy that played a pivotal role among German Jews. Nor could they have been unaware that the orthodox Ashkenazi Jews of Frankfurt, no less than the moderate conservatives and the radical reformists, despised the Yiddish language and followed Mendelssohn in championing the use of written and spoken German for secular matters, and Hebrew for issues religious. By the time Dik—and, with a different emphasis, Trunk—came to rework the pope myth, the city of Frankfurt, like the city of Mainz earlier, had become both literally and figuratively the centre of the struggle for independent Jewish identity and survival in respect of both Christian and orthodox Jewish interpellation. Christian definition of what was of political and economic importance became unconsciously displaced on to Jewish evaluation of what was of spiritual and cultural value, so that it became necessary to show Jews fighting for survival on Christian territory and in Christian terms.

Once again, however, the battleground for this *Kampf* is as much chosen for, as chosen by, the writers through social, political and economic factors over which Jews themselves exercised little control. Christians still set up its parameters, and defined its terms. Supremely ironic—and utterly inevitable—is therefore the fact that on the first day of Hitler's promulgation, on 7 April 1933, of the 'Law for the Restoration of the Professional Civil Service', ordering the dismissal of all civil servants 'not of Aryan descent', it was Frankfurt that moved first to implement its provisions. German Jewish academics were forbidden to teach in Frankfurt universities, Jewish actors to perform on Frankfurt stages, and Jewish musicians to play in Frankfurt concerts. Frankfurt, so rich in Jews who proudly regarded themselves as Germans first, led the vanguard in making Germany *judenrein*. Frankfurt—despite, or because of, its long Jewish history—became the first German city to insist that in the New Order one could not be both a German and a Jew.[4]

This is manifestly why Singer, concerned with radical disidentification from all forms of subjectification to Christian values, insists on shifting the locale of his own investigation of the pope myth completely away from assimilationist Germany to Janov, an undeniable *farvorfener hek tsvishn yidn* (Y 279), 'dump in the sticks among Jews'. The counter-transposition away from metropolitan Europe and back to Pale of Settlement Poland effects the concomitant repudiation of what Singer insists is the grandiose fantasy of enlightenment, and the destructive secular aspirations of Jews. Rejecting Christian hegemony and the identity Christians have forced upon Jews, Singer chooses his setting precisely to disidentify his tale's concerns from all Christian evaluations of what is important. He insists on measuring values exclusively according to Jewish criteria.

Of the different potential modes of responding to the way Christians had constructed and enforced the identity of Jews who lived among them, Yiddish writers clearly found counter-identification the most difficult to attempt, as this investigation has attempted to show. The only period in which this might have been possible was in the disillusionment which followed Europe's failure fully to complete its emancipation and equalization of its Jews—in 1897, for example. In that year, the year of the First Zionist Congress, the year of the foundation of the Jewish Labour *Bund*, the year of Gustav Mahler's conversion to Christianity, the Viennese Jewish parliamentary deputy Joseph Karels could complain to his colleagues:

When you consider the way in which the poor Jews strive to gain your favour in the ranks of the Germans, how they try to accumulate the treasures of German culture, how they work in the sciences, some perhaps dying young as a result—and all the thanks they get is that they are not even accepted as human beings.[5]

Jews who wished to identify with their people without joining the Gentiles had no choice but to remain linguistically Jewish, however much they themselves attempted to redefine that condition. Individual Jews might dismiss the strictures of the *Halakhah* as ideologically indispensable in defining their identities as Jews, but they could not dismiss their enemies' categorization of them as belonging to an identifiable and abhorrent group of outsiders. As one of Bernard Malamud's characters has mordantly pointed out in our own time, 'If you ever forget you're a Jew, a Gentile will remind you.'[6]

What Yiddish writers could, and did, attempt to do was to challenge the ideology of traditional rabbinism. But as long as these writers addressed their readership in the discourse of Jews, they were forced to remain complicit with the identity-defining system imposed on them by the dictates of orthodoxy. Herein lies one of the sharpest ironies of Yiddish literature. That branch of Yiddishism which attempted the secularization of its language and literature was an attempt at counter-identification that was doomed from the start. Since it was linguistically impossible to construct a secular literature out of materials rooted in religious discourse, the efforts of such writers came increasingly to demonstrate that the more they struggled to escape ideological subjectification, the more they became enmeshed in its toils. Central precursors here are the pope myth versions of Dik and Trunk. Dik rewrites the pope myth in the warm glow of emancipation and enlightenment in an attempt to show that one could now be both a Jew and a European. Trunk, eighty years later, deliberately chooses to rewrite Dik's version, not simply to show that this idealism was naïve, but—what was more important for him— to show that the condition of being Jewish is both unalterable and unendurable. The choice may indeed have ceased to be either/or for Jews, but Trunk perceives that its parameters have shifted—one can either be a Jew or be nothing, for there is no accommodation for Jews in a Gentile world. However painful it might be, Jews must cling for identity to a conception of the self as one member of, and inseparable from, a people bound together not only by a common religion or ancestry, but also by a common culture, ideology and set of mutual obligations that creates a nation consciously concerned to preserve its uniqueness and cohesion.[7] The alternative is the surrender of identity to a concept of self devised and enforced by an alien other who is hegemonically stronger.

It is here that the discourse employed in all Jewish writing becomes most self-revealing. Jewish writers who moved outside Jewish languages and sought literary recognition in the great languages of Europe, if they attempted at all to preserve a Jewish identity in subject matter and theme, were compelled to adopt a mode of discourse which of necessity interpellated Jews according to Gentile values. A clear case in point is the work of Israel Zangwill, whose crafted English style—sometimes consciously, sometime unconsciously—is saturated with late Victorian English prejudices against, and distaste for, Jews. Writing about Jews in the language of Gentiles, Zangwill is involuntarily forced to identify the very Jews he wishes to portray with sympathy in the negative terms imposed by the discourse he employs. Efforts to transfer meaning from Jewish into Gentile language unavoidably involves some degree of alienation of subject matter from writer, since readers receive what is written in discourse resonant with non-Jewish ideological values. This accounts in some measure for the jarring discrepancies between the Yiddish originals and the authorized English versions of Singer's work. Singer is forced to identify Jews and Christians in one way for his Yiddish readers and in quite another—often misleading—way for his English readers, a phenomenon that is only in part the author's conscious choice. This difficulty is in fact evident in almost every attempt to translate Yiddish texts into English. Each must of necessity be constrained by the unavoidable connotational and ideological demands inherent in the discourse peculiar to the language into which the translation is being made. The transference of the nuances of discourse inherent in one language to those inherent in another may well be impossible.[8]

This point receives shocking negative reinforcement from one of the 'twelve theses' that the official organization of students in Germany, preparing for a bonfire in which to burn the intellectual publications of the Weimar Republic, posted up throughout Germany, and thus on the campus of Berlin University, on 13 April 1933 in support of Hitler's 'Professional Civil Service' *diktat* mentioned earlier: 'Our most dangerous opponent is the Jew. The Jew who can only think Jewish but writes German lies. He who is German and writes German but thinks anti-German is a traitor. The student who speaks anti-German and thus writes anti-German is thoughtless and is untrue to his obligations.'[9] In their 'twelve theses', the students went on to suggest a programme through which to identify and remove this 'corruption' of the German language:

1. We wish to take the Jews seriously as strangers, and we wish to respect the idea of race.
2. We therefore demand from the censor:
3. That Jewish works appear in Hebrew. If they appear in German, they are to be labelled as translations.
4. The strongest control in the use of German script.
5. That German script be used only by Germans.
6. That the anti-German spirit be removed from public libraries.

Jews were thus to be denied not only the use of the German language, but even the typeface in which to print it. In response, Max Herrmann, one of the Jewish professors at Berlin University, wrote a letter of protest to the German ministry of culture on 1 May 1933, which in hindsight reveals both the dilemma and the tragedy of the assimilated Jew: 'My honour is offended [...] by the reference to that group with which I am associated by birth, and about which it is publicly stated that the Jew can only think Jewish, that if he writes German, then he lies. [...] I write German, I think German, I feel German and I do not lie.'[10] In the summer of 1933, Herrmann was removed from his post together with all the other Jewish academics in German universities, and perished in 1942 in Theresienstadt.[11] He was but one of thousands of Jews who found that no degree of linguistic or cultural assimilation was enough to guarantee them either acceptance or life from an ideologically slanted culture determined to reject them.

If it can conceivably be thought that Jews speaking about things Jewish in a non-Jewish tongue use a 'damaged' discourse, then it would seem self-evident that the only discourse in which they might speak authentically about matters Jewish would be that of a Jewish language, namely Yiddish or Hebrew. Yet its centuries of denigrators have charged Yiddish with being a 'jargon', a patois that bears all the hallmarks of corruption and is unregenerately marked with the brand of inferiority and Diaspora subservience. What then of Hebrew, the language and discourse of Scripture? Hebrew was revived as a modern language to serve the specific purposes of Jewish nationalism as defined by the Zionist movement, which argued that Hebrew alone was the only true and authentic language of the Jews, free from any Diaspora accretions and wholly independent of Gentile influence.

Unlike Yiddish, which the Zionists dismissed as the language of *Galut*, Exile, the tongue of 'a people of dust' who went spinelessly like sheep to the Nazi slaughter, modern Hebrew is, in the Zionist definition, the virile language no longer of the scholar but of the warrior. None of this can possibly be true, as students of language have long known. All languages grow and develop under the influences of other languages and the use to which they are put by those who articulate them. It is not scientifically possible to speak of 'purity' of discourse in any single human language. Yet it remains equally true that every language has elements that are not directly transferable in translation to another, and in this resides their uniqueness. These elements are determined by cultural contexts that are themselves not transferable, but are dependent upon a set of customs, rituals, practices, norms and values shared in common among particular social, national or religious groups, all of which must be acquired by those who wish to know another's tongue fully. It is surely not necessary to share Hitler's racist fantasies about the inability of foreigners ever to acquire the genuineness of another tongue to suggest, as does this tentative drawing together of some threads about the pope myth and the language in which it is re-developed over several centuries, that the discourse of Yiddish is unalterably 'Jewish' in a way that the discourse of Christian languages can never be. Each attempt at translating one of these tales must of necessity be constrained by two kinds of unavoidable connotational and ideological demands: those inherent in the discourse of the 'source' language, the language in which each text was written, and those peculiar to the 'target' language, that language into which the translation is being made. The transference of the nuances of discourse inherent in one language to those inherent in another may well be impossible. If this is so, it is axiomatic that from the subjectifying effect of conflicting discourses, whether Gentile or Jewish, no Jewish literature, even in our own time, can ever escape.

How far Gentile subjectification of Jews—and the Jews' acceptance of that subjectification in using Gentile language—continued to influence the Jews' own self-definition can be seen in a disquieting illustration from the life of the German-Jewish social and religious philosopher Martin Buber (1878–1965). In his disputation, in German, with the Protestant theologian Karl Ludwig Schmidt on 4 January 1933, Buber pointed to a contrast between the Church and the Synagogue which, though it was intended to demonstrate the durability of the Synagogue, recalled in a distressingly similar way the terms employed by Rozenzweig nearly twenty years earlier:

I live not far from the city of Worms [...] and from time to time, I go [...] to the cathedral. It is a visible harmony of members, a totality in which no part deviates from perfection. I then go over to the Jewish cemetery consisting of crooked, cracked, shapeless, random stones. I station myself there, gaze upward from the jumble of the cemetery to that glorious harmony, and seem to be looking up from Israel to the Church.[12]

Buber was, of course, seeking to demonstrate the cohesiveness of the Jewish people even in their scattered diasporic existence. Nevertheless, the language and imagery in which he tries to make this point startles a contemporary Jewish reader. It evokes—deliberately, no doubt—that ancient contrast between Church and Synagogue that positions the latter in a perpetually inferior relation to the former. Buber seeks to achieve the antithetical rhetorical effect, but is essentially defeated because the language he employs is incapable of rendering it persuasively. He makes no mention of the fact that Worms was the oldest Jewish community in Central Europe—its synagogue, burnt down on *Kristallnacht*, 9 November 1938, was built in 1034—and that in the very cemetery he describes were to be found some of the oldest extant Jewish tombstones in Europe.[13] Preceding Hitler's first major anti-Jewish decree by barely two months, the picture Buber paints is redolent of an implied sense of Jewish inferiority which, if he himself did not feel it, was certainly imposed upon him unconsciously by his choice of imagery and language. These are the products of centuries of Christian dominion, internalized by Jews and heightened by their belief in the innate superiority of Christian over Jewish culture.

If the four reworkings of the pope myth in Yiddish literature demonstrate anything beyond Diaspora Jews' abiding dread of assimilation and its obliterative consequences for continued Jewish existence, it is the fact that this fear was most effectively expressed through the medium of Yiddish, the pre-eminent discourse of a subaltern people. It is not of the Yiddish but of the Hebrew versions of this tale that David Levine Lerner can boldly assert:

This defiant story expresses the confidence of medieval Jewry both in the ultimate truth of Judaism and in the Jews' potential for success in the Gentile world [...]. The world view of [medieval European Jewry] was indeed constructed of [binary oppositions], most notably those between Judaism and

Christianity, and between this world and the World to Come, the two dyads on which the legend of the Jewish Pope is based. [...] [The tale] reveals these irreconcilable oppositions as the foundations of the powerful medieval Jewish faith, which strengthened the Jews in their resolve never to succumb to the oppression that they suffered at the hands of the religious majority which surrounded them.[14]

The effectiveness of successive Yiddish versions of this tale in putting forward, with all its terrors and dangers nakedly exposed, quite the contrary possibility, is as much due to the uncertain, underdetermined nature of the Yiddish language as it is to the insight and awareness of the individual writers who tackled it. Faith, as the *Mayse-bukh* version shows, is never so strong that it does not need continual bolstering; and never so weak, as Isaac Bashevis Singer demonstrates, that it cannot be relied upon when materialism fails. And between the waverings of faith and doubt, it is the Yiddish language that best articulates the still, small voice of Jewish resignation and Jewish hope.

Notes to Chapter 8

1. Paul Johnson, *A History of the Jews* (London, 1987), 253.
2. Max Weinreich, *History of the Yiddish Language*, trans. Shlomo Noble, with the assistance of Joshua A. Fishman (Chicago and London, 1980), 343.
3. All this information is provided by the research of Max Weinreich. See Weinreich, *Yiddish Language*, 331–41, 439–41.
4. Martin Gilbert, *The Holocaust: The Jewish Tragedy* (1986; London, 1987), 36.
5. Cited in Barry Rubin, *Assimilation and its Discontents* (New York, 1995), 38.
6. This quotation, from one of Malamud's short stories, is used as the epigraph to Joseph Heller's satiric novel about the problems of maintaining a Jewish identity in modern WASP America, *Good as Gold* (1979; repr. London, 1984).
7. Rubin, *Assimilation and its Discontents*, 5.
8. In the light of his own translated work, it is ironic to note that Singer himself made the same point forcefully in condemning the attempt of Yiddish communist ideologues to purge the Yiddish language of its 'petty bourgeois religious' connotations in a scathing review he wrote of the first post-war issue of the newly revived Soviet Yiddish journal *Sovietish Heymland*. See Isaac Bashevis Singer, 'A New Use for Yiddish', *Commentary* 33/2 (Mar. 1962), 267–9.
9. Cited in Sander L. Gilman, *Jewish Self-Hatred: Anti-Semitism and the Hidden Language of the Jews* (Baltimore and London, 1986), 309; also Gilbert, *Holocaust*, 37.
10. Gilman, *Self-Hatred*, 309.
11. Ibid. 310.
12. Cited in *Encyclopaedia Judaica*, vi. 101.
13. Weinreich, *Yiddish Language*, 328.
14. David Levine Lerner, 'The Enduring Legend of the Jewish Pope', *Judaism* 40/2 (Spring 1991), 148–9, 170.

APPENDIX

❖

R. Shimen Barbun, the Rabbi of Mainz or *The Tripartite Dream*

by
Ayzik-Meir Dik
translated and annotated by
Joseph Sherman

1. The Ghetto in the City of Mainz

Until now, my dear lady readers, we have related spirited stories of our present times which are so much better than those earlier times in which our forefathers lived. These are times in which, at last, we receive equal treatment with all other peoples of Europe; times in which we are permitted to dwell in every city and in all their streets, in which we too may become officials[1] and turn our hands to all occupations; times, praise God, in which we are even in a position to criticize ourselves and to ridicule various of our stupidities, in exactly the same way in which all civilized nations of Europe censure their own people. We no longer need fear to expose our divers shortcomings wholly publicly, even in the newspapers. In this way, not concealing our unworthy aspects from Christians, we assuredly demonstrate our great desire to improve ourselves, so confident and easy are we at present in regard both to the government, and to the native inhabitants who have grown civilized and humane.

Now, however, my dear lady readers—in order that you too may appreciate your good fortune in living at this juncture, in this happy place and time in civilized Europe, and not in previous centuries in places of barbaric Asia like Arabia, Persia, or Morocco—we wish here to relate an event which took place a century ago, one from which you can gain a clear understanding of the wild and savage times from which our parents suffered so greatly that they composed the long prayer, 'And he being merciful' and those tragic liturgical poems, full of deep sighing and heavy groans, which are recited on the Sabbaths between *Peysekh* and *Shvues*.[2]

In those times there were many lands and cities in which no vestige of Jewish life was permitted to manifest itself, and even in those cities in which Jews were indeed permitted to dwell, they were confined in a segregated quarter called a 'ghetto'.[3] This quarter was surrounded by a high stone wall. It had only one portal bearing iron gates that were locked every evening as well as on the Sabbath, on Sunday, and at times when a Christian procession went through the city.[4] A Jewish sentinel stood on guard within, and a Christian without. To this day, one such ghetto exists in Rome,[5] and hundreds more survive elsewhere, even in Frankfurt am Main and in Mainz, an old city ruled over by a prince-bishop.

It goes without saying that folk lived there in very cramped and dirty conditions. The dwellings were small, squat and dark, the streets narrow and crooked, the Jewish population as closely packed and huddled together as one can imagine, yet gainfully employed and busy all the same. Their chief commerce consisted in old clothes, antiques, and bills of exchange, and they plied a thriving trade with the Christians. Although an appearance of great poverty prevailed, the Jews grew rich in secret. They assumed the appearance of beggars, however, so that the government would not plunder them. About five thousand Jewish families lived in that place, but they dwelt as one household, since they intermarried and hence became distantly related one to another. Thus the joys and sorrows of each individual affected the whole community.

Among them were great Talmudists and pious men, learned scholars and cabbalists and mathematicians. Better than anything else, they understood the game of chess. In this the Christians took instruction from them, and the finest players among the Jews would be summoned to play chess with the most powerful nobles. Truth to tell, this was their chief purpose in playing chess, since thereby they gained excellent opportunities to perform good works—sometimes for themselves, sometimes for one another, and sometimes for the community as a whole. By this means they established firm acquaintanceships with persons of influence through whom they were able to accomplish whatever could be accomplished. Can anything else in the world bind the great to the humble more closely than this complex game, during which one forgets who one is? Nay, more—one is absorbed as if in a duel. Each of the two sides seeks to protect himself and to be victorious over the other, yet at the same time admires the prowess of his adversary despite himself, and when the game is concluded, cordially befriends him and esteems him more highly on account of his exceptional skill at play. Because the Jews were always the victors, they acquired wide renown as the best chess players in the realm, with the result that many young Christian princelings came to learn the game from them.

2. R. Shimen Barbun

For a hundred years in this Jewish settlement, no Jew was better known than R. Shimen Barbun. He was one of the most erudite Talmudists of his time; in addition he was a notable cabbalist and a man deeply and widely read in many fields and in many languages. Moreover he was a man of striking handsomeness, resembling a holy patriarch both in appearance and in behaviour. He was profoundly God-fearing and upright, a man communally very active in the performance of the commandments and in providing loans without interest. A numismatician, he was a specialist dealer in old coins, a trade through which he soon established extensive contacts with men of the highest rank in the Christian world. Even more, however, his ability at chess gained him a great reputation among the ruling aristocracy, for herein he had no equal, not even among the Jews of that quarter. He was possessed of so many secrets and innovative moves that no one could anticipate them, and in consequence they called him the king of all chess players.

This great man was so far contented with himself and with the world at large that he had no desire to assume a rabbinical position, though both there and elsewhere they would willingly have appointed him to the rabbinate. 'I am grateful to God', he used to say, 'that I have my sustenance, and the leisure I enjoy after my business affairs I do not wish to sell for any amount of money. Secondly, were I to become a rabbi, it would no longer be seemly for me to visit various high-ranking clergymen to play chess, and through these games I can benefit members of our community far more than through my rabbinical function, since I am often able to win many favours for them through my playing.'

But the old proverb tells us that no happiness ripens to maturity on this earth. Our Sages in Midrash add further that Abraham was not contented with his life, Isaac was not contented with his life, Jacob was not contented with his life, and—if the expression be permitted—even the Creator, Blessed be He, was Himself also not contented with His Creation, for it is not written, 'And God rejoiced in all the creations that He had made'; it is only written, 'He will rejoice', that is to say, the time of His rejoicing is still to come.[6] It goes without saying that, for all his serenity and self-sufficiency, R. Shimen Barbun proved no exception to this rule. With diminishment he grew deeply unhappy in his declining years, as unhappy indeed as our father Jacob and considerably more unhappy than he. Jacob mourned a son fully two and twenty years, being yet father to eleven children; while he of whom we speak mourned an only son for many more years, and recognized him withal in circumstances far more dreadful than those in which Jacob recognized his son Joseph, as we shall here recount.

For thirty five years, R. Shimen Barbun lived childless in this Jewish colony. A life with children is indeed a life filled with trouble. But without children there is no life at all.[7] One finds oneself alone in the greater community. One looks upon oneself as forgotten, particularly when one is in middle age. It is hard to live this way, but worse to die thus. As we Jews believe, after the death of parents, a child is like a good emissary who effects the annulment of all evil decrees passed on a good friend; when one has no child, however, one is obliterated without trace. This weighty thought pressed like a heavy stone on R. Shimen's noble heart, and on this account, in the still nights he would pray that God might rejoice him with a son. In time his prayer was accepted and, to boot, a wonder came to pass.

A wonder indeed, but would it be a wonder for our new enlightened world which does not believe even in truths? In those days, however, it was quite natural on occasions for an individual to dream that which was true, for in time past to receive sleeping visions was quite commonplace, as we find in our holy books, and in the *Gemore*, and most indisputably in the Book of Job (33:14–16) where it is written, 'For God speaketh in one way, yea in two, though man perceiveth it not. In a dream, in a vision of the night, when deep sleep falleth upon men [...] Then He openeth the ears of men, and sealeth their instruction.' This means as follows: God speaks once to men, and when men pay no attention, God speaks to them once more, but only in dreams; in nightly manifestations, when slumber falls over mankind, then God reveals to their ears His decision to direct them aright. In consequence, since dreams were greatly believed in those days, God employed them to instruct mankind. Thus it was no wonder that R. Shimen Barbun—who was certainly a great believer in visionary revelations, for he was also a cabbalist who was assuredly in chimerical contact with the spirit world—should dream that which was true. In so short a space, my dear lady reader, draw no specific conclusions at present concerning this possibility, and believe in this tale which has been taken from true historical sources, and envy earlier generations which were far closer to God than we are today.

3. The Fearful Dream

On the Eve of the New Moon of the month of Elul, in the thirty-fifth year of his life, returning at night from synagogue after *Yonkiper Koton*[8] during which he had fasted, R. Shimen was deeply troubled. His heart seemed as if it had been ripped out, his eyes overflowed with tears. He felt distinctly uneasy, as if the whole world had grown narrow for him, and he himself did not know what ailed him. Consequently he ate very little, and soon lay down to rest. Almost immediately his eyelids shut like heavy leaden gates. No sooner had he fallen asleep, however, and the real world with its weighty burdens had rolled away from under his feet, than his spirit carried him over to a better world. In this world of dreams, a slave can become a king, a pauper a rich man, a sick man well, and a childless man the father of a fine son. There it soon appeared that his wife, too, bore him a son; he prepared a fitting celebration for the boy's circumcision; and the child grew up strong and healthy with him, knowing neither teething pains nor any other of the sicknesses of children, and was withal very handsome, clever, possessed of every talent, and above all gifted in studies and in knowledge of languages, so that when he grew to *barmitsve* he was arrayed in the Crown of Learning.

Grew to *barmitsve*? How is this possible, you will certainly ask me, my dear lady reader. This was a dream of one night. Must one imagine that fully thirteen years passed? I should like to respond to that by saying that such a question is entirely childish, since time in itself is in truth neither short nor long: it only appears so according to our individual conception of it, as we see clearly when some hour passes so rapidly that we are hardly aware it has gone, and by contrast another hour seems to last an eternity for us. This is because time is a delicate matter which our human understanding cannot comprehend.

Regarding time, the great commentator R. Yedaya Pnini, in his golden book, *The Examination of the World* (Chapter 11),[9] observes: 'Time is something divine, the true reality of which we humans cannot grasp.' This is clearly proved by the fact that a dream of the greatest import is perceived in the thousandth part of a second. Thus, in a momentary slumber, a man once dreamed that he married a king's daughter, and in little more than ten years, after the death of his father-in-law, he himself became a king. Subsequently he begot a child with his wife, and when the child was about nine years old and fell into a well, his great grief awakened him, and he remained disturbed on this account for several weeks.

Now, my dear lady reader, let us return to our tale. R. Shimen perceived in his dream that, in his thirteenth year, his son was arrayed in the Crown of Wisdom, which is the Crown of Torah, whereat, moreover, he was so greatly overjoyed that he started up in pure happiness, but soon drifted off again into a sweet sleep, as was the case with the Prophet Jeremiah, who relates, 'Upon this I awaked, and beheld; And my sleep was sweet unto me' (Jeremiah 31:25).

He dozed and dreamed again that he saw his son at the age of about twenty, beautiful as an angel, with his forehead now adorned with a golden crown on which were inscribed in black letters the words 'Crown of Priesthood', and thousands upon thousands of people kneeled to him. The father wished to approach his son, but he was not permitted to do so, and this caused him such pain that in slumber he began to weep so bitterly and for so long that his wife heard and roused him, inquiring what troubled him. His response was terse. 'I dreamt something dreadful,' he told her, and slept again. Scarcely had he shut his eyes, however, than he dreamed a third time, and again about his son. He imagined that he saw him at the age of some thirty years, grown pale and clad in sackcloth and ashes like a penitent, sitting in a small house of prayer poring over the pious book, *The Duties of the Heart*,[10] and studying. Anew it seemed that he desired to speak with his son, to question him about this shocking transformation. But his tongue was to all intents trammelled and tied, and he was forced to strain every nerve before he could tear those bonds asunder and recover his speech. Then he burst forth with that long repressed question pent up in his breast from the first moment he had glimpsed his son in so pitiful a situation, a time which had been an eternity to him.

'In what, my child, have you sinned so greatly,' he demanded, 'that you have become so rigorous a penitent? Have you transgressed so gravely against God or men that in order to make peace with them you must cut yourself off entirely from the world, and in your youth, no less?'

'And it will remain thus until the last day of my life,' was his son's answer.

And immediately hereupon R. Shimen Barbun awoke. It was already broad daylight.

For more than three full months after this dream, he went about like one confused, and discussed it with no one. He believed this dream to be nothing more than a trick of the fantasy, like the majority of other dreams, and was consequently not worthy of regard.

4. The Fulfilment of the First Dream

Our Sages in Midrash (Chapter 64)[11] observe that three things grow stale in the course of time and disappear from our notice: mournful predictions, immoderate mourning and sad dreams. Such was the case with R. Shimen Barbun, too. In the space of three months, R. Shimen had almost forgotten his dream, and had begun to feel more cheerful. Perhaps he might never have recollected that period of his life, had not his wife reminded him of it with glad tidings. She informed him that she was with child. With this intelligence she freshly inked over the faded letters of an old manuscript—in other words, she reawakened his disregarded dream, and in his heart sorrow and joy blended one with another. Then he recounted his fearful and wonderful dreams to his wife and to his close friends, all of whom interpreted it for the good. He did not lightly allow himself to rest, however, and thereafter he held this gift from God—to have begotten a child—to be a false benefaction, for his heart warned him that it would bring him more sorrow than consolation.

Thereafter he would secretly pray that he might be fortunate and blessed in the child that was soon to be born to him, and that he might be found worthy enough to bring up his son to Torah, to marriage, and to good deeds. His wife, too, no less than he, also prayed that the child she would bear might sweeten their lives and ornament their old age. Every day of her pregnancy she would recite the Three Hundred and Sixty Supplications[12] and withal she vowed, as Hannah did of old (1 Samuel 1:11) that if she were to bear a son, she would sanctify him only to Torah and to the service of God, and would then consider herself the happiest woman in the world.

Thus, with devout prayers, the nine months of her pregnancy sped by, and were, in the fullness of time, gladdened with a son who was as beautiful and lovely to look upon as a newly created angel. Even his puling and squalling seemed as dulcet and mellifluous as the harmonies of a better world, so that it became a pleasure to see and to hear this child, and it did the heart even more good to fondle and to kiss him. The boy grew more beautiful and more brilliant with every passing day. When he started to talk, the city resounded with the aptitude and wondrous ideas which purled from his mouth; when he entered *kheyder* to commence his studies, his teacher was beside himself with astonishment, for so far from appearing as if he were learning for the first time, it seemed more as if the child were reminding himself of what he had learnt long ago. In barely a few years, his thorough familiarity with the whole of the *Tanakh* and the Mishnah, and his perfect understanding of intricacies of calculation, led all the learned men of Mainz to observe of him that the angel had neglected to slap him at his birth, in consequence whereof he had not forgotten what had been taught him in the other world. (*Author's Note*: The *Gemore* notes, Tractate *Niddah*, chapter *Hamapelet*, as follows: 'As soon as it [a newborn child] sees the light an angel approaches, slaps its mouth, and causes it to forget all the Torah completely', that is, everything he has learnt there, in the other world.)[13] Since in study he strode rapidly forward with every year that passed, he soon had no teacher capable of instructing him; by his twelfth year he had exhausted all his father's sources of learning and Torah; in his thirteenth year he had risen to such heights both in scholarship and in erudition that the most distinguished rabbis of France and Germany conferred on him rabbinical *smikhe*, and the greatest sages of both these countries acknowledged him as pre-eminent among the learned. This fortunate child was called Joseph, and this name, coupled with the surname Barbun, began so to resound in both the East and the West that the most influential, the most eminent and the most learned men of the time longed to acquire him for a son-in-law, and envied R. Shimen Barbun for having been found worthy to beget such a son.

All this notwithstanding, R. Shimen was not as joyful and content as the world believed, for the degree to which the benevolent promise of the first dream had been fulfilled moved him with grave disquiet regarding the issue of the last dream, and consequently, in moments of his greatest joy, bathed him in tears, and forced deep sighs from his oppressed heart.

5. The Fulfilment of the Second Dream

Our Sages explain in Midrash *Kohelet* how far Gehenna is from Paradise. One says a hand's breadth; another says that only a thin partition separates them. Our Sages say they are so close to each other that it is possible to look from Gehenna into Paradise and from Paradise into Gehenna.[14] This teaching apart, its truth is evident also from vivid examples in the chance events of our lives. Happiness and unhappiness, joy and sorrow border closely on one another and, by common consent, dog each other's heels so nearly, that while yet living in the greatest joy, in the highest happiness, one can already descry that unhappiness which hastens onward so rapidly that one treads upon the other. Elsewhere it is expressed even more clearly: 'Do not give up the belief in retribution' (*Ethics of the Fathers* 1:7), that is to say, man should constantly prepare himself for trouble and misfortune. As the old proverb says, man has not been created content, hence his eyes are filled with tears even at the moment in which he laughs. Such was precisely the case here. In a time of greatest happiness, a sorrow comes to pass quite unexpectedly, like thunder which cracks sharply in the loveliest weather, and a downpour drowns the sheaves and the haystacks which have been gathered together with sweat and effort over many months. The husbandman sees this and turns aside and holds his peace. Such was the course of events during the week in which preparations were being made to receive as a relative by marriage one who was alike a great prince and a great scholar. A certain Don Menachem of Orleans was to have come to bend his looks upon this Joseph Barbun and to examine him in learning, in order to take him into his family as a bridegroom. Just as his parents were hoping to see Torah and worldly grandeur joined in their home, their son, who was their whole joy, their whole hope, vanished. He had gone bathing with his servant, and neither of them had returned.

Now, my dear lady reader, who can describe the grief of the parents? Who can depict their weeping, their unutterable sorrow? No child was ever more deeply mourned by his father and mother than this Joseph. The whole city wept with them; even Christians came to condole with them. They refused to be comforted, however. For fully two weeks, all the waters of the place were sounded to the depths, but absolutely no traces were to be found. A month passed before the boy's little hat was found, borne with sand to the river bank. It was brought to the father as once the coat of Joseph had been brought to his father Jacob. The father seized it with both hands, drenched it with his tears, and cried out, 'Alas the day! My child is drowned! Now I know I shall never see you more! You are drowned! False are the visions which dreams bring! That which death has once possessed, is never surrendered! O unhappy father that I am, it has not been granted to me to console myself with my child's grave. O, I would have planted it with flowers, I would have watered them with my tears! Daily, as on a holy site, I would have recited my prayers there! You were a saint, and you would have solaced me with the happiness that some day I would be buried beside you! Now, my beloved child, you have become a meal for fish. The belly of a shark is doubtless your resting-place!'

In this way his parents grieved and wept over him for him for many days and many years. The father grew prematurely grey, and the mother went blind from weeping. On this account, they also came down in the world, and R. Shimen was unwillingly forced to become a rabbi there in the ghetto. He lived on for more than twenty years in distress and heavy affliction. He forsook all worldly pleasures; no light-hearted expression was ever to be seen on his face, and no cheerful word ever left his lips. He wore mourning continually, and would recall the name Joseph both in eating and in studying, and on every occasion when he missed him—even at chess, the only recreation in which he indulged to alleviate the severity of that anguish which would otherwise have consumed his body and his soul.

And it came to pass on a certain day, the seventh day of the month of Nisan in the twenty-third year after these events, when the ghetto was bustling with preparations for the Passover, and the entire Jewish population of that place, like bees in a hive, were hard at work making ready the *matse* and other necessities of the holy days, and R. Shimen Barbun, who was then rabbi in that place, was occupied, according to custom, with providing Passover flour for the poor, that the leader of the community approached him with tear-swollen eyes and related some shocking news.

'You should know, Rabbi,' he exclaimed, 'that I have this day received a command from our Prince-Bishop that all we Jews who dwell here in this ghetto must, within only four weeks, quit this place as one man. Should we tarry longer, they will dispossess us of everything we own, and will pitilessly drive us forth like dogs with sticks and whips.'

A long silence ensued. Then R. Shimen lifted up his voice with a deep groan, 'What can help us in this?'

'The only thing to do now,' cried the leader of the community, 'is for your honour to take upon yourself the burden of approaching the Bishop and pleading with him, for he regards you as a man of considerable consequence, and you are, after all, acquainted with him, for in your youth you used to play at chess with him. Even though he was then only a minor official, he has surely not changed despite that. He is still the same good man he was then. He will surely receive you most cordially.'

'That is why I cannot understand it,' cried out R. Shimen. 'What could have moved him to issue so harsh a dictate? Surely one of our community must have sinned greatly against him. Thus my advice is that we should issue a communal injunction that whoever has done this, or whoever knows anything about it, should immediately confess it to me so that I may know how to account for it to him. Then my visit will certainly not be made in vain.'

'I agree,' answered the leader of the community, 'and it should take place during this afternoon's prayers, for to lose even a day in so dangerous a matter is too much.'

And thus it was done. But no one presented himself, either to take responsibility or to impart the slightest information. So it remained for R. Shimen, in company with the leader of the community, to approach the Bishop to enquire of him the cause of this stern decree and to beg him immediately to annul it. Meanwhile the community imposed a fast and recited the Penitential Prayers, as the practice has always been among us Jews.[15] First we come to terms with God, and then we seek the assistance of man. The deputies presented themselves to the Bishop who admitted them to his presence and received them with great friendliness, but they achieved naught with him.

'I have nothing personal against you,' he answered them. 'Not one of you has insulted me. Quite the contrary. It pains me greatly to have to treat you so tyrannically. Secondly, I stand to suffer considerable loss from this, since I receive my greatest revenue from you. You have brought great trade to my city. But what can I do when I have been commanded thus by the Pope? Should you indeed wish to plead, you must travel to Rome and fall down before the Pope himself. Perhaps you will be fortunate enough to effect a change of heart in him.'

Then R. Shimen replied, 'Inasmuch as you have been good enough to have compassion on us, and advise us to travel to the Pope, I beg you, gracious and holy ruler, to give me a letter of recommendation from yourself to the Pope in which you may represent to him who I am, so that he may hear my pleas. Without such a letter they will assuredly not admit us into his presence.'

'I shall do that,' the Prince-Bishop replied. 'I shall also introduce you to him as a great chess player, since the Pope is very fond of the game. It seems to me that you will secure your object far more effectively with him through this means than through any other.'

In passing, the Bishop enquired of R. Shimen Barbun the position regarding his son, and whether he had heard anything of him. In the same breath, he comforted him, giving him good hope that his son might still be alive and might yet be found, and that he might ultimately be a source of proud pleasure to his father. The Bishop went on to adduce numerous examples of rediscovered children, chatting on for more than an hour about all sorts of irrelevances. When his ruler had produced the letter, R. Shimen Barbun, prior to his departure, reopened his discussion regarding the fiat, and importuned the Bishop at least to give them his own opinion regarding it—in other words, what displeasure he felt the Pope might harbour against the local Jewish community to have made him promulgate so bitter an edict. The Bishop responded, half-laughing, 'Without doubt you will discover that there,' and immediately hereupon withdrew to his private room, bidding them adieu.

With heavy and grieving hearts, R. Shimen and the leader of the community returned to the Jewish quarter. They immediately summoned a great assembly and explained how matters stood—namely that it was necessary to travel to Rome, expenses for which purpose more than a thousand thalers were needed. Furthermore, those who should accompany them had to be elected, because a delegation from any community had to consist of more than two. All these problems were solved in a moment—both money and men instantly appeared. The morrow was again declared a day of fasting, and prayers were offered that their emissaries might be successful in Rome. R. Shimen recited the *Tokheha* [the catalogue of divine punishments listed in Leviticus 26:14–39 and Deuteronomy 28:15–68] in reprimand to the community, among whose members rivers of tears were shed. Thereafter their five dignitaries journeyed to Rome with R. Shimen Barbun.

Since the distance was great and the time was short, they travelled even on the holy days, and arrived in Rome just as the Christian

Easter had ended. Thus they could soon approach the Pope. But before they made their way to him, they met with the leaders of the Jewish community in Rome to enquire from them what sort of man the Pope was, how he treated them, and how they were to gain access to him. In passing, they told of the injunction on account of which they had just come. The Roman Jews, however, were astounded at this report.

'How can this be?' they exclaimed. 'The present Pope is among the best of men. During the time he has been on the Papal throne, he has shown only favour towards us. We cannot therefore understand what he has against you. Assuredly your community must in some way have transgressed against him.'

In short, they did not know what to make of it. And how can one find means to be of assistance when one does not know the cause of the trouble? All agreed that they should meet with the Pope, and offered advice about when they should go, and whom they should bribe to admit them. The Roman Jews placed an interpreter at their disposal. R. Shimen, however, declined the offer with thanks. 'I have no need of it,' he answered, 'because I myself speak Latin fluently.' Within a few days the Jewish community of Rome declared a day of fasting among themselves in support of the Mainz delegation when they set off to the Pope, in the hope that their mission would prosper.

Thus the deputies from Mainz made their way to the Vatican, to the great palace of the Pope. They caused themselves to be announced to him, and he admitted them into his presence. He received them in his audience hall clad in his papal vestments, with the holy crown on his head and the golden sceptre in his hand, as if he were about to receive a royal embassy. He seated himself on his holy three-legged chair and beckoned them to draw closer and state their desire.

'Our desire,' called out R. Shimen, approaching closer and falling to his knees, 'O Holy Father, is that the full measure of your compassion, prevailing over the full severity of your law, may annul the decree against the Jewish community of Mainz, which does not know for what sin it has deserved this punishment at your hands. In Mainz we are the most complaisant and orderly people, and the most serviceable besides. I can prove it to you with a letter from our Prince-Bishop, Lord Gilbert, in which moreover my own character is described and presented to you.' Thus saying, he submitted the letter to him.

The Pope perused the letter, and bade R. Shimen rise. 'So? You are the famous R. Shimen Barbun?' he observed. 'Until now I have only heard of you. Now I have the pleasure of speaking with you. You are a man of great account, and I have long wished to try conclusions for some hours on religious matters with such a one as yourself. If they speak true, you are the greatest Talmudist among the Jews, and the most learned among them. I thank God for this opportunity to meet you personally and to spend time in your company. As for the rest of you representatives from the Jewish community of Mainz, go you peacefully home. You will receive my decision in three days' time. And you, Barbun, tarry awhile in my private room.'

In this manner the delegation left, and Barbun, at the Pope's instance, retired to his study. There the Pontiff received him as an equal, invited him to be seated, regaled him with costly juices and rare fruit, and engaged him in a deep debate on matters of faith. R. Shimen Barbun could not cease marvelling at how it was possible for a Pope, a young man, to possess such deep knowledge of the Jewish faith, to show such proficiency, such profundity in it, that there was scarcely a holy book whose contents were not intimately familiar to him, no single tractate of the Talmud whose quintessence was not at his command, no branch of the Kabbalah wherein he was unversed.

This disquisition lasted more than three hours and ended with the victory of R. Shimen Barbun, who finally gained mastery over the Pope. When the disputation had ended, the Pope said to him, 'Now I wish to play at chess with you. In the letter you brought me, Gilbert, your Prince-Bishop, praises you as a great chess player, and you are similarly renowned throughout all Germany and France.'

'Our Prince has not written you a lie,' replied R. Shimen Barbun, 'for I truly excel at this game.'

A golden chess set was then produced, and sitting down to the game, R. Shimen was even more dumbfounded by the Pope's shrewdness and skill at play than by his theological proficiency.

'Why are you so astonished?' asked the Pope. 'Is chess playing, like your religion, the exclusive property of you Jews as well, that my good understanding of the game so startles you?'

'No, Holy Father,' responded R. Shimen, 'I am not so stupid as to think that. I wonder only at how you discovered moves that no other player comprehends or will ever learn. I alone know them, having gained possession of them from a manuscript, and only one other, having acquired them from me—and he has been dead long since.'

'And who was that other,' enquired the Pope, 'that you found none but him worthy of your instruction?'

'O Holy Father,' R. Shimen Barbun cried out, 'do not exacerbate old wounds which have bled within me for more than twenty years. This was my only son, a child whose like could be found only in the mirror. He was called Joseph, and was lost to me as Joseph was lost to his father Jacob. As it appears, he was drowned with his servant, and I mourn for him as Jacob mourned for his Joseph.'

'And you will yet live to see him,' exclaimed the Pope, 'in great glory, as Jacob lived to see his son Joseph.'

'O, may Almighty God fulfil your blessing,' groaned R. Shimen. 'Then I would echo the very words Jacob uttered when he recognized his Joseph: "Now let me die, since I have seen thy face, that thou art yet alive" ' (Genesis 46:30). And he wept greatly before the other. (*Author's Commentary*: To me, the interpretation of this verse appears that Jacob prayed to the Lord that the words he had spoken when they first brought the coat of his son before him, 'I will go down to the grave to my son mourning' [Genesis 37:35], might be annulled. Jacob meant, 'He will not return to me, but I will go down to him', just as King David said: 'I shall go to him, for he will not return to me' [2 Samuel 12:23]. Jacob prayed that, at the very moment in which he saw his son Joseph alive, his former words should be reversed, and thus he said, 'Let me die now.' He meant, in other words, 'Let me die at this very moment in which I see that you are still alive, in accordance with the natural order of the whole world, which ordains that the father should die during the lifetime of his son, and not the son in the presence of his father, as was the case with Terah and his son Haran [the father and the brother of Abraham]. Haran died in the presence of his father Terah, who was the first upon whom this punishment was visited, as can be seen from the scriptural genealogy' [Genesis 11:27–8].)

'Do not weep, dear father!' the Pope called out to him in a loving and tender voice, falling instantly upon his neck with a great cry. 'I am your son Joseph. I am still alive. I have been raised to the Papacy, and I give thanks to God that I am in a position to sweeten your old age and to still your tears.'

No wonder, my dear lady reader, that this news had an even more powerful effect upon this old man than upon our father Jacob. The latter, after all, recognized his son Joseph as a Jew, while the former recognized his son as the Catholic Pope. He was on the point of collapse. Two conflicting feelings simultaneously shot their arrows into his wounded heart. Each one individually is capable of overpowering the strongest spirit in the world; how much more such an old man as this? Since one can sometimes die from sudden joy, what more needs be said about sudden grief? And what more evil tidings could such a pious father as R. Shimen Barbun receive than that his son had become a Pope? He fell senseless to the ground, and when they revived him, he swooned again and again. When he came to himself, he cried out to his son the same words that Hezekiah cried out when the Prophet Isaiah, imparting the glad tidings that he would recover, added the sharp rebuke that God would bring this to pass only for the sake of David's merit, and not for Hezekiah's sake alone. Then Hezekiah exclaimed, 'Behold, for my peace I had great bitterness' (Isaiah 38:17). This was the case here too. With the revelation that he had become the Pope, the son turned to gall the joyful tidings that he was alive.

Well, my dear lady reader, who is in a position to record the first words that passed between such a father and such a son, who reached out to each other across a gulf of some twenty years? A human pen is too deficient, too commonplace for such an interchange that sprang from soul, heart and viscera. So you will have to be content with the little I will here report to you of that colloquy. After they had both composed themselves a little, and their emotions had subsided somewhat, the son began to render an account to his father of what had befallen him, and how he had come to this pass.

'That catspaw, my servant,' he began, 'whom you ordered to remain with me and serve me, as we went to bathe together, led me astray into a narrow alley which lay between two churches, and passing a small door, he pulled on the bell-rope which hung outside it. As soon as it rang, several priests sprang out and dragged us both into a cloister. They soon separated me from him, and locked me in a cell containing only a bed, a table, and two chairs. The barred window overlooked a garden. There I was totally isolated, save that twice a day a serving-boy brought me food and drink, and with it, on every occasion, another of their religious books. For the first two weeks I wept and clamoured. I ate nothing more than bread, drank only water, and slept on the ground because I did not want to lie on fabric made of the forbidden mixture of linen and wool. There was no question of even touching one of their tracts. My sensations were those of one buried alive, waiting in his grave. My only thoughts were for you and my mother. I pictured to myself your great grief, your weeping and your sorrow over me. Would that a tenth of my curses might fall upon the false friend who abducted me thither: I damned and reviled him for days on end. The kidnapper certainly received enough money for his treachery in that monastery, where one of his uncles is a baptized priest. He himself was doubtless subsequently baptized, although I cannot be sure of this, for they soon packed him off to Spain. A few weeks later, after I had fallen ill, a doctor visited me in company with two priests, offered comfort, and represented how happy I could be if I were to become a devout Christian and betake myself to their religious studies, for they knew who I was and what great gifts I possessed. On the other hand, he intimated, if I remained obdurate I would make myself unhappy in the highest degree. I would fall into the hands of the Inquisition and their like.

'I received such visits two or three times a week, and on each occasion the callers spoke in the same terms. At that time I was still very young, barely thirteen years old. I had a great lust for life. I was terrified of the tortures and cruelties of the Inquisition. (*Author's note*: The Inquisition was a secret court of justice composed of clerics who used to spy out Christians or baptized Jews who were not strict in their religious observance, and similarly persons whom they could falsely accuse of having intended to receive baptism but had recanted. On such persons they would inflict all the tortures in the world; when these proved of no avail, they would burn the obdurate alive.) So I allowed myself to be forcibly baptized. Done as it was against my will, I wept bitterly at the moment of its execution. Soon after this christening, I was sent to Ferrara in Italy. There, little by little, I began to forget you, my home, my religion. I sought comfort only in learning, studying their works of theology until I surpassed all my fellow students in scholarship. In a few years I became a postulant among them, and rose steadily from one rung to another until I became a canon, then a bishop, and thereafter, Pope. My riches, my great eminence, and my enormous gratification seduced me so thoroughly, impressed me so deeply, that it soon became very difficult for me to tear myself from my spiritual height to become a despised Jew again, and be exposed to the terrible danger of falling victim to the fearful Inquisition.

'This year, however, your Prince-Bishop Gilbert visited me. Because I had long suspected him of having had a hand in my abduction, I invited him to my table. At the meal I opened a discussion with him regarding your Jewish community in his city of Mainz and, in passing, I enquired about you: whether you were still alive, and how you fared. "This Rabbi Shimen Barbun," he replied, "lives yet. He has become the rabbi there, is held in great esteem, and labours under heavy affliction, for he mourns his only son who was lost to him." He went on to inform me of the dream centred upon me which came to you before I was born, about which I knew nothing. This account moved me so deeply that I rose from the table. I retired to a private room and wept until I could weep no more. I resolved that I would meet with you. Since I could not do so in the normal way, by writing asking you to come to me—for the matter would certainly have become common knowledge and I could not afford this, since it would have done great harm both to you and to me—I consequently issued the command that all Jews should be expelled from Mainz. From the outset, I foresaw that this decree would unfailingly drive you hither to plead for them, since you are the greatest man there, celebrated among Jews and Christians alike. This calculation has gained my objective. So, dear father, be not heart-stricken on my account, for I am guilty of nothing in being lost to you—neither in receiving baptism, nor in keeping silence until now. Joseph, who was far more righteous than I, also concealed his glory from his father. Nay more, he named his son "Manasseh" ['making to forget': Genesis 41:51], for God caused Joseph to forget as one both his loneliness and the house of his parents. No one is to blame for all this. It was simply a determination of Providence and nothing more, as was possible to infer from your dream. Even the faithless servant was only an instrument of God in this affair, only part of a predetermined process: "An obligation must be fulfilled by those who are obligated."[16] In other words, God causes evil to come about only through evil persons.

'Now, holy father, all that remains for me to comfort you is to set about fulfilling your last dream as well. I will become a penitent. I will return to our Jewish faith. The only question is whether God will accept my repentance.'

'O, my child!' the father answered him, 'God is merciful, and His hand is ever open to receive those who return to the faith in which they were born: the more so for you, who are blameless in all this. You are a Marrano. Do it, my child, and thereby sweeten my last years, as Ishmael sweetened the life of his father Abraham by doing penance for his death.' (*Author's Note*: Our Sages say that with the words God spoke to Abraham, 'Thou shalt be buried in a good old age' (Genesis 15:15), He implied that Ishmael would do penance for

Abraham's death, and our Sages support this with several other scriptural verses (see, for example, Genesis 25:8–9).)

'But this, dear father,' responded the son, 'cannot happen so soon. God grant it may come to pass in a year's time. Since I suspect Gilbert, your Prince-Bishop, of having been involved in my abduction, if I were to vanish immediately he would certainly surmise that you had persuaded me to become a Jew again, and he would persecute us both. Then, on our account, all other Jews would suffer as well. The matter must in consequence be delayed for at least two years.'

'Why for two years?' asked the father.

'Firstly, because I have many affairs to put in order before my flight; secondly, I must grow a beard and sidelocks, not only that I may go unrecognized, but also that I may look like a true Jew once more. Then I will come to you as a fervent penitent, clad in sackcloth and bestrewn with ashes, and I will pass my days with you in the ghetto. I shall live under cover among the Jews to prevent anyone from knowing me to be your son. Failing this, my presence among you could occasion great harm.[17] All the same, I shall maintain myself in the guise of a Marrano who fled the Inquisition in Spain in order to live out his life with you as a penitent, as indeed, many Spanish Marranos actually do who wish to lead a devout Jewish life and make atonement for their former wicked deeds. And what God will subsequently do with us, I know not.'

This, my dear lady reader, was the gist of their conversation. The father spent three days in Rome with his son, and on each of his visits, their discussions ranged fully and widely over various subjects that are not relevant to our story. On the fourth day, the Jews of Mainz received a benign dispensation commanding that they should be left in peace in their ghetto, with several valuable privileges added thereto, and they returned home with great rejoicing.

6. The Fulfilment of the Third Dream

The two whole years which had to pass before his son would return to him seemed far longer to R. Shimen than the interminable time that had elapsed before he discovered what had befallen him. Now every day his son spent as Pope of the Catholic belief was a day of sorrow and punishment for him. He could never resolve within himself why and wherefore a great and just God had ordained this for him. From his dream it was plain to perceive that this had been an imposition from Heaven. But for what purpose had this thing been revealed to him in a dream? All these questions were, however, soon put to rest a couple of years later when his son came to him, as we will now relate.

'A human being,' says the old proverb, 'survives everything,' and thus our R. Shimen Barbun survived the two years. His son returned to him on a dark night, heavily bearded, dressed in sackcloth, his head scattered with ashes.

'Now I am yours once again,' the son told his father. 'No one has ever made such a sacrifice to God for his faith as I have made. Remember what sort of glory, what sort of riches, what sort of honour I have allowed to roll away from under my feet, only to remain a Jew. (*Author's Note*: In those days, no king or emperor dared act without the consent of the Pope. Should the Pope need to mount his horse, either the Roman emperor or the German emperor would hold the stirrups of the saddle for him.) Thousands have knelt before me. Kings have prostrated themselves in the dust before me. With blood have I torn all this from my heart, only to make peace with my conscience. When I have succeeded in doing this, I shall be perfectly content.'

'Surely,' cried the father, 'you will be inwardly at peace. Indeed, your sin is not as great as you imagine, because in committing it you were nothing other than a Marrano. Secondly, as I perceived from our discussions, you have not forgotten your learning, something which was not the case even with Joseph the Righteous, who himself observed, "For I have forgotten all my toil" (Genesis 41:51), a statement that our Sages interpret to mean, "I have entirely forgotten the Torah which I studied with great effort." '

'This is true, dear father,' replied the son. 'I have not forgotten my learning, for I used to study every day. I was a Pope only in appearance. In my heart, however, I was a Jew in the highest degree, and believed that I had become a Pope only in order to benefit our brothers. I regularly re-read that sentence that Joseph spoke to his brothers, "For God did send me before you to preserve life [...] to give you a remnant on the earth, and to save you alive for a great deliverance" (Genesis 45:5/7). I have annulled countless harsh decrees against Jews, the majority, however, in the last two years which have passed since your recognition of me.'

He also related to his father in detail the form his favours to the Jewish people had taken, but this is not the place to recount them. His father was so delighted at this that he fell upon his son's neck and kissed him and wept for joy. 'Now, my child,' he exclaimed, 'both great questions regarding the conduct of the Creator, Blessed be He, which perplexed me all through the two hours which passed after you made yourself known, have been resolved for me by your narrative. In the first place, why did He determine that you should become a Pope? And secondly, why did He reveal this to me beforehand in a dream? The first is soon explained by the fact that, just as through the biblical Joseph, so through you great benefits should accrue to the whole people of Israel. The second is answered by the fact that I have only the dream to thank for your having remained piously observant even as Pope. For solely as a result of that dream did I ensure that I implanted in you, through all available means, a reverence for purity so absolute that you might not be led astray into sins such as would later force you into massive repentance. Thus, my child, is the honour of God preserved, my mind is set at rest, and I can say with my whole heart, "The Lord is righteous in all His ways, and gracious in all His deeds."[18] Now, too, do I understand the true meaning of that passage in Scripture (Exodus 33:13/23) which recounts the answer God gave to Moses our Teacher when Moses asked, "Show me now Thy ways." God replied, "Thou shalt see My back; but My face shall not be seen." In other words, mortal men can only understand the meaning of God's purposes in their conclusions, but not in their inceptions. To be even more plain, everything that the Compassionate One does with man is done in man's best interests.'

7. The End

Shortly thereafter the alarm was raised that the Pope had disappeared. Extensive investigations were undertaken, but it was impossible to discover a trace of him. Some maintained that he had been murdered and cast into the Tiber. This was hardly credible, for the man had no enemies. All were well disposed towards him. Some maintained that he had fled. But this was also not really believed. Firstly, why should he flee from a princeliness so great that millions pursued it? Secondly, in that case surely he would have taken with him precious objects and riches, and here not even a groschen was missing. The only one who surmised the truth was Gilbert, the Prince-Bishop of Mainz, who realized that the Pope had returned to Judaism. Gilbert, however, was prevented from even uttering such a thought lest through it the Catholic belief might be discredited. Hence in six months' time they created another Pope. With the passing of time the matter was so effectively put to rest that our Joseph could live quite undisturbed in the ghetto, particularly since his identity remained a secret even from all other Jews. He would sit and study quite openly, clad in sackcloth and ashes. He would eat only with the rabbi, his father. In cash, he had brought with him only a thousand ducats, money he had saved from his salary. He brought nothing else away with him. In this manner he passed his life there for several years.

In the process of time, when his father had grown very old, he summoned Joseph one evening and spoke thus: 'Know, my child, that my days in this world are numbered. Therefore I wish to exercise a father's right to make a request of his child before his death. Firstly, I implore you to marry soon, while I am still alive. Secondly, you should now put off your sackcloth and ashes, for you have made atonement for your sin twice twofold. Thirdly, you should assume the rabbinical chair in my place, here in this ghetto. I have already discussed this with the present community. I have borne witness to them on your behalf that you are the only one worthy to stand in my place. And they concur. You must fulfil these three things now, while I yet live.'

'These three requests I will indeed fulfil, speedily and soon,' his son answered him. And God favoured the father to see all with his own eyes. He lived on for a few years thereafter, and died in contented old age, rewarded with some sweet and pleasant days after so long and difficult a life. And he was buried there with great honour.

His son survived him for many years, and until the last hour of his life no one knew who he was. Even then he never acknowledged it verbally, for at the end his speech had been taken from him. He simply made over to the leader of the community his private papers wherein this whole history was related. These papers themselves were kept secret for many decades. Only a century later were they included in the annals of that place. There this history is extensively described. We have extracted only a summary of it. A small part of it was also reported in the Russian-Jewish newspapers, but with minor alterations, as is the custom with journalists who are concerned less with writing the truth than with what accords with their bias.

Notes to the Translation

The notes which follow are factual expansions of information given by Dik in his tale. The tragic correspondence of Dik's historical information with the evidence adduced by Raul Hilberg in defining the precedents which the Nazis carried to their logical conclusion has already been noted. Dik was very well informed about matters of Jewish history, a clear demonstration of his integrity as a reformer and bringer of *Haskalah* to the masses. As an educator, Dik was also concerned to inform his unlearned readership on all subjects, particularly Jewish ones, and his numerous references to biblical, Talmudic and midrashic sources are accompanied with exegeses and simple expositions leading to short homilies on the passages quoted, all of which are designed to serve as moral instructions and practical examples for use in daily life. These are often added as footnotes to the main body of his story. For the most part, Dik is at pains to provide Yiddish translations of all the quotations he makes in Hebrew. In general, all sources quoted by Dik in the body of his Yiddish text are more fully identified within brackets in the body of my translation itself. Only longer, more expanded extra-textual notes and some obscure references are included here.

1. Throughout Europe, from the time Christianity became the state religion of Rome following the conversion of Constantine in 312, Jews were prohibited by law from holding public office. The first Church proclamation to this effect was made by the Synod of Clermont in 535. Seven centuries later, in 1237, Emperor Frederick II excluded Jews from public office in his kingdom on the following principle: 'Faithful to the duties of a Catholic prince, we exclude Jews from public office so they will not abuse official power for the oppression of Christians.' In 1940, Hitler insisted that his campaign against the Jews 'was a battle against a Satanized power which had [...] grasped in its hands all key positions of scientific, intellectual, as well as political life' (quoted in Raul Hilberg, *The Destruction of the European Jews* (New York, 1985),10, 12). The neo-Nazi right-wing movements in South Africa during the 1980s, in so far as they were prepared to tolerate Jews (as 'whites') at all in their cloud-cuckoo land of 'restored Boer Republics', publicly announced that they would do so only on condition that 'Jews refrain from interfering in politics'. Thus does the ancient and archetypal stereotype of the Jew perpetuate itself in the mindset of Jew-haters.

2. The prayer, 'And He being Merciful' (*ve-hu rahum*), was introduced into the daily evening (*ma'ariv*) service during the Gaonic period (tenth century). It is taken from the book of Psalms (Psalms 78:38 and 20:10) and speaks of God's abundant mercy: 'And He being merciful forgives iniquity and does not destroy; frequently He turns his anger away, and does not stir up all His wrath. O Lord, save us; may the King answer us on the day when we call.' According to the commentators, Psalm 78 was selected because it contains all thirteen words which allude to the Thirteen Attributes of Divine Mercy enumerated in Exodus 34:6–7 in the passage beginning *El rahum ve-hanun* (Lord God, Merciful and Gracious). It is characteristic of the category of *piyyutim* whose nature is supplication, to which Dik's narrative here refers, always to include the Thirteen Attributes of Divine Mercy, as is evident from the Penitential Prayers or *Slihot* recited on Fast Days, Days of Penitence, and on *Yom Kippur*. Even more significant is the fact that in Ashkenazi communities on the Sabbaths between *Peysekh* (Passover) and *Shvues* (The Feast of Weeks), the prayer *Av ha-rahamim* (Father of Mercies) was recited from the eleventh century onwards in memory of those Jews of the Rhineland

communities, which included such cities as Mainz, Worms and Speyer, who laid down their lives for the Sanctification of the Holy Name during the First Crusade of 1096.

3. Ghettos were made compulsory dwelling-areas for Jews in Church law, first promulgated at the Synod of Breslau in 1267. See Hilberg, *Destruction*, 6.
4. The Synod of Orleans in 538 forbade Jews from showing themselves in the streets during Passion Week. This injunction was then repeated and steadily enforced throughout Christendom. See Hilberg, *Destruction*, 5.
5. On the ancient ghetto of Rome, Raul Hilberg provides the following information:

> No summation of the canonical law can be as revealing as a description of the Rome ghetto, maintained by the Papal State until the occupation of the city by the Royal Italian Army in 1870. [...] The ghetto consisted of a few damp, dark, and dirty streets, into which 4700 human creatures had been packed tightly [...] To rent any house or business establishment outside of the ghetto boundaries, the Jews needed the permission of the Cardinal Vicar. Acquisition of real estate outside the ghetto was prohibited. Trade with industrial products or books was prohibited. Higher schooling was prohibited. The professions of lawyer, druggist, notary, painter, and architect were prohibited. A Jew could be a doctor, provided that he confined his practice to Jewish patients. No Jew could hold office. Jews were required to pay taxes like everyone else and, in addition, the following: (1) a yearly stipend for the upkeep of the Catholic officials who supervised the Ghetto Finance Administration and the Jewish community organisation; (2) a yearly sum of 5250 lira to the Casa Pia for missionary work among Jews; (3) a yearly sum of 5250 lira to the Cloister of the Converted for the same purpose. In return, the Papal State expended a yearly sum of 1500 lira for welfare work. But no state money was paid for education or the care of the sick. (Hilberg, *Destruction*, 6)

6. 'He will rejoice ...': the source of this passage is *Midrash Rabbah* 20:2 on Leviticus 16:1 (*Parshe Aharey Mot*, Leviticus 16–18). Although Judaism generally eschews asceticism, the passage sets out to show how, in certain instances, the Lord might defer the happiness of the pious, so that they might better enjoy their share of bliss in the World to Come. In translation, the passage in *Midrash Rabbah* reads as follows:

> Abraham was not happy in this world of Mine [...] A son was born to him when he was a hundred years old and in the end the Holy One, blessed be He, said to him: Take now thy son [...] and offer him [...] for a burnt offering (Genesis 12:2). [As a result of this trial, Sarah died after having heard of what had transpired.] It has been said: she had scarcely finished speaking when she died. [Therein lay Abraham's unhappiness, not in the actual trial.] Abraham came to mourn for Sarah, and to weep for her (Genesis 23:2). [...] Israel did not enjoy happiness in this world of Mine, as may be inferred from the fact that it does not say: 'Israel *rejoiced* (*samakh*) in his Maker, but *shall rejoice* (*yismakh*)' (Psalm 149:2) as much as to say: 'They are destined to rejoice in the works of the Holy One, blessed be He, in the Time to Come.' The Holy One, blessed be He, if the expression be permitted, did not enjoy happiness in this world of His, as may be inferred from the fact that it does not say, 'The Lord *rejoiced* in

His works' (*samakh hashem bema'asav*) but: 'The Lord *will* rejoice [in his works]' (Psalm 104:31), as much as to say: the Holy One, blessed be He, *will in the Time to Come rejoice (*yismakh*) in the works of the righteous.* This passage might give some consolation to those who bear the burden of unhappiness in this world.

See H. Freedman and M. Simon (gen. eds.), *Midrash Rabbah*, Leviticus, trans. J. Israelstam and Judah J. Slotki (London, 1951), 252–4.

7. 'But without children there is no life at all.' Rachel preferred death to childlessness, which prompted the comment of the *amora* Joshua ben Levi that to be without children is death (*Nedarim* 64b).
8. Gershom Scholem notes (*Encyclopaedia Judaica*, xvi. 846) that the eve of every new month became for the pious a day of fasting and repentance. The custom of observing this 'minor day of atonement' is a late one and is not mentioned in the *Shulhan Arukh*. It began among the cabbalists of Safed in the second half of the sixteenth century. Special Penitential Prayers (*Slihot*) were written for the afternoon (*minkhah*) service, based on the themes of exile and redemption. This custom became popular among the pious, who observed this day as though it were sanctioned by *Halakhah* and not—as it actually was—an outgrowth of the study of the Kabbalah. The custom remained in popular force until the nineteenth century. The beginning of the month of Elul ushers in the month of preparation for the Days of Awe, culminating in the celebration of *Rosh ha-Shanah* and *Yom Kippur*. The *Rosh Chodesh* Elul commemoration therefore takes on additional significance, since it commences the period of the daily recitation of *Slihot* and the daily blowing of the *shofar* in call to Jews to repent and prepare to make the annual *heshbon ha-nefesh* or accounting of the soul on the holiest days of the Jewish calendar.
9. Yedaya ben Abraham Bedersi Ha-Pnini (*c.*1270–1340) was a poet and philosopher. Possibly a native of Beziers, he is known to have spent time in Perpignan and Montpellier, and may have been a physician. Little else is known of his personal history. His best literary work is *Sefer Bekhinot Olam* ('The Book of the Examination of the World'), a monograph expatiating on the futility and vanity of this world, by contrast with the greater benefits of intellectual and religious pursuits. Although noted for its religious fervour, the book often tends towards the ascetic and pessimistic. It was first published in Mantua between 1476 and 1480; an English translation appeared in London in 1806 under the title, *An Investigation of the Organisation of the World*. Yedaya wrote several other important philosophical works including *Theories Concerning the Material Intellect* and *A Treatise Upon Personal or Individual Forms*, as well as a commentary on the twenty-five propositions with which Maimonides opened the second part of the *Guide to the Perplexed*. Yedaya is best known for his epistle addressed to Solomon ibn Abraham Adret after the latter had pronounced a ban on philosophic study in Barcelona in 1305, accusing the Jewish communities of Provence of heresy and disrespect to the Torah. Yedaya argued in response the benefits of the study of Greek philosophy, which strengthen rather than weaken religious beliefs. See *Encyclopaedia Judaica*, ix. 1308–10.
10. *The Duties of the Heart* was for centuries the most beloved of Jewish ethical treatises, particularly among Ashkenazi Jews. Written in Muslim Spain during the eleventh century by Bahya ibn Pakuda, it was translated into Hebrew from its original Arabic during the twelfth century by Judah ibn Tibon, and became

192   THE JEWISH POPE

the favourite devotional reading of generations of pious Jews. Maimonides records in a letter that 'this book was never removed from the desk of my father and teacher.' For a comprehensive summary of its contents, see Rachel Puterman, '*Duties of the Heart*: The Quest for Spiritual Perfection', *Jewish Affairs* 47/2 (July 1992), 19–26.

11. This reference is to *Midrash Rabbah* 64:5, and is part of the commentary on Genesis 26:8 (*Parshe Toldot*). It reads as follows: 'R. Johanan said: A bad dream, an evil prophecy, and unreasonable mourning (that is, mourning protracted beyond human reason) are nullified by the lapse of time.' The mourning in question cited here was Isaac's protracted mourning for his father Abraham. The verse (Genesis 26:8) reads: 'And it came to pass, when he had been there a long time, that Abimelech, king of the Philistines, looked out at a window, and saw, and behold, Isaac was sporting with Rebecca his wife.' The Sages explain that Isaac resumed his marital relations with Rebecca 'because time had brought him healing [from his grief over Abraham's death]'. In connection with 'an evil prophecy', and a bad dream, which was held to be a form of vision and therefore on the same footing as a prophecy, the Israelites replied to the prophet Ezekiel: 'The days are prolonged, and every vision faileth' (Ezekiel 12:22), that is, 'they assumed that since a long time had passed and the prophecies were still unfulfilled, they would remain so.' See H. Freedman and M. Simon (gen. eds.), *Midrash Rabbah,* Genesis, trans. H. Freedman (London, 1951), 575–6. Of interest here is the fact that in his Yiddish text, Dik asserts that the Midrash he quotes refers to *Parshe Vayishlokh* (Genesis 32:4–36:43), whereas in fact it refers to *Parshe Toldot* (Genesis 25:19–28:9). Presumably Dik is quoting from memory. If so, while his memory is normally excellent, it has failed him here.

12. Since barrenness was regarded as a curse and a punishment from God (Leviticus 20:20–1; Jeremiah 22:30), and was the most painful disaster that could befall a woman, an extensive tradition grew up among both Sephardi and Ashkenazi Jewish women of using magical treatments and incantations to seek a cure for this affliction. I can find no specific information regarding these Three Hundred and Sixty Supplications, although the number may have some connection with the days of the year. One particularly favoured biblical verse which was regularly recited to cure barrenness was Deuteronomy 7:12, the opening verse of *Parshe Ekev* (Deuteronomy 7:12–11:25). See J. Trachtenberg, *Jewish Magic and Superstition: A Study in Folk Religion* (New York, 1939).

13. Tractate *Niddah* (Purity), chapter *Hamapelet*: On Stillborn Children, in the order *Tohorot* 30b–31a. Consult *Niddah*, trans. I. Slotki in *The Babylonian Talmud: Seder Tohorot* (London, 1948), 212.

14. Midrash *Kohelet* is the Midrash on Ecclesiastes, here specifically Ecclesiastes 7:14: 'In the day of prosperity be joyful, and in the day of adversity, consider: God has made even the one as well as the other, to the end that man should find nothing after him.' Midrash expounds on this verse thus: 'Even the one as well as the other: this is, Gehinnom and Paradise. What is the distance between them? A handbreadth. R. Johanan said: [They are divided by] a wall. The Rabbis say: They are parallel [literally, equal], so that one should be visible to the other.' See H. Freedman and M. Simon (gen. eds.), *Midrash Rabbah*, Ecclesiastes, trans. A Cohen (London, 1951), 197.

15. In his narration of this sequence of events, Dik again unquestioningly presents as a self-evidently correct Jewish response a reaction that makes the Jews of his Mainz ghetto complicit with the persecutions visited upon them. As Dik presents it, the immediate reaction of R. Shimen and his community—automatically to assume that they are indeed guilty of some (unspecified) crime, and to hasten their efforts to atone for it—epitomizes what Raul Hilberg has identified as 'alleviation attempts' on the part of Diaspora Jewry against threatened Christian persecution which were continually repeated for nearly two thousand years of ghetto existence. As Hilberg defines them,

> alleviation attempts are typical and instantaneous responses by the Jewish community. Under the heading of alleviation are included petitions, protection payments, ransom arrangements, anticipatory compliance, relief, rescue, salvage, reconstruction—in short, all those activities which are designed to avert danger, or, in the event that force has already been used, to diminish its effects. [...] One of the most sagacious alleviation reactions in the Jewish arsenal is anticipatory compliance. In this type of alleviation attempt, the victim foresees the danger and combats it by doing the very thing demanded of him. But he does so *before* he is confronted by ultimatums. He is, therefore, giving in on his own terms. In a sense, this is the action of a man who—sensing a fatal blow—wounds himself. With this wound he seeks to demonstrate that the blow is unnecessary. (Hilberg, *Destruction*, 14–15)

16. 'An obligation must be fulfilled by those who are obligated'. The sources for this quotation are Talmud *Bavli*, Tractate *Shabbat* 32a and *Tosefta Yoma* 5:12. The passage in question reads: 'Reward is brought about through a person of merit (*zakkai*), and punishment (*hovah*) through a person of guilt.' The teaching refers specifically to the legal culpability of one who builds a house without a parapet, in consequence of which someone else falls from his roof. According to the juridical conclusion arrived at here, the first, while guilty of having caused harm to his neighbour, is also used as the divine instrument for fulfilling the second man's destiny to fall as a punishment for his sins.

17. Return by a baptized Jew to his original Jewish faith was defined as heresy by the Synod of Mainz in 1310. The Inquisition identified and tried all such offenders but then, since the Church held that it could not itself shed human blood, handed the condemned over to the secular arm of the law for the standard punishment, burning at the stake. Earlier, the Fourth Lateran Council of 1215 had expressly called upon the secular powers to 'exterminate' all heretics. See Hilberg, *Destruction*, 6, 10.

18. 'The Lord is righteous in all His ways, and gracious in all His deeds'. The primary source of this quotation is Psalms 145:17. Preceded by two verses taken from Psalms 84:5 and 144:15, 'Happy are they that dwell in Thy house; they are ever praising Thee. Happy the people that is so situated; happy the people whose God is the Lord', this psalm appears in its entirety in the daily liturgy. Great importance is attached to its recital; as the Talmud (*Berakhot* 4b) notes: 'He who repeats Psalm 145 three times daily is assured of his share in the World to Come.' This psalm was from earliest post-Exilic times introduced twice into the liturgy for the morning (*shaharit*) service, and once into that of the afternoon (*minkhah*)

service. As an aid to memory, this psalm is an acrostic, each verse beginning with one of the letters of the Hebrew alphabet arranged successively, with only the letter *nun* omitted.

SELECT BIBLIOGRAPHY

❖

ADLER, H. M. (trans.) *Mahzor le-Yom ha-Kippurim/Service of the Day of Atonement* (New York: Hebrew Publishing Company, 1938).
ALTER, ROBERT, *The Art of Biblical Narrative* (New York: Basic Books, 1981).
AUSUBEL, NATHAN (ed.), *A Treasury of Jewish Folklore* (New York: Crown, 1948).
BARON, SALO W., *A Social and Religious History of the Jews*, iv (Philadelphia: Jewish Publication Society of America, 1957).
BELSEY, CATHERINE, *Critical Practice* (London and New York: Methuen, 1980).
BURGIN, RICHARD, 'Isaac Bashevis Singer's Universe: The Second of a Two-Part Series', *The New York Times Magazine* (3 Dec. 1978), 39, 40, 44, 46, 50, 52.
—— 'A Conversation with Isaac Bashevis Singer', *The Michigan Quarterly Review* 17/1 (Winter 1978), 119–32.
CHAZAN, ROBERT (ed.), *Church, State, and Jew in the Middle Ages* (West Orange, NJ: Behrman House, 1980).
COHEN, A. (ed.), *The Soncino Chumash* (London: Soncino Press, 1979).
DAVID, ABRAHAM, 'Jewish–Christian Relations, Past and Present: Notes on the Legend of the Jewish Pope', *Immanuel* 15 (Winter 1982/3), 85–96.
DIK, AYZIK-MEIR, *R. Shimen Barbun, oder der drayfakher troym* (Vilna: Romm, 1874).
DUFFY, EAMON, *Saints and Sinners: A History of the Popes* (New Haven, CT: Yale University Press, 1997).
Encyclopaedia Judaica, 26 vols. (Jerusalem: Keter, 1971).
ENDELMAN, TODD M. (ed.), *Jewish Apostasy in the Modern World* (New York and London: Holmes and Meier, 1987).
FARRELL, GRACE (ed.), *Isaac Bashevis Singer: Conversations* (Jackson and London: University Press of Mississippi, 1992).
FLEISCHNER, EVA (ed.), *Auschwitz: Beginning of a New Era? Reflections on the Holocaust* (New York: Ktav Publishing Co., 1977).
GASTER, MOSES (ed. and trans.), *Ma'aseh Book* (Philadelphia: Jewish Publication Society of America, 1934).
Gesta Romanorum, translated by Charles Swan, rev. and corrected by Wynnard Hooper (1876; New York: Dover Publications, 1959).
GILBERT, MARTIN, *The Holocaust: The Jewish Tragedy* (1986; London: Fontana/Collins, 1987).

GILMAN, SANDER L., *Jewish Self-Hatred: Anti-Semitism and the Hidden Language of the Jews* (Baltimore and London: Johns Hopkins University Press, 1986).
—— *Inscribing the Other* (Lincoln, NB, and London: University of Nebraska Press, 1991).
GINZBURG, LOUIS, *The Legends of the Jews*, trans. from German by Henrietta Szold, ii: *From Joseph to the Exodus* (Philadelphia: Jewish Publication Society of America, 1913).
GORR, SHMUEL, *Jewish Personal Names: Their Origin, Derivation and Diminutive Forms*, ed. Chaim Freedman (Teaneck, NJ: Avotaynu Inc., 1992).
HERTZ, J. H. (trans. and ed.), *The Pentateuch and Haftorahs* (London: Soncino Press, 1958).
HILBERG, RAUL, *The Destruction of the European Jews* (New York: Holmes and Meier, 1985).
HIRSCH, SAMSON RAPHAEL (ed.), *The Pentateuch*, i: Genesis, rendered into English by Isaac Levy, 2nd edn. (Gateshead: Judaica Press, 1989).
HOTZ, BARRY (ed.), *Back to the Sources: Reading the Classic Jewish Texts* (1984; New York: Simon and Schuster, 1992).
HUGHES, PHILIP, *A History of the Church; An Introductory Study*, ii (New York: Sheed and Ward, 1947).
JOHNSON, PAUL, *A History of the Jews* (London: Weidenfeld and Nicolson, 1987).
KELLY, J. N. D. (ed.), *The Oxford Dictionary of Popes* (Oxford: Oxford University Press, 1986).
KUGEL, JAMES L., *In Potiphar's House: The Interpretive Life of Biblical Texts* (San Francisco: Harper, 1990).
LEFTWICH, JOSEPH, *Israel Zangwill* (New York and London: Thomas Yoseloff, 1957).
LERNER, DAVID LEVINE, 'The Enduring Legend of the Jewish Pope', *Judaism* 40/2 (Spring 1991), 148–70.
LIPTZIN, SOL, *The Maturing of Yiddish Literature* (New York: Jonathan David, 1970).
Ma'ase-bukh, St. 3902, Opp. 40. 1410, Bodleian, listed Cowley p. 406.
MCCABE, JOSEPH, *A History of the Popes* (London: Watts and Company, 1939).
MACDONELL, DIANE, *Theories of Discourse* (1986; Oxford and New York: Basil Blackwell, 1989).
MADISON, CHARLES A., *Yiddish Literature: Its Scope and Major Writers* (New York: Schocken, 1971).
MAITLIS, JACOB, *The Ma'aseh in the Yiddish Ethical Literature* (London: Shapiro, Vallentine and Company, 1958).
—— (ed.), *Mayse-bukh: 84 dertseylungen*, vol. 36 in Shmuel Rozhansky (gen. ed.), *Musterverk fun der yidisher literatur* (Buenos Aires: YIVO, 1969).
MARCUS, JACOB R. (ed.), *The Jew in the Medieval World: A Source Book 315–1791* (New York: Atheneum, 1974).

MASTERS, BRIAN, *A Student's Guide to Sartre* (1970; London: Heinemann Educational, 1979).
MENDES-FLOHR, PAUL R., and REINHARZ, JEHUDA (eds.), *The Jew in the Modern World: A Documentary History* (New York and Oxford: Oxford University Press, 1980).
NEUGROSCHEL, JOACHIM (trans. and ed.), *Great Works of Jewish Fantasy: Yenne Velt* (London: Cassell, 1976).
New English Bible: New Testament (Oxford and Cambridge: Oxford University Press and Cambridge University Press, 1961).
PHILIPS, A. T. (trans. and ed.), *Mahzor l'Rosh ha-Shanah / Prayer Book for the New Year* (New York: Hebrew Publishing Company, 1931).
PRINZ, JOACHIM, *Popes from the Ghetto: A View of Medieval Christendom* (New York: Dorset Press, 1966).
RAPPAPORT, SALO, *Perspectives on Judaism: Essays on Jewish Culture and Personalities* (Johannesburg: B'nai B'rith, 1985).
REYZEN, ZALMEN, *Leksikon fun der yidisher literature, prese un filologie*, 4 vols. (Vilnius: Boris Kletskin, 1929).
ROSKIES, DAVID G., *Against the Apocalypse: Responses to Catastrophe in Modern Jewish Culture* (Cambridge, MA, and London: Harvard University Press, 1984).
—— *A Bridge of Longing: The Lost Art of Yiddish Storytelling* (Cambridge, MA, and London: Harvard University Press, 1995).
RUBIN, BARRY, *Assimilation and its Discontents* (New York: Random House, 1995).
SAMUEL, MAURICE, *In Praise of Yiddish* (New York: Cowles, 1971).
SCHOLEM, GERSHOM, *The Messianic Idea in Judaism* (1971; New York: Schocken Books, 1978).
SEIFERTH, WOLFGANG, *Synagoge und Kirche im Mittelalter* (Munich: Kösel-Verlag, 1964).
SHALIT, LEVI, 'Joseph in Egypt: The Beginning of Jewish Dualism', *Jewish Affairs* 49/2 (Winter 1994), 6–8.
SHARON, MOSHE, *Judaism, Christianity and Islam: Interaction and Conflict* (Johannesburg: Sacks Publishing Co., 1989).
SHERMAN, JOSEPH, 'Reforming through Fiction: An Appreciation of Ayzik-Meir Dik', *Jewish Affairs* 48/4 (Summer 1993), 27–33.
SIMON, MARCEL, *Verus Israel: A Study of the Relations between Christians and Jews in the Roman Empire (135–425)*, trans. from French by H. McKeating (Oxford: Oxford University Press, 1986).
SINGER, ISAAC BASHEVIS, 'Zeydlus der ershter', *Der sotn in goray un andere dertseylungen* (1943; Jerusalem: Hebrew University, 1972).
—— 'A New Use for Yiddish', *Commentary* 33/2 (Mar. 1962), 267–9.
—— 'If You Could Ask One Question About Life, What Would the Answer Be? Yes ...', *Esquire* (Dec. 1974), 95–6.

SINGER, ISAAC BASHEVIS, *Der shpigl un andere dertseylungen* (1975; Jerusalem: Magnes Press, 1979).
—— *Short Friday and Other Stories* (New York: Fawcett Crest, 1980).
STERN, DAVID, *Midrash and Theory: Ancient Jewish Exegesis and Contemporary Literary Studies* (Evanston, IL: Northwestern University Press, 1996).
TRUNK, Y. Y., 'Der yidisher poypst: historishe dertseylung', *Kvaln un Beymer* (New York: CYCO, 1958).
UDELSON, JOSEPH H., *Dreamer of the Ghetto: The Life and Works of Israel Zangwill* (Tuscaloosa: Alabama University Press, 1990).
WAAGENAAR, SAM, *The Pope's Jews* (La Salle, IL: Library Press, 1974).
WALSH, MICHAEL J., *The Popes: An Illustrated History* (London: Marshall Cavendish, 1980).
WEINREICH, MAX, *History of the Yiddish Language*, trans. from Yiddish by Shlomo Noble, with Joshua A. Fishman (Chicago and London: Chicago University Press, 1980).
YERUSHALMI, YOSEF HAIM, *Zakhor: Jewish History and Jewish Memory* (New York: Schocken Books, 1989).
ZANGWILL, ISRAEL, *Children of the Ghetto*, 3rd edn. (New York: Macmillan, 1895).
—— *Dreamers of the Ghetto* (London: Globe Publishing Company, 1925).

INDEX

❖

Abraham 8, 65, 184–5, 190 n. 7
Ahasuerus 69
Alexander I 86
Alexander II 85
Alter, Robert 42
Althusser, Louis 4
Ambrose 6–7
Amnon, R. 15
Anacletus II 18
Ashkenazi, R. Jacob ben Isaac 69, 157
Augustine 3, 6

Balaam 108, 111
Balfour Declaration 154
Bathsheba 99
Beiles Affair 20
Belloc, Hillaire 153
Benjamin 43, 44, 46–7, 48, 49, 53
Bernard of Clairvaux 11, 18
Blood Libel 19, 20–1, 95
Börne, Ludwig 155
Buber, Martin 164–5

Canaan 6, 40, 52, 57, 61, 62, 63
Caro, R. Joseph 15
Catherine II 86
Chamberlain, Joseph 152
Chess 71, 76–7, 95, 97, 108, 117, 118, 168–9, 177, 178, 180
Chesterton, Cecil 153
Chesterton, G. K. 153
Christiani, Pablo 69
Chrysostom, John 6
Compulsory missionary sermons 13, 118
Constantine 2
Coward, Noël 154
Crusades 10, 11, 158

Damascus Affair 20
David (king) 99, 123, 124
David, Avraham 14
Destruction of the Second Temple 7–8, 9, 113
Diaspora 1, 3, 7–9, 11–12, 13–24, 26, 27–8, 46–50, 69, 81, 96, 107, 109–10, 122, 157, 163–4, 165
Dik, Ayzik-Meir 23, 83–105, 112, 113, 159, 161, 189, 193 n. 15
Dinah 45
Dominicans 13, 19, 147
Donin, Nicholas 29, 42
Dothan 29, 42
Dubnov, Shimen 107

Eder, David 153
Emico, Count 10
Ephraim 38, 60–1

Frank, Jacob 20
Frankfurt am Main 108, 109, 111, 114, 115, 117, 135, 144, 155, 157, 158–60, 168
Freud, Sigmund 132

Gabriel (angel) 31, 37
Galveston Plan 153
Gaster, Moses 81 n. 5, 150
Gesta Romanorum 67, 69–70, 71
Ghetto 12, 58, 69, 111, 113, 119, 140, 141, 143, 144, 145
Gilman, Sander L. 155
Ginzburg, Louis 22, 23, 66 n. 6
Gordon, Y. L. 84, 85
Goshen 49, 52, 55, 56, 58, 59, 62, 113
Graetz, Heinrich 140, 144

200 INDEX

Gregory I 70
Gregory IX 19
Gregory XIII 13

Hadrian (emperor) 113
Hamor 45, 64
Hamsun, Knut 106
Hannah 101, 173
Haran 99, 181
Harkavy, Alexander 85
Hasidism 83, 85, 91, 143
Haskalah 83, 84–5, 86, 88, 89, 91, 92, 93, 96, 98, 104, 107, 121, 123–4, 125, 126, 127, 129, 130, 135
Heine, Heinrich 125, 143
Hellenism 2, 146
Heller, Joseph 166 n. 6
Herrmann, Max 163
Hertz, J. H. 6, 103
Herzl, Theodor 143, 151, 152
Hezekiah (king) 99, 182
Hilberg, Raul 92, 93–4, 189, 190, 193 n. 15
Honorius III 12

Ibn Eza, R. Abraham 36–7, 77
Ibn Habib, R. Jacob ben Solomon 68
Ibn Pakuda, R. Bahya 191 n. 10
Innocent II 18
Inquisition 16, 183, 185, 193 n. 17
Isaiah 99, 117, 118, 126, 182
Ishmael 184
Islam 2, 12
Isserles, R. Moshe 15, 77

Jabotinsky, Vladimir 154
Jacob (patriarch) 15, 28, 29, 40, 46, 50, 51, 53, 54, 55, 58, 59, 60, 61–2, 71, 76, 98, 99, 111, 112, 170, 181
Janov 128, 131, 134, 157, 160
Jeremiah 112, 172
Jerome 6, 8
Jerusalem 8, 116, 122, 139, 145
Jesus 2, 3, 8, 11, 12, 17, 20, 21, 118–19, 126, 130, 141, 142, 143, 145
Jewish Territorial Organisation (ITO) 152
Job 170

Joseph (in Genesis) 1, 17, 18, 22, 23, 26–66, 71, 72, 76, 91, 102, 103, 111, 112, 127, 130, 131, 132, 144, 170, 181, 184, 186, 187
Judah 45, 46–9, 50, 54, 55
Judah *he-Hasid*, R. 68
Julius III 13

Karels, Joseph 160
Kugel, James 22, 54

Lawrence, D. H. 153
Lerner, David Levine 14–16, 78, 118, 165
Levi 45
Lévi-Strauss, Claude 16
Lothar (emperor) 18
Louis IX 19
Luzzatto, R. Jacob 67

Maccabees 2, 140
Maimonides (R. Moses ben Maimon) 77, 127, 129
Maitlis, Jacob 72–3, 75, 78–9, 81 n. 5
Mainz (Mayence) 10, 15, 75, 80, 94, 102, 104, 157, 158–9, 168, 174, 179, 183, 184, 185, 187, 190, 193 n. 17
Malamud, Bernard 161, 166 n. 6
Manasseh 38, 49, 60–1, 102, 144, 184
Marrano 185, 187
Mayse-bukh 23, 67–82, 130, 134, 158, 159, 166
Mendele Moykher Sforim (S. Y. Abramovitsh) 90
Mendelssohn, Moses 158, 159
Messiah 1, 2, 7, 8, 18, 140
Midrash 1, 3, 9, 17, 18, 22–3, 24 n. 2, 26–66, 68, 86, 170, 173, 175, 190, 192 nn. 11 & 14
Montefiore, Sir Moses 84
Moses 19, 64, 65, 103, 124, 129, 138, 141, 142, 143, 187
Muslims 10, 11, 12

Nahmanides (R. Moshe ben Nahman) 20, 33, 36, 42, 43, 51, 52, 53, 69
Nazis 12–13, 58, 92, 93, 107, 110, 115, 117, 160, 162–3, 164, 165, 189

Nicholas I 86, 105 n. 3
Niger, Shmuel 90
Paris 19, 20, 69, 158
Pascal, Blaise 4
Paul III 13
Paul IV 12
Pêcheux, Michel 5
Peretz, Y. L. 106
Pharaoh 17, 34, 35, 36, 37, 39, 41, 47, 49, 50, 52, 53, 54, 55, 56, 57, 58, 61, 62, 63, 64, 71, 112
Pius IX 13
Pnini, R, Yedaya 172, 191 n. 9
Pollak, Jacob 67
Potiphar 31, 33, 47
Potiphar's wife 30, 31, 32–3

RaSHbaM (R. Shmuel ben Meir) 36
RaShI (R. Shlomo Itzkhaki) 28, 31, 32, 34, 40, 41, 45, 51, 56, 57, 63, 72, 123
Reuben 44, 45
Reyzen, Zalmen 89–90, 98, 105 n. 1
Rome 9, 13, 18, 75, 79, 112, 113–14, 115, 116, 117, 143–4, 145, 146, 147, 178–9, 190
Romm Publishing House 87
Rosenzweig, Franz 3, 4, 14, 24 n. 3, 165
Roskies, David G. 88, 91, 105 n.1

Saladin 10–11
Samuel, R. 68
Sartre, Jean-Paul 109, 110
Schechter, Solomon 140, 150
Schiff, Jacob 153
Schmidt, Karl-Ludwig 164
Scholem, Gershom 9, 191 n. 8
Sforno, R. Ovadyah ben Yakov 33, 35, 45, 46, 51, 52
Shechem 42, 45, 47, 64
Sholem Aleykhem (S. Y. Rabinovitsh) 90, 106

Simeon 42, 45
Singer, Isaac Bashevis 23, 90, 121–36, 160, 162, 166 n. 8
Solomon, King 91
Spain 13, 15–16, 20
Straus, Oscar 153
Sulzberger, Judge Meyer 140

Talmud Disputations 16, 19–20
Terah 99, 181
Tertullian 6
Theodosius (emperor) 6
Theresienstadt 163
Titus 113
Trunk, Y. Y. 23, 106–20, 121, 122, 135, 159, 161

Udelson, Joseph 150
Uvarov, Count Sergius 84
Ussishkin, Menachem 150

Vilna Gaon (R. Elijah ben Solomon) 77

Ward, Mrs Humphrey 140
Weimar Republic 162
Weinreich, Max 7, 13–14, 125–6, 158
Weizmann, Chaim 150
Wilde, Oscar 106
World Zionist Organisation (WZO) 152, 154
Worms (city) 67, 158, 165, 190

Yehiel, R. 20

Zangwill, Edith 149, 150
Zangwill, Israel 23, 137–56, 162
Zeitlin, Aaron 122
Zohar 133